Criminal Justice

and retribution, deterrence, rehabilitation, incapacitation). The chapter then returns to the notion of crime and reviews the three primary methods of measuring crime. Next, the chapter addresses different competing tensions in the criminal justice system, such as the tension between due process and crime control in processing, discretion, and four decision points in the system. Finally, the chapter concludes with a review of some recent trends in criminal justice.

Web Activity

See a translation of the earliest written criminal code, the Code of Hammurabi, at http://avalon.law.yale.edu/subject_menus/hammenu.asp

---

WHAT IS CRIME?

Understanding crime is best begun with a discussion of a concept called **deviance**. Deviance refers to human behaviors or actions that are considered by others to be wrong, bad, or inappropriate. Some inappropriate acts are relatively minor, such as spitting on the sidewalk, while others, such as killing a person, are seen as being seriously deviant. Not all deviant acts are illegal. For example, in most places it is not illegal for men to wear women's clothing in public, but a man in a dress will usually draw stares and scorn from onlookers.

Deviance is location, time, person, and event specific, meaning that some behaviors could be considered normal or deviant depending on the circumstances. For example, it is considered normal to yell at a football game, but deviant to yell in a library. This simply means that deviance is more than just a particular act; the person committing the act, the surrounding events, the time, and the location all help others define if someone's behavior should be deemed deviant.

Societies rely upon **informal social control** to influence people's behavior. Indeed, throughout most of history, social control was vested in the individuals (and their families) who were harmed and communities would take informal actions, such as shaming and ostracizing violators of the community's norms. Examples of informal social control include staring, scorn, the cold shoulder, shunning, and telling people that they are doing something wrong. Societies still rely very heavily upon informal social control to keep people in conformity. Although anyone may attempt to engage in informal social control, some common agents of informal social control are parents, schoolteachers, employers, classmates, and fellow employees.

Informal social control can be very successful in family and small group settings where everyone knows one another. The great growth of cities and the shift to large, diverse communities has diluted the impact of informal social controls. As a response to this social change, more formal means of dealing with unwanted behavior have been developed. In addition, some deviant acts are too serious to be managed via informal social control.

Serious deviance is prohibited by societies with written laws. These laws identify the prohibited deviant behaviors, the circumstances that make such behaviors illegal, and the possible punishment for violating them. For example, it is not illegal to kill another person in self-defense, but it is illegal to do so with premeditation. In modern society, laws are generally written and approved by elected legislators at either the federal or state level. Local governments (such as towns and cities) may also pass their own laws. Crimes can be classified as either **mala in se** or **mala prohibita**. Mala in se acts such as murder, robbery, and rape are viewed as inherently evil and are thus often classified as serious crimes. Mala prohibita acts are less serious offenses such as underage drinking, speeding, and loitering. Mala prohibita acts are still considered crimes, but they are not viewed as inherently bad, only as behaviors that should be prohibited by law. A law is usually classified as either a **felony**, which is a serious breach of law usually carrying a penalty of more than one year in prison, or a **misdemeanor**, a less serious crime usually carrying a sentence of less than one year in prison. When someone engages in an illegal act, and the conditions of the act are not excused by a law, that person has broken the law and thus committed a crime.

Critical Thinking Exercise

Think about a time when someone used informal social control in response to your behavior. What were you doing, and what did the agent of informal social control do? Think about a time when you applied informal social control on another person. What was that person doing, and what did you do in response?

CRIMINAL JUSTICE SYSTEM POLICY

Policies are created to set a standard of how a problem or issue will be addressed. The criminal justice system engages in policy on a daily basis. From arrest policy to prosecution policy to sentencing policy, the system engages in practices to deal with crime. Throughout the history of the criminal justice system, various policies have been supported more than others, and the justification behind these policies has varied over time.

Public policy is *"A relatively stable, purposive course of action followed by an actor or set of actors in dealing with a problem or matter of concern. This definition focuses on what is actually done instead of what is only proposed or intended; differentiates a policy from a decision . . .; and views policy as something that unfolds over time"* (Anderson 2003: 2, emphasis in original). Simply, if crime is a problem, the criminal justice system and its policies represent society's response to that problem.

Historically, criminal justice policy, or lack thereof, first centered on revenge on the part of the victim. In Europe, between the collapse of the Roman Empire and 600 A.D., it was common for individuals and families to act as their own criminal justice systems (Johnson and Wolfe 1996). These societies relied upon informal social control to keep order because they lacked contemporary elements of criminal justice, such as prisons and paid, full-time police. If a person was harmed by another the victim had to seek his or her own justice, often violently, and if a person was killed, the victim's family had to seek justice from the offender or the offender's family. Since the government was not involved in this system of justice, there was little criminal justice policy.

As society changed and became more complex, the victim-centered system of justice did not work well and was replaced by governmental control of justice. Under governmental control of justice, the government assumes the role of deciding what behaviors are considered illegal, who are considered offenders and victims, and what the punishments are. As a result, when a law is broken and a crime is committed, the government acts as the victim, as it is the government's law that has been violated.

Public policies are created at different levels of government. At the highest level are policies created by the federal government, which apply to the federal criminal justice system, but could also apply to state and local systems. These are macro-level policies. Public policies at the local level, called micro-level policies, are also used to enact or change criminal justice. Thus, state laws differ in the acts they prohibit and the punishments for violating these laws. Policies may also be created by governmental entities other than federal and state legislatures. The judicial branch creates policy by issuing court rulings, and the executive branch creates policy through executive orders. Within each of these branches, various agencies are able to create policies that are far-reaching or that apply only to the agency at hand. For instance, the Ohio Public Defender Commission outlines standards and guidelines that must be followed for its public defenders. At the local level, some towns and cities create their own policies, such as local ordinances banning loud car stereos. Finally, individual criminal justice organizations like jails and prisons or police agencies create their own internal policies, such as visitation requirements or minimum education requirements for police officers.

Web Activity

You can see a description of the three branches of the federal government (judicial, legislative, and executive) at https://en.wikipedia.org/wiki/Federal_government_of_the_United_States.

CRIMINAL JUSTICE SYSTEM PHILOSOPHY

Initially, the relationship between policy and crime sounds simple. Crime is a problem, so society chooses how to solve the problem and implements policy to effect the necessary solution. Unfortunately, combating crime is not so simple. Part of this complication is caused by differences in society's philosophies about what the criminal justice system *should* do. Because society is not unanimous in how it should respond to crime, criminal justice policy becomes more complicated. In some instances, certain criminal justice organizations will implement one type of policy, while other agencies will adopt other policies. Sometimes these policies compete with or contradict each other. Part of this complication is due to different philosophies of criminal justice.

The Classical School

The **Classical school** of criminal justice stemmed from the mid-18th-century writings of Cesare Beccaria. Beccaria argued that humans possess free will, are rational, and make choices about how to behave. Human behavior is influenced by each person's weighing of the costs of an action and the benefits he or she expects to receive. For example, someone contemplating robbery will weigh the possible rewards (getting money) against the possible costs (arrest and imprisonment) and decide whether to rob or not rob. Thus, criminals choose to commit crime by a process of rational thought.

Beccaria argued that punishments should be harsh enough to deter potential offenders, but not overly punitive or cruel. Laws should be clearly written in advance and should specify the punishments for each crime. Mitigating factors, such as the criminal's personality, social circumstances, or financial need, should not be weighed by a judge or jury. Simply, the law should be applied evenly to everyone who breaks it. Deterrence is the cornerstone of Classicism.

The Positivist School

The **Positivist school** of criminal justice developed after the Classical view was established. Positivists claim that human behavior is influenced by conditions and situations external to individuals that are beyond the control of individuals. For example, poverty and abusive parenting influence the likelihood that a child will grow up poor and abusive as well. The law would likely hold little deterrent value for this child, since he or she may have learned only deviant behaviors and never learned pro-social behaviors.

Positivists contend that preventing crime results from intervening in the conditions that cause crime and not in stricter laws. Crime can be combated best by eliminating poverty, providing opportunity, improving parenting, or reducing contact with delinquent peers. Positivists disagree about the exact causes of crime, however, so their particular prescriptions for attacking the roots of crime differ. Under Positivism, no single cause of crime exists. Rather, different factors influence different people to act in different ways. This means that no single response will be effective in solving crime. Each situation and individual needs to be evaluated for the cause and an intervention or response needs to be implemented. Two individuals may commit the same act (such as robbery) but do so for different reasons (one person does it to get money to feed his family, while another person does it in response to a previous conflict with the victim).

The Classical and Positivist schools provide a general overview of the potential causes and solutions to crime. Although some solutions involve an overhaul of social conditions, most come in the form of punishment. There is disagreement, however, over why, how, and to what extent punishment should be used. These disagreements are illustrated in four punishment philosophies: retribution, deterrence, rehabilitation, and incapacitation.

Retribution

Retribution is a philosophy based on the belief that criminals should be punished because they have violated the law. Thus, the criminal justice system exists to punish wrongdoers. Punishment should be commensurate with the harm committed by the criminal (an "eye for an eye"), which is in accord with the beliefs of those who follow the Classical school. Retribution, however, does not punish in order to prevent potential criminals from committing crime. Rather, advocates of retribution argue that punishment is the proper and just thing for a society to do, regardless of its effectiveness in preventing crime. This is sometimes called **just desserts**.

Retributivists favor the use of incarceration as a way to punish offenders. Lesser punishments such as probation and policies such as plea bargaining may not result in the punishment fitting the crime. Retributivists also favor the use of capital punishment, in accordance with the "eye for an eye" edict.

Deterrence

Like retribution, **deterrence** is the belief that offenders should be punished; however, punishment should have some other goal besides just desserts. Proponents of deterrence contend that punishments should prevent crime by making potential offenders aware of the costs of crime. In effect, potential offenders will know that they will be punished if they commit a crime. Because of the belief that people seek pleasure and avoid pain, deterrence advocates argue that costs of crime need to outweigh its benefits, thus individuals will refrain from crime. This belief is also drawn from the Classical school.

There are two types of deterrence: specific and general. **Specific deterrence** refers to deterring a particular offender. For example, a juvenile punished for skipping school will not skip again in order to avoid future punishment. **General deterrence** prevents people from committing crime by showing them, through the experiences of other punished criminals, that crime does not pay. For example, fellow students at the truant's school will probably not skip school in the future if they have learned of the punishment received by their friend for skipping. Thus, general deterrence predicts that a person does not need to be directly punished in order to be deterred.

Deterrence appears to work best when the punishment is *certain*, *severe*, and *quickly applied*. Offenders must be punished every time they commit a crime (*certainty*). Furthermore, the punishment must be *severe* enough to make punishment outweigh the benefits or fruits of the crime. Finally, the punishment must be inflicted soon after the crime is committed, which is sometimes called *celerity*.

A system dedicated to deterrence would try to maximize the certainty, severity, and celerity via policy. A deterrent system would find ways to increase the rate at which crimes are reported and offenders are caught. This might involve policies requiring that crime victims report their victimizations to authorities. A deterrent system would also have to ensure that the severity of punishment was painful enough to outweigh the benefits of crime. This could entail policies and laws that limit the discretion of workers in the criminal justice system, abolish pleas bargains, and apply the law evenly to everyone, no matter what their status, gender, or other nonlegal factors. Finally, the system would value speedy processing of suspects. There should be little delay between arrest, trial, and punishment.

Rehabilitation

Rehabilitation, which falls under Positivism, seeks to prevent crime by rectifying individual problems that are thought to be responsible for the criminal behavior. Simple punishment is not seen as an effective solution to crime. The philosophy of rehabilitation views criminals as "broken" and seeks to "repair" them by reformation and treatment. This philosophy assumes that criminals can be reformed. Once reformed, criminals will no longer engage in crime. Examples of rehabilitation include drug treatment, mental health counseling, changing how offenders think cognitively, and job training. Prisons and jails would be structured to be more therapeutic, rather than punishment oriented.

Rehabilitation requires some flexibility in the criminal justice system that allows for an individual focus on the offender. Each offender should be held in prison or jail or kept under supervision in the community until he or she is rehabilitated. Some offenders will be quickly rehabilitated while others will require long periods of treatment. This individual focus requires differential sentences based on the needs of the offender and not solely on the crime. The staff of correctional facilities should also decide when an offender is rehabilitated and can be released. Rehabilitation would also entail the use of community supervision of offenders during which they receive treatment that will assist in their rehabilitation and reintegration into society.

Incapacitation

Incapacitation is the belief that the role of the criminal justice system is to separate or segregate criminals from the rest of society in order to protect society. If known criminals are removed from society, there should be less crime. Unlike retribution, incapacitation does not see segregation as a form of punishment. Rather, incapacitation is designed to keep offenders away from society. Incapacitation also differs from rehabilitation in that it does not necessarily advocate treating offenders.

Incapacitation comes with its own policy implications. First, it entails an emphasis on using secure facilities, such as prisons and jails, rather than community corrections like probation. This is not to say that community corrections cannot be used as part of incapacitation; rather, pure incapacitation would emphasize physical segregation. This segregation restrains offenders from engaging in further criminal activity. Incapacitation is the goal behind laws such as habitual-offender and "three-strikes" laws that incarcerate individuals if they continue to commit offenses. The idea is that previous punishment (if any) was not sufficient to deter or reform the offenders, so the system must resort to keeping them away from society for a long time in order to prevent further crime.

Critical Thinking Exercise

Each of these philosophies entails its own policy, to impel criminal justice employees to adhere to the policy's intent. Choose one of the philosophies above and write a policy designed to implement that philosophy at a particular step of the criminal justice process (that is, to be implemented by the police, courts, or corrections). If you find this task easy, try writing a policy that satisfies the dictates of two or three of these philosophies. Do you find this to be easy or difficult?

MEASURING CRIME

Defining crime is relatively easy when compared to the task of measuring crime, but crime is central to the existence of any criminal justice system, and measuring crime accurately is important. Accurate measures of crime are important because these measures give us better insights into the nature and extent of crime. For instance, we can determine if crime is increasing or if certain types of crime are becoming less common. Further, measuring crime lets us predict crime trends and plan for future demands on the criminal justice system. Valid and reliable crime statistics also permit researchers to craft better theories of crime and criminal justice, which in turn help guide the administration of justice. Finally, good crime statistics can be used to evaluate criminal justice policies and programs. For example, we could use crime statistics to see if a mandatory minimum sentencing policy prevents crime.

It is difficult to determine the amount of crime that actually occurs because many crimes do not come to the attention of the criminal justice system. For instance, many victims do not report their victimizations to the police. In addition, some victims may not even realize that they have been victims of crime. Research reveals that on average, less than half of all victimizations are actually reported to authorities (Morgan and Kena 2018: 5). Because of this underreporting of crime, criminologists often refer to the total number of unreported crimes as the **dark figure of crime** (Biderman and Reiss 1967). Underreporting means that authorities in the criminal justice system often have great difficulty producing accurate crime statistics.

Web Activity

Look at data from Americans about their crime reporting practices at the *Sourcebook of Criminal Justice* website (http://www.albany.edu/sourcebook/tost_3.html#3_l). Do rates of crime reporting differ for different types of crime? How much do reporting rates change from one year to another?

Crime is usually expressed in one of two ways. The first way of expressing crime statistics is as a count. Counts simply report the total number of crimes reported over a given time span. Thus, a city might report that it had three homicides last year. Using raw counts is not without problems. Raw counts do not facilitate comparisons of different places with different populations. For example, in 2018, New York City reported a total of 295 murders and nonnegligent manslaughters. During that same year, Kansas City, Missouri reported a total of 137 murders and nonnegligent manslaughters (Federal Bureau of Investigation 2019). At first blush, Kansas City seemed like a safer city in 2018. Kansas City, however, has fewer inhabitants than New York, so it would seem natural for it to have fewer homicides. A raw count of homicides does not allow us to fairly compare the two.

It is sometimes better to use a **crime rate** instead of a raw count. Rates are usually expressed as the number of events per 1,000 or 100,000 people (or residents) per year. For example, a city with a population of 100,000 people where three people were murdered in one year would report a homicide rate of 3.0 homicides per 100,000 population. Using the New York and Kansas City numbers, the homicide rate in New York in 2018 was 3.46 per 100,000 population, while the homicide rate for Kansas City in 2018 was 27.7 per 100,000. Not only do rates permit better comparisons of different cities or states, they also allow better analysis of crime trends over time. Cities and states grow and shrink over time. Rates control for these differences in populations. Regardless of the measurement, there are three general sources of crime statistics: official (reported) statistics, self-report statistics, and victimization statistics.

Web Activity

The Bureau of Justice Statistics' website (http://www.bjs.gov/ucrdata/) has an easy-to-use data access program. You can look at crime statistics by state, region, or city, for different years and crime types.

Official Statistics
Official statistics are gathered from criminal justice agencies and represent the total number of crimes and cases brought to or handled by the agency. The number of crimes reported to the police and the number of arrests made

are the most commonly reported official crime statistics. Other official statistics include those from the courts and corrections. While police data are the most commonly reported, it is important to recall that only about 40 percent of crime victims report their victimization to the police. In addition, research indicates that police officers do not arrest all persons they encounter who are suspected of committing a crime (see Smith and Visher 1981). These facts mean that both reported crimes and arrests are imperfect measures of crime.

The largest and best-known sources of official statistics in the United States are the Federal Bureau of Investigation's (FBI's) Uniform Crime Reports (UCR), which is now referred to as the Summary Reporting System (SRS). The UCR collects police data on 29 crime categories and reports the numbers of crimes reported to the police and the number of arrests for many of the police agencies in the United States (Maltz 1999). The UCR also provides demographic information on arrestees and circumstances of the more serious personal crimes. Starting in 2021 the primary data collection will take place under the National Incident-Based Reporting System (NIBRS). The NIBRS still collects data on crimes reported to the police, but the NIBRS captures data on 49 offenses falling into 23 offense categories, as well as detailed information on 50 data elements related to offenders, victims, and the crime incidents for all offenses (see Box 1.1). Rather than abiding by the hierarchy rule in the SRS (which only counts the most serious offense when multiple offenses occur at the same time), the NIBRS counts up to 10 offenses per criminal incident. The FBI has been transitioning police agencies from reporting to the UCR, and instead reporting via NIBRS, but the transition has been slow and many agencies do not report to NIBRS. According to the most recent published account, only 43 percent of the police agencies participate in the NIBRS (Federal Bureau of Investigation 2019). As of January 2021, the FBI plans to move all agencies to reporting to NIBRS and then phase out collecting crime and arrest data by UCR.

Web Activity

The textbook website has tables from the UCR SRS for your inspection (www.oup.com/he/lab6e).

Official arrest statistics or crimes reported to the police can sometimes provide a reasonable estimate of crime, but one should always be careful when interpreting these official statistics. Police agencies can change their attention to certain events, and thus change their overall number of arrests, regardless of the true crime rate. For example, a police agency may deploy many officers in a red-light district in order to crack down on prostitution. This crackdown may yield a considerable increase in arrests for prostitution, although the true incidence of prostitution has not changed. An uninformed observer might wrongly conclude that the incidence of prostitution is increasing, when in fact the increase in arrests is a result of the police initiative designed to combat prostitution.

BOX 1.1

Information Collected by NIBRS

Offense Information	Arrestee Segment
Bias motivation	Arrest date
Location type	Type of arrest
Number of premises entered	Multiple arrestee segments
Method of entry	indicator
Type of criminal activity/gang information	Arrestee was armed with
Type of weapon/force involved	Age, sex, race, ethnicity
	Resident status
Property Segment	Disposition of arrestee under 18
Type of property loss/etc.	Victim Segment
Property description	Type of victim
Value of property	Age, sex, race, ethnicity
Date recovered	Resident status
Number of stolen motor vehicles	Aggravated assault/homicide
Number of recovered motor vehicles	circumstances
Suspected drug type	Additional justifiable homicide
Estimated drug quantity	circumstances
Type of drug measurement	Type of injury
Offender Segment	Relationship of victim to offender
Age, sex, race, ethnicity	

SOURCE: Federal Bureau of Investigation (2015). *National Incident-Based Reporting System*. Washington, DC: FBI. https://ucr.fbi.gov/about-us/cjis/ucr/nibrs/2014/resource-pages/incidents-and-offenses_f.pdf.

Similarly, crimes reported to the police represent just that—crimes where the victims have notified the police of their victimization and the police chose to record them as victimizations. If the crime is not reported, if the police do not make an arrest, or if police choose to not record an incident as a crime, official statistics will not provide an accurate estimate of the true crime rate. This problem carries through to the court and correctional statistics, which receive most of their cases from the police.

Self-Report Statistics
Self-report statistics overcome some of the limitations of official statistics. Self-report statistics are gathered from people by asking them to report the number

of times they have committed a crime during a set period of time in the past. For example, since 1975, the Monitoring the Future project has surveyed youths about a range of attitudes and activities, including alcohol and drug use and delinquent behavior. These types of surveys may ask high school seniors how many times they have smoked marijuana during the past year. The respondents are usually promised **confidentiality**, which means that the reports cannot be linked to specific individuals.

Self-report statistics avoid some problems associated with official statistics. For example, they are often better at discovering crimes that the victim did not bother reporting to authorities. Further, self-report statistics are good for exploring crimes where there is no victim, called **victimless crimes**, such as illegal drug use or underage drinking. Self-reports are also good for uncovering less serious offenses such as drug use or shoplifting and for learning about crimes where an arrest is unlikely (Hindelang, Hirschi, and Weis 1979).

Web Activity

Data from the Monitoring the Future project, a major source of self-report data, can be found at http://monitoringthefuture.org.

Unfortunately, there are problems associated with self-report statistics. First, respondents may exaggerate or underreport their criminal behavior. Respondents may exaggerate their criminal activity in order to reinforce their self-concept as tough characters. Conversely, respondents may underreport because they forgot their criminal activities, because they did not know that what they had done was illegal, or because they are afraid to reveal their past criminal activities. Second, *who* is surveyed about their criminal activity is important. Most self-report surveys target high school populations, since they are easily identified and available. Self-reports are much more rare from adults, thus the data is typically useful only for understanding youthful misbehavior. Giving a self-report survey to high school seniors at their school is also likely to lead one to underestimate the true incidence of crime committed by 17- and 18-year-olds. This is due to the fact that serious criminals in this age range are more likely to be suspended from school, might be skipping school on that day, or might be locked up in secure juvenile facilities. Thus, self-reports have limitations and do not yield a completely accurate estimate of the true crime rate.

Victimization Studies

The third type of crime statistic comes from **victimization studies**. In victimization studies people are asked if they have been victims of crimes during a past time period. One example is the National Crime Victimization Survey (NCVS). The NCVS is a nationally representative survey of more than 134,000 US households designed to measure criminal victimization. The survey is conducted annually by the Bureau of the Census for the Department of Justice's Bureau of Justice Statistics. As with self-report studies, victimization studies sometimes encounter problems. For example, respondents may forget victimizations, lie, or fail to tell the interviewers about their victimizations. Sometimes victims will "telescope" a victimization from outside the survey time span. For example, a victimization survey may only be concerned with crimes committed during 2016, but a respondent may report that a 2015 assault occurred during 2016. The dangers of lying, underreporting, and telescoping can all be combated by various methodological techniques. For example, the NCVS uses a technique called *bounding* to mitigate the likelihood that a respondent will telescope.

Web Activity

Data from the NCVS can be found at the textbook website (www.oup.com/he/lab6e).

Overall, these three techniques for measuring crime provide estimates of the dark figure of crime. It is important, however, to keep in mind their limitations when using each one. Each method is subject to problems that may affect the accuracy of the estimate derived.

Critical Thinking Exercise

Which type of statistic would be best suited to study homicide in US cities? What about the sexual abuse of young children? What statistic would be best suited to studying drug use by high school students? In general, for each of the three types of data (official, self-report, and victimization), what types of crime is each best suited to capture? What types of crime is each poorly suited to capture?

A SYSTEM OF CHECKS AND BALANCES

Some believe that the criminal justice system in the United States is too punitive when dealing with offenders, while others feel it is not punitive enough. The criminal justice system in the United States attempts to strike a balance between these two concerns.

Individual Liberty Versus Societal Civility

The first important characteristic of criminal justice in the United States is that it represents a balance between a number of opposing forces. First, the system tries to balance the rights of people to do what they want with the requirement that society remains civil, calm, and relatively crime-free. Thus the government imposes restrictions on individual behavior through laws and creates the agencies designed to enforce them in an attempt to keep society orderly. This desire for order must be balanced, however, with the public's desire for freedom to do what it wants. If there is too much governmental restriction, people are oppressed. On the other hand, society will veer toward disorder and chaos if there is too much individual freedom. The competing forces of individual liberty must be balanced with the desire for societal order at all levels of criminal justice and all stages of the system.

Crime Control Versus Due Process

Writing in 1968, Herbert Packer noted that the criminal justice system balances the competing philosophies of crime control and due process in its operations. The **crime-control model** advocates the aggressive and quick apprehension, trial, and processing of criminals. Briefly, this crime-control orientation seeks to prevent crime via a number of processes, such as deterrence and incapacitation, and cares less about ensuring that suspects are given specific legal rights. Crime control emphasizes that the system efficiently processes suspects in order to suppress crime. On the other hand, the **due-process model** is more concerned with the process of justice and grants suspects many rights to protect them from overzealous investigation and prosecution. In a due-process model the system should carefully ensure that individual rights are not violated. In other words, a due-process perspective is concerned less with suppressing crime than with ensuring that individuals are not unfairly harmed by their government. In reality, the criminal justice system embodies a balance between these competing philosophies via the creation of policy, although the system constantly swings between these two extremes.

Other Competing Ideologies

Balancing competing ideologies also applies to the philosophies of criminal justice discussed earlier. In effect, the system constantly oscillates among these four competing philosophies and, in many cases, decisions are based upon satisfying two or three of these ideologies. This constant mixture of philosophies means that advocates of one philosophy are never completely happy, for the system never fully implements their version of justice. Instead, the system operates under all four philosophies in most situations. A mix of philosophies is sometimes evident when individual criminal justice employees make decisions. For example, a judge might decide upon a defendant's sentence length based on the amount of time required for rehabilitation but may also want to punish the offender and send a deterrent message to the community. The criminal justice system cannot be viewed as being committed to any one philosophy; rather, the operation of criminal justice is a simultaneous combination of these different ideologies.

A Loosely Coupled System

Unlike many nations, where there is one national criminal justice system, criminal justice in the United States is composed of many loosely coupled, semiautonomous organizations. For example, instead of one national police force, there are over 18,000 separate police agencies, each acting as a separate, independent agency. Likewise, instead of one court system, there are county, state, and federal courts, and cities and towns have municipal courts. There are thousands of local jails and hundreds of prisons (both state and federal). Likewise, there are thousands of probation and parole agencies, as well as thousands of juvenile courts. Why have Americans created so many organizations to deal with crime and disorder?

This loosely coupled system reflects Americans' distrust of large government and their preference for local control. In some states, certain criminal justice positions are elected, such as sheriffs and judges, while other positions on parole boards are appointed. In this way, citizens exercise local control over their criminal justice system. This loosely coupled system also facilitates a system of checks and balances, where the decisions of one criminal justice agency are reviewed by later criminal justice agencies. For example, prosecutors usually conduct pretrial screenings with arrestees to decide if charges will be filed or the case dropped. In effect, prosecutors review the work of the police officers responsible for an arrest and decide if the suspect should be charged. There is less pressure for prosecutors to rubber-stamp arrests and charge suspects, for prosecutors do not work for their local police agencies.

The separation of these criminal justice components facilitates the review of decisions. Likewise, the prosecutor's decision to charge is not the final decision. Judges have the opportunity to review this decision and, if the case goes to trial, either a judge or jury will evaluate the defendant's guilt. In this way, criminal justice in the United States embodies a system of loosely coupled agencies that check the decisions made by other agencies. Although it may appear cumbersome and inefficient at times to have so many different agencies dispensing justice, the system protects citizens from a single, all-powerful state. It allows local areas to tailor their criminal justice systems to their own local needs and permits the creation of particular balances of competing forces, such as crime control and due process and rehabilitation and retribution, for example.

Discretion

Discretion is an important attribute of the criminal justice system; in fact, the system could not function without it. Prior to the mid-1950s, however, few people understood or appreciated the nature or importance of discretion (Walker 1993: 6–8). Discretion involves decision-making by people involved in criminal justice—most often but not always employees of criminal justice agencies. These people are usually referred to as criminal justice actors. For example, a police officer decides to stop one motorist but not another. A judge imposes a longer sentence on one convicted criminal than on a criminal with a similar record who has committed the same crime. A parole board releases one prisoner early, but not another. These choices represent discretionary decision-making by criminal justice actors.

Discretion involves legal and permissible decisions by criminal justice actors, including acting and choosing to not act (Klockars 1985: 93).

Discretion does not include decision-making where actors break agency rules or the law, such as instances of corruption or misconduct. But within the bounds of permissible decision-making there are a wide range of possible actions available for both actors and agencies. Discretion is fundamental to the criminal justice system; it is like the thread that constitutes the cloth of the criminal justice system. The next section treats the criminal justice system as a series of four decision points that involve discretionary decisions.

The Four Cs of the Criminal Justice System (Citizens, Cops, Courts, and Corrections)

The American criminal justice system can be viewed as a conglomeration of quasi-independent organizations, each processing the outputs of the previous agency. The system can also be viewed as a process model, whereby decisions made by one system component influence the following components. This system model can be called "the four Cs of the criminal justice system." The process model highlights the importance of decision-making by individuals in the system.

Citizens

The first of the system's Cs are people not employed by the system, called citizens. The decisions made by crime victims, complainants, and offenders are crucial for understanding how the system works, for citizens provide the vast majority of inputs for the rest of the system. For example, research indicates that the majority of people arrested by the police are arrested based on the complaint of another citizen. Further, as stated earlier, research indicates that victims do not always call the police to report crimes. This rate of reporting varies depending on the seriousness of the crime, as victims of serious crimes are more likely to report their victimizations. Reporting rates also differ depending on the type of crime. For example, roughly 73 percent of vehicle theft victims report their loss to the police, compared to 29 percent of theft victims (Morgan and Kena, 2018: Table 4, p. 7).

Web Activity

You can investigate reporting rates by crime types using the NCVS Victim Analysis Tool at https://www.bjs.gov/index.cfm?ty=nvat.

Some states have responded to the underreporting of crime by using two different policies. The first policy involves passing laws that require people to report specific crimes to authorities. In many states, physicians, teachers, and social workers are mandated by law to report suspected cases of child abuse. Some states have also sought to eliminate victims' unwillingness to press charges by requiring that police officers arrest certain types of offenders, even if the victims do not request arrest. This is particularly common in domestic violence cases.

Cops

The second decision-making point of the system consists of the police and other law enforcement agents. Police officers do not patrol the streets arresting everyone suspected of committing a crime; rather, officers selectively enforce the law. In many instances, an officer chooses *not* to arrest, even when there is probable cause. Not fully enforcing all the laws all the time is a good thing; the full enforcement of every law is not possible, and society would probably not tolerate it (see Klockars 1985). Again, the police exercise considerable discretion about what situations to get involved in and how to resolve these situations. The police decision to arrest is influenced considerably by the seriousness of the suspected offense, the wishes of the victim or complainant, and the demeanor of the suspect (Smith and Visher 1981). The letter of the law only plays a part in an officer's arrest decision and, in the majority of cases, the police do not make arrests.

Policies have been implemented in the hopes of controlling how police officers act. As mentioned earlier, some state laws require that police officers arrest suspects who are believed to have committed domestic violence. In this way, policymakers hope to control the unwillingness of some victims to press charges. Such policies also take discretion away from police officers, who will often not arrest in such situations. Individual law enforcement agencies can also create rules and regulations to control employee behaviors. Many agencies have rules mandating when officers may use deadly force and engage in vehicle pursuits, for example (Walker 1993).

Courts

The third decision-making point is composed of court workers, such as pretrial intake workers, prosecutors, defense attorneys, and judges. This third decision point is unique, for not all of the people who work in this area are employed by a particular court, nor are they necessarily employed by the criminal justice system. For example, defendants may employ their own defense attorneys who are not employed by the government. Thus, courtroom decisions are not made by members of the same organization, but rather by a range of actors who meet in a court "arena." This is known as the **courtroom workgroup**. The workgroup members exercise considerable discretion about a range of decisions, such as whether cases should be plea bargained, sent to trial, or dismissed. The workgroup often negotiates the charges to be brought and the possible sentences. For example, a prosecutor may negotiate a plea agreement with the defense attorney, reduce the charges against a suspect, and recommend a possible sentence to the judge. Likewise, defendants and defense attorneys can also decide to accept a plea bargain or invoke their right to a trial. Finally, judges make important decisions concerning such things as the admissibility of evidence and sentencing.

Decisions made by court workers are also affected by policy. For instance, a judge will set policy regarding the way in which his or her courtroom will operate. Further policies, in the form of laws, mandate a range of activities, such as how soon a trial must be held, how plea bargaining and trials are conducted, and how defendants are sentenced.

Corrections

The final decision-making point is composed of criminal justice system employees who work in corrections and includes probation and parole officers, correctional officers, and workers who provide services to offenders, such as social workers. Probation and parole officers are responsible for the supervision of offenders in the community and correctional officers are responsible for maintaining security in a correctional institution, whether it is jail or prison.

The behaviors of correctional workers are also shaped and constrained by policy. For instance, state and federal laws mandate that prisoners have the right to adequate medical care while incarcerated. In other instances, the policies are created by individual correctional agencies and might cover such activities as how often probationers are drug tested or what happens to probationers who fail drug tests. Policies also cover such things as appropriate dress codes for employees and the procedures for dealing with offenders who do not follow the conditions of probation or the rules of the institution.

Each of these decision points is composed of multiple people and actors, all of whom influence the future of the criminal case, the suspect, and the victim. Thus, if a crime victim chooses to not report a crime, it is unlikely that the system will become involved. Likewise, the actors at each of these decision points interact and often negotiate the outcome of that decision point. Such negotiation is common during these discretionary interchanges. Discretion is important for running the system, and understanding discretion is crucial to understanding the system. Despite this, society has long been concerned with controlling and guiding these discretionary decisions in criminal justice (Gottfredson and Gottfredson 1988; Walker 1993). Controlling discretion is an important goal for the system, as it hopes to ensure fair and uniform processes. These attempts at controlling discretion often take the form of policies that are found throughout the system.

RECENT TRENDS IN CRIMINAL JUSTICE

The criminal justice system, like other social entities, responds to new or emerging issues in society at large. Four recent issues of note are criminal justice reform, disproportionate minority contact, restorative justice, and the role of victims in the justice system.

Criminal Justice Reform

The criminal justice system is constantly undergoing change. At times, calls for change and actual change are more evident than at other times. Since about 2010, reform across the criminal justice system has become prominent. The calls for reform have mostly originated from groups advocating for less criminal justice involvement and contact with people across a range of situations. For example, in the wake of protests in Ferguson, Missouri in 2014, public attention focused on the ways that policing and courts issue monetary fines on citizens and then threaten (and use) criminal justice sanctions, such as additional fines, arrest, and imprisonment, when citizens do not pay those fines. In some communities fines and the resulting increased involvement with criminal justice spiraled in tandem and were viewed as oppressive and unfair by community residents.

Related to fines and sanctions has been a recent focus on decreasing prison populations and reforms in sentencing laws, to shrink prison populations. The United States maintains one of the largest prison populations in the western world—an expensive and socially costly way of responding to crime. In recent years reformers have questioned the fairness of imprisoning people for relatively minor offenses (especially drug offenses) and the effectiveness of prison at changing behavior. Others have noted the burdensome monetary costs of warehousing people in prison, while others note how incarceration has harmed communities of color. Many of these reform efforts are a response to the outcomes, reaped decades later, of the war on crime and "get-tough" criminal justice policies and legislation.

Disproportionate Minority Contact

Recent years have seen increasing attention on the degree of criminal justice system contact with minority members and communities. The issue of race and ethnicity and criminal justice are about as old as the criminal justice system itself. Recently the issue has become framed as how and why the criminal justice system has greater presence in minority communities and has increased contact and involvement in the lives of people of color. One example is a process called the school-to-prison pipeline. Over the past 20 years, police officers are increasingly present in schools, often as school resource officers (SROs). Because the police are present in school, detractors argue that minor misbehavior by students at school is now more likely to involve the police. Students are more likely to build a formal record, even for minor misdeeds, but over time this formal record can influence later decision-making by criminal justice actors. For example, a student who has a few encounters with their SRO for minor rule violations may later be referred to juvenile probation based on this minor prior record. In turn, the probation sentence may increase punishments at a later time in the criminal justice system, a process called cumulative disadvantage. The solution, according to some reformers, is to remove police officers from schools and let school administrators handle misbehavior by students, unless it clearly involves a crime.

A second area of disproportionate minority contact involves differences in the rates at which the police stop motorists (driving while Black) and citizens on the street and choosing to search some motorists and citizens while not searching others. To be clear, with more than 18,000 police agencies there is tremendous variation in the rates at which different agencies stop and search. In other words, some agencies engage in numerous stops and searchers, others relatively few. Studies tend to find differences based on citizen sex and race. For example, a recent study of data from more than 55 million traffic stops found that Hispanic men and Black men had the highest rates of motor vehicle searches in the 16 states studied (Baumgartner et al. 2017).

Restorative Justice

Restorative justice is a philosophy that advocates for less punishment of offenders and instead, a process during which the offender, victim, and community meet to discuss the harm caused by the crime and an acceptable response. Restorative justice shifts some control over the response to the crime to the victim and community, which empowers them. It also forces the offender to admit their wrongdoing and accept the harm they have caused. Finally, under ideal circumstances, the victim, community, and offender meet and decide on a suitable way to resolve the harm caused by the crime. Instead of focusing on punishment and the state's response to crime, restorative justice allows for a tailored and individual response to crime and justice.

Victims

Although the police are often referred to as the gatekeepers of criminal justice (because they decide about arrest), decisions made by victims are hugely important across the entire system. In some ways, victims are the true gatekeepers of criminal justice. For example, research consistently finds that victims report their victimization to criminal justice authorities only 40 percent of the time. Even after a crime is reported, victims continue to influence the process. When the police respond to the scene of a crime, research shows that officers are more likely to arrest a suspect if the victim asks for an arrest. Conversely, police are less likely to arrest when the victims ask for leniency from the police. If an arrest is made, victims still influence the process. For example, victims may help the police and prosecution by cooperating with the investigation, appearing for hearings and trial, and sometimes by prodding police and prosecutors to persist in the investigation or prosecution. On the other hand, victims may choose to slow or even halt the process, by not talking with investigators or prosecutors, asking to drop charges, or disappearing (that is, moving and not providing forwarding information). It is difficult to prosecute a case when the witness no longer wishes to cooperate with the prosecution.

After an investigation, victims may also influence the process by being visible in the media (for example, by sitting in court during the trial and appearing on TV) and by providing victim impact statements in court during sentencing. And victims may continue to exert pressure during parole hearings (when offenders are eligible for release from prison). In some states, legislation requires that victims be notified whenever their offender is eligible for parole or has been released from prison. Compliance with victim notification laws, that is, ensuring that prosecutors or correctional authorities notify victims, can be difficult. In some instances the crime occurred decades prior to the offender's parole hearing or release, and authorities can no longer locate the victim.

CONCLUSION

As evidenced above, the criminal justice system is a rather complex mix of philosophies and policies. These philosophies and policies cannot exist, however, without individuals whose job it is to keep the criminal justice system operational.

Individuals create policies based on their own philosophy of how they feel the criminal justice system should operate. The individuals who shape these policies represent a broad spectrum of society—legislators, judges, prosecutors, police, victims—who have different ideas as to how to deal with the crime problem. What is evident is that no philosophy or policy is perfect for every individual, so the system must continually try to improve itself by creating and enacting more policy—a cycle that never ends.

Critical Thinking Exercise

This chapter has outlined four very large historical trends in criminal justice. What trends do you think we will see over the next 20 to 30 years? How will the system react to these larger social trends, and how will justice be affected?

KEY WORDS

Classical school
confidentiality
courtroom workgroup
crime-control model
crime rate
dark figure of crime
deterrence
deviance
discretion

due-process model
felony
general deterrence
incapacitation
informal social control
just desserts
mala in se
mala prohibita
misdemeanor

official statistics
Positivist school
rehabilitation
retribution
self-report statistics
specific deterrence
victimization studies
victimless crime

SUGGESTED READINGS

Bittner, E. (1970). *The functions of the police in modern society: A review of background factors, current practices, and possible role models.* Bethesda, MD: Center for Studies of Crime and Delinquency, National Institute of Mental Health.

Gottfredson, M., and D. Gottfredson. (1988). *Decision-making in criminal justice: Toward the rational exercise of discretion.* New York: Plenum Press.

Holtfreter, K., and K. A. Wattanaporn. (2013). An examination of gender responsiveness for female offender reentry. *Criminal Justice and Behavior,* 41(1), 41–57.

Johnson, H., and N. Wolfe. (1996). *History of criminal justice,* 2nd ed. Cincinnati, OH: Anderson Publishing.

Klockars, C. (1985). *The idea of the police.* Beverly Hills, CA: Sage.

Morgan, Rachel E., and Grace Kena. 2018. *Criminal victimization, 2016: Revised.* Washington, DC: US Department of Justice, Office of Justice Programs, Bureau of Justice Statistics.

Pew Center on the States. (2011). *State of recidivism: The revolving door of America's prisons.* Washington, DC: The Pew Charitable Trusts.

Walker, S. (1998). *Popular justice: A history of American criminal justice,* 2nd ed. New York: Oxford University Press.

CHAPTER 2

Issues of Law

CHAPTER OUTLINE

After reading this chapter, you should be able to:

- Discuss the historical bases of law in the United States
- List and discuss the sources of law in the United States
- Point out the differences between constitutional, legislative, executive, and judicial sources of law
- Define substantive law and provide two examples
- Distinguish between mala in se and mala prohibita
- List and define different types/categories of crimes
- Identify two defenses to criminal liability
- Discuss how the internet has affected substantive law
- Point out how terrorism has affected criminal law
- Define procedural law
- List and discuss the amendments to the US Constitution that outline criminal procedural rights
- Tell what incorporation means
- Discuss how the internet and national security have affected procedural law

---

INTRODUCTION

Laws are sets of rules that govern the conduct of individuals, groups, businesses, government entities, and the like. Laws are created and enforced by the power of the state—that is, local, state, and federal government bodies. The US Constitution gives the responsibility of law creation to the federal legislature, the US Congress. The Constitution also allows the federal court system to "interpret" the laws created by the federal legislature. In doing so, the federal courts work to ensure that the laws that are created are fair and applied equally to all citizens.

The various state constitutions also give the responsibility of law creation to their respective state legislatures. Just like the federal system, states allow their court systems to interpret the laws in much the same way as the federal courts. Within states, legislative bodies such as county commissions and city councils create laws that apply to their geographic areas.

As stated above, the federal and state legislatures create laws that govern the behavior of a variety of entities. Individuals are subject to laws that prohibit certain types of conduct, such as killing a person or burning down a house. Groups of individuals who assemble are required by law to do so peacefully and not to incite riots. The conduct of businesses is regulated so that these businesses do not engage in fraudulent practices or environmental harm. Government entities are required to follow the law as well, in that they cannot engage in discriminatory practices when they enforce the law. In addition to these prohibitions, the law ensures that violators will be punished. These are just a few examples of the law in effect, but the main point is that the law applies to everyone, even those government bodies that are responsible for its creation. This is known as the "rule of law" and is traced back to the early origins of American law (see Rembar 1989).

HISTORY OF LAW IN THE UNITED STATES

American law is rooted in European, particularly English, law. Historically, English law was largely unwritten and parochial, in that communities relied on local customs and norms to guide conduct. These customs were transmitted from generation to generation and were altered occasionally if necessary. After the Norman Conquest in the 11th century, William the Conqueror instituted a practice of collecting these customs and norms and recording them so that they could be applied to the country as a whole. This practice of transforming unwritten local customs into written codes of behavior for the entire country established the English tradition of **common law**, or law that was common to all throughout the country. Local judges were responsible for applying the common law, and their decisions were recorded to help guide future judges when making their decisions. This is known as **precedent**, and this practice continues to exist today.

Over time, local English judges refined and recorded many laws, many of which were criminal laws. By the 17th century, these judges had created the crimes of murder, robbery, arson, and rape, among others. Judges also created less serious crimes such as libel, perjury, and disturbing the peace (see generally Blackstone 2002).

The criminal law that exists today is taken from the English tradition of common law. The United States was founded by British colonists who brought their legal tradition to American shores. After declaring independence from England in 1776, the new states incorporated the English common law and adopted many of the criminal laws that had been defined. The newly created federal government chose not to incorporate English common law; instead, Congress established its own laws, including criminal laws, that were similar in content to common law, but not directly taken from it. An exception to the incorporation of common law is Louisiana, which bases its law on the Napoleonic Code, a uniform system of laws adopted by Napoleon from ancient Roman law.

SOURCES OF LAW IN THE UNITED STATES

Although English common law is the root of most of the law in the United States, various government bodies are responsible for shaping, applying, and interpreting the law. As stated earlier, the responsibility for law creation lies with legislatures, which create **statutory law**. Other government entities, however, are also involved in the creation of the law. The most important entities, state and federal constitutions, are the highest sources of law in the country. Other entities represent all branches of government—legislative, executive, and judicial.

Constitutions

Constitutions are considered the highest sources of law in this country. All other laws that are created must abide by constitutions. Each state and the federal government have their own constitutions, which outline the structure of the governments and how they will operate. These constitutions designate government power, indicating what the government can and cannot do. This is called **constitutional law**. For instance, California's constitution specifies that tax money cannot be used to support religious schools (see Constitution of California, Article 9, Section 8), and the federal constitution specifies that the federal government cannot abridge an individual's freedom of speech (see US Constitution, Amendment 1). State constitutions are the highest form of law in each state, but the US Constitution is the highest form of law in the country; that is, all laws (state and federal) and state constitutions must abide by the US Constitution. Any law or constitution that conflicts with the US Constitution is not allowed to stand.

Web Activity

For links to and interesting facts about the US Constitution, go to https://www. archives.gov/founding-docs

---

Legislative

Aside from the actual legislature, the legislative branch creates government bodies that carry out some lawmaking responsibilities. These bodies are typically referred to as agencies, bureaus, and so forth. These administrative agencies include federal bodies such as the Federal Communications Commission and the Food and Drug Administration (FDA), as well as state bodies such as the Ohio Public Defender Commission. Administrative agencies have the responsibility of enforcing **administrative law**. These agencies create rules and policies that govern their responsibilities. For example, the FDA establishes guidelines for allowing medicines to be available to consumers either by prescription or over the counter. The Ohio Public Defender Commission establishes guidelines for its public defenders to follow when representing poor defendants. Although created by the legislature, these agencies typically fall under the executive branch due to their regulatory and enforcement activities.

Web Activity

See www.fda.gov and www.fcc.gov for more information about the Food and Drug Administration and the Federal Communications Commission, respectively. Also, see https://opd.ohio.gov/wps/portal/gov/opd/home/ for more information about the Ohio Public Defender Commission.

Executive

The executive branch also has some law-creation responsibility. The executive branch is composed of individuals such as mayors, governors, and the president. These individuals have limited lawmaking ability, and the laws that are created are usually quite narrow and issue specific; however, they are important, nonetheless. For example, a mayor may impose a curfew in a particular city, or the president may impose regulations on driving cars through national forests. In recent years, the use of executive orders by President Trump is seen as a "sharp departure" from previous presidents. These orders feature broad policy proclamations, especially on issues on which the President and Congress disagree, such as immigration and environmental policy (see Waslin 2020: 54).

Web Activity

For more information about a particular lawmaking ability of the president—the executive order—go to www.archives.gov/federal-register/executive-orders/disposition.html.

Judicial

The judicial branch of government, embodied by the various state and federal courts, engages in law creation. During the early period of common law in England, local judges were primarily responsible for creating and disseminating laws throughout the country. Today, however, judges have been stripped of most of their lawmaking authority. Whenever a judge makes a decision in a particular case, he or she is engaging in law creation. This type of law, called **case law**, is usually based on laws that were created by some other body. For instance, in the early 1960s, the state of Florida did not allow a poor defendant to have an attorney provided to him or her. In 1963, the US Supreme Court ruled that Florida and other states must provide poor defendants with an attorney in certain criminal cases (*Gideon v. Wainwright* [1963]). Recently, the US Supreme Court ruled that LGBTQ employees cannot be discriminated against in the workplace due to their sex, based on the Civil Rights Act of 1964 (see *Bostock v. Clayton County, Georgia*, 2020). As a result, the US Supreme Court engaged in law creation by forcing the states to adopt its mandate.

Web Activity

For more information about the US Supreme Court, go to www.supremecourt.gov.

SUBSTANTIVE LAW

Regardless of which government body creates the law, the law is either substantive or procedural in nature. **Substantive law** is often called the "what" of the law, in effect, the law that defines rights and duties. Substantive law is distinguished from **procedural law**, which describes the procedures that must be followed when carrying out the law. An example of substantive law is law that defines first-degree murder as the deliberate, premeditated killing of another. An example of procedural law is law that states that poor defendants must be given an attorney if charged with certain crimes. Procedural law will be discussed later in this chapter.

Two primary examples of substantive law are civil law and criminal law. Civil law deals with issues pertaining to private matters between two individuals. Civil law encompasses torts (e.g., wrongful injury), contracts and property issues, and domestic relations. Civil law allows individuals who feel wronged by another to take their cases to court for a remedy. For example, if person A is involved in an automobile accident with person B, who is uninsured, person A may sue person B in civil court for the money needed to replace the disabled car. Civil law also governs issues such as divorces, child custody, inheritance, wills, and the like.

Criminal law is another primary example of substantive law. Criminal law concerns issues between the government and individuals who are accused of violating government-created laws. Unlike civil law, in which an individual is responsible for finding a remedy to his or her problem, criminal law involves the government prosecuting an individual if that individual has committed a crime.

Substantive criminal law is defined by government bodies, and it specifies what individuals can and cannot do and the punishments for wrongdoing. This is called the **principle of legality**; in effect, the government cannot punish individuals for wrongdoing unless a law exists to define the conduct as a crime and to prescribe a punishment for it. Traditionally, individual conduct has been defined as **mala in se**, or inherently bad, and **mala prohibita**, or prohibited but not necessarily bad. Governments have considered acts such as murder and rape as mala in se and acts such as gambling and speeding as mala prohibita. As a result, behaviors that are considered inherently bad are typically punished more severely than others.

Critical Thinking Exercise

Develop a list of mala prohibita laws and discuss each one. Should they be pro-hibited? Why? What impact does enforcement of such laws have on the criminal justice system? What value do these laws have for society in general? What nega-tive effect might these laws have on society?

When governments specify which behaviors to deem criminal, the crimes must have two elements: act and intent. The act, called **actus reus**, is the most important element of criminal liability; it represents the physical action involved in conduct. The act must be voluntary, in that it is not the result of coercion or some condition that affects voluntary movement (such as a seizure). For example, for the crime of larceny, the act would be the taking of another's property.

Although a voluntary act is needed to establish actus reus, there are in-stances in which a failure to act constitutes actus reus. In these cases, an act of omission can result in criminal liability. The act of omission comes into play when individuals are required by law to act but fail to do so. For example, life-guards are required by law to aid drowning individuals; failure to do so can result in criminal liability. The same is true of physicians, who are legally bound to tend to patients in their care.

Critical Thinking Exercise

Some states have proposed legislation called Good Samaritan Laws, which impose criminal liability on individuals who witness crimes but do nothing to stop them. This would create a type of act of omission. For instance, while person X is walking down the street, he sees a mugger attack a woman and steal her purse. If he continues on his way without acting, he would be breaking the law. What are the advantages and disadvantages of having such laws in place? What would be the difficulties in enforcing such laws? Do you feel they are a good idea?

In addition to an act, a crime must also have intent, called **mens rea**. In effect, an individual must intend to commit the act in question; that is, the indi-vidual must have a blameworthy state of mind. Establishing intent is rather dif-ficult; in fact, intent is usually inferred from the act. For example, if an individual grabs someone's purse and runs away, we can infer that the individual intended to commit theft. This may seem obvious, but the issue of intent is most impor-tant when an individual's *degree* of liability is in question. Take the following example: Person A points a gun at person B in an attempt to scare person B. The gun accidentally discharges, killing person B. Person A can be held liable for the death of person B, even though person A did not intend to kill person B. In effect, even though person A will be held liable for murder, he would not be held liable for the more serious crime of first-degree murder, since he did not intend to commit murder in the first place.

As with actus reus, there are instances when intent need not be present in order for an individual to be held liable for a crime. This is called **strict liability**, in which liability is imposed without intent. Strict liability applies to behaviors that are typically considered mala prohibita (not inherently bad), such as serving alcohol to minors and committing traffic offenses. In these instances, it makes no difference whether an individual intended to engage in the act or not; he or she can still be held liable. A common example of a strict liability crime is statutory rape; if an individual engages in intercourse with a person who is below the age of consent, that individual will be held liable for his or her behavior, even if he or she had no intent to engage in intercourse with a minor. Historically, statutory rape laws were created to punish males who had intercourse with young girls, as this devalued the girls before their eventual marriage. Even after girls were no longer considered the property of their fathers, statutory rape laws stayed on the books, punishing males for having intercourse with underage girls. With the rise of the #MeToo movement, a number of states have removed this distinction, paving the way for males *and* females to be charged with the statutory rape of a minor (see Tenzer 2019).

Along with the actus reus and mens rea, **causation** must also be present. In other words, an individual's conduct causes a particular result; for example, a person causes death in a homicide case. Causation can take a number of forms. The first and most obvious is called a **direct cause**, or **"cause in fact."** Also called "but for" causation, a direct cause occurs when an individual's behavior is the direct cause of harm; essentially, but for an individual's behavior, harm would not have occurred. An example of a direct cause would be an offender shooting a gun at a victim and the victim dies immediately of the gunshot wound. A second form of cause is **concurrent cause**. In this instance, two independent causes happen at the same time and either cause could have resulted in harm. For example, if two individuals shoot a victim simultaneously, either of these wounds could result in harm. Third, harm can result from a **proximate cause**. In proximate cause, something other than the individual's behavior caused the harm, but the individual began the series of events that led to the harm. For example, if an individual shoots a victim in the foot, but an incompetent surgeon operates on the victim and the victim dies, an individual can still be held responsible for the victim's death, even though the individual is not the direct cause of harm. Related to direct cause, this type of cause is called the "but for" cause—an individual causes a chain of events that, but for the individual's behavior, harm would not have resulted.

As mentioned in causation, the concept of **harm** must be present for criminal responsibility. Engaging in an *act* must *cause* some sort of *harm* to a protected person, place, or thing. The criminal law exists to protect people from harm (in the form of murder or robbery), to protect property (in the form of burglary or arson), or thing (in the form of larceny or shoplifting). Despite this, harm can be absent in some crimes, such as drug use, in which no other person, place, or thing is actually being harmed (beyond just the individual engaging in the behavior).

TYPES OF CRIMES

Throughout this chapter, specific crimes have been used as examples to illustrate various concepts in criminal law. The following discussion expands this, describing the various categories of crimes that exist in criminal law. This discussion will not, however, provide a detailed discussion of all of the crimes on the books; it merely provides an overview and uses a couple of states as examples.

Web Activity

For more information about your own state's laws and the laws of the federal government, go to www.law.cornell.edu/lii/get_the_law.

Crimes Against the Person

Personal crimes are generally considered the most serious crimes and are treated as such by the criminal justice system. Homicide, rape, assault, and kidnapping are crimes that come to mind when discussing personal crimes. Although these crimes may seem fairly straightforward, they are not so easily categorized. Each crime carries with it differing degrees of liability. For instance, killing another person could carry a sentence anywhere from probation to the death penalty; the circumstances surrounding the killing determine how an individual is to be handled by the system. The crime of homicide will be used as an example.

As seen in Box 2.1, there are varying degrees of liability when it comes to the killing of another. The same is true for other personal crimes as well, but time and space do not permit an examination of them all. Each state defines its crimes and establishes punishments for their violation; these statutes are available for public consumption either at the local library or on the internet.

BOX 2.1

Degrees of Liability for the Crime of Homicide

Homicide laws vary from state to state, but each state allows for differing degrees of homicide to account for attendant circumstances. The most serious form of homicide is typically called first-degree murder or aggravated murder, depending on the state. This typically involves the deliberate, planned killing of another person. In Ohio, aggravated murder has a number of definitions, one of which is the following: "No person shall purposely, with prior calculation and design, cause the death of another" (Ohio Revised Code, §2903.01 (A), 2020). In California, first-degree murder also has a number of definitions, one of which is "the unlawful killing of a human being . . . with malice aforethought" (California Penal Code, §187 (a), 2020). In these examples, the actus reus is causing the death of or unlawful killing of another person, while the means rea is found in the prior calculation and design and malice aforethought elements. In these states, aggravated or first-degree murder carries the possibility of a death sentence, although a death sentence is not mandatory. Other punishments for this crime include life imprisonment without the possibility of parole or life imprisonment with the possibility of parole after a certain number of years.

A less serious form of homicide is called second-degree murder. This form of homicide is not as easily definable as first-degree murder. In second-degree murder, an individual typically has no specific intent to kill another, but engages in extremely harmful conduct that runs the risk of the victim being killed. For example, an individual can be charged with second-degree murder if, during the course of a severe beating, the victim dies. The intent was not to kill the victim; however, the individual engaging in the beating should have known that death was possible, but chose not to stop his or her conduct. In Ohio, second-degree murder is defined as "purposely causing the death of another" and carries a punishment of a minimum of 15 years in prison up to life (Ohio Revised Code, §2903.02 (A), §2929.02 (B), 2020). In California, second-degree murder is largely defined by what it is not; in effect, various types of first-degree murder are defined, while second-degree murder is defined as all other kinds of murders that are not listed in the first-degree murder category. This crime is punished by a minimum of 20 to 25 years in prison up to life (California Penal Code, §189, §190, 2020).

Other less serious forms of homicide include voluntary manslaughter and involuntary manslaughter. Voluntary manslaughter is homicide that is provoked or is committed in the heat of passion. Ohio defines voluntary manslaughter as being committed "under the influence of a sudden passion or in a sudden fit of rage" and sets the punishment as up to 10 years in prison (Ohio Revised Code, §2903.03, §2929.14, 2020). In California, voluntary manslaughter is defined as "unlawful killing . . . upon a sudden quarrel or heat of passion" and is punishable by up to 11 years in prison (California Penal Code, §192, §193, 2020).

Involuntary manslaughter is the unintentional killing of another that involves reckless behavior on the part of the perpetrator. Ohio defines involuntary manslaughter as "causing the death of another as a result of the commission of certain lower-level felonies or misdemeanors" and punishes the act with up to 10 years in prison (Ohio Revised Code, §2903.03, §2929.14, 2020). California specifies that involuntary manslaughter occurs during the commission of a lawful or unlawful act "without due caution and circumspection" and punishes the act with up to 4 years in prison (California Penal Code, §192, §193, 2020).

Crimes Against Property

Property crimes are not treated as severely by the criminal justice system as personal crimes, but they are considered serious nonetheless. Typical property crimes include larceny and theft, burglary, arson, embezzlement, and trespass. One type of property crime, robbery, is also considered a personal crime, since force or the threat of force is used to steal an individual's belongings. Property crimes typically do not involve harm to individuals, and thus the punishments are less severe. For example, an individual cannot receive the death penalty for engaging in a property crime.

Like personal crimes, individual property crimes have varying degrees of liability. An example of this is seen with the crime of burglary. In Ohio, burglary involves trespass into an occupied structure with the intent to commit a crime. If an offender is carrying a gun or inflicts physical harm on a person within the structure, he or she is committing "aggravated burglary." If the structure is not occupied, he or she is engaged in "breaking and entering." Aggravated burglary is the most serious charge of the three, resulting in a punishment of up to 10 years in prison. Breaking and entering is the least serious charge, resulting in a punishment of up to one year in jail. Although intent is present, the degree of liability differs depending on specific circumstances (see generally Ohio Revised Code, §2911.12, §2911.13, 2020).

Crimes Against Public Order

Public order crimes are categories of offenses that do not necessarily harm other persons or property. These offenses are largely victimless crimes, where there is no readily identifiable victim. Public order crimes are seen as harming society as a whole, and the criminalization of such conduct aims to maintain social order. In comparison to personal and property crimes, public order crimes are committed by far more people, although they are not punished as severely. Examples of public order offenses are driving under the influence of alcohol, disorderly conduct, vagrancy, and loitering.

Related to public order offenses are public morals offenses. These offenses are those that offend the morality of certain groups in society. Many public morals offenses involve sexual behavior—behavior that is not necessarily bad but is considered immoral and deviant by some. Prostitution is perhaps the most common example of a morals offense.

Drug Offenses

Laws that criminalize the use of drugs and alcohol could probably be categorized as public order offenses, but they deserve a section of their own. The reason is that the government's reaction to illegal drug use has dramatically altered how the criminal justice system deals with these offenses. The "war on drugs" has led to an increased focus on drug offenses, sometimes to the exclusion of other offenses.

Numerous criminal behaviors are associated with the use of drugs. Possession of illegal drugs, such as marijuana and cocaine, and possession of paraphernalia, such as needles, constitute perhaps the largest number of drug offenses, but laws are in place that focus on all levels of the illegal drug trade, such as trafficking, manufacturing, and selling. Punishment for drug offenses depends on a variety of factors. These include the type of drug being used, the amount of drugs involved, and where a drug transaction takes place (for instance, near a school). Because of increased attention to drug offenses by both state and federal governments, the punishments for drug offenses have increased, ranging from probation to the death penalty. In recent years, a number of states have enacted legalization or decriminalization statutes with regard to marijuana; however, the federal government has not followed the states' lead on this matter (see Rosen 2019).

White-Collar Offenses

A final category of offenses concerns those that are committed by individuals during the course of their jobs. The term *white collar* refers to the idea that individuals from a higher socioeconomic status are more likely to commit these types of crimes. It should be noted, however, that individuals of a lower socioeconomic status are capable of and do commit white-collar offenses.

The better-known white-collar offenses are committed by individuals who use their job positions as a mechanism to engage in illegal behavior. Lower-level offenses such as employee theft do not receive as much attention as other white-collar offenses, although these lower-level offenses are perhaps more frequent. Tax evasion, price fixing, and insider trading are better known and more widely publicized. See Box 2.2 for an illustration of white collar crime and the Wells Fargo account fraud case.

BOX 2.2

White Collar Crime and the Wells Fargo Account Fraud Case

Between 2002 and 2016, employees of Wells Fargo bank opened accounts for customers without their knowledge and signed up customers for credit cards they did not request. Additionally, these employees forged signatures and transferred customers' money. All told, employees opened over one million checking and savings accounts and more than 500,000 credit cards without customers' authorization. The employees engaged in this behavior to meet staggering sales goals of the bank; the employees received bonuses for opening new credit cards and checking accounts and enrolling customers in products such as online banking, resulting in customers losing money and suffering a blow to their credit ratings. After an investigation, this fraudulent activity led Wells Fargo bank agreed to pay $3 billion to settle criminal charges and civil actions connected to this activity (see Flitter 2020).

Web Activity

For other white collar crime examples, see money.cnn.com/news/specials/enron for more information about the Enron scandal, http://www.economist.com/node/12818310 for more information about the Bernie Madoff scandal, and https://www.thoughtco.com/martha-stewarts-insider-trading-case-1146196 for more information about the Martha Stewart case.

Many other crimes are defined in state and federal statutes, but they are simply too numerous to mention here. All states and the federal government publish their statutes or place them online for public access. The next section deals with an issue that has already been addressed—liability—and instances in which individuals are not held liable for engaging in criminal behavior.

DEFENSES TO CRIMINAL LIABILITY

Throughout this chapter, the issue of liability has arisen to describe when an individual is held accountable for illegal behavior. The notion of criminal liability rests on the assumption that an individual knowingly commits a crime and has the intention of doing so. There are some situations, however, in which an individual is not held responsible for a criminal act and is not punished for wrongdoing. These situations constitute defenses to criminal liability.

Justification

In some situations, a crime is justified based on an individual's belief that what he or she did was the right thing to do. Perhaps the best-known **justification** is self-defense. Self-defense is used to deter an unwanted attack—force is used if an individual *reasonably* believes it is *necessary* for *protection* against an *impending* attack. The italicized words indicate what must be proven by an individual who claims self-defense. *Reasonable* means that an ordinary person would believe that force is to be used. *Necessary* indicates that force is needed to defend oneself. *Protection* suggests that the only reason that force is to be used is to protect oneself from harm, not to inflict harm needlessly on another person. *Impending* implies that an attack must be imminent and immediate, that there is no time to escape. The amount of force used must also be reasonable; for example, an individual cannot use **deadly force** if an offender merely steals a purse. Individuals who claim self-defense must prove that an ordinary, reasonable person would have acted in the same way if attacked. In some states, individuals have a "duty to retreat" if they can reasonably do so. In these situations, if individuals do not retreat when it is reasonable to do so, they cannot use self-defense as a justification. Additionally, the defense of one's home is a prime concern for most citizens. Under the "castle doctrine," individuals have no duty to retreat if an intruder enters their home and may use self-defense to protect themselves. For example, in North Carolina, an individual can claim self-defense if a person "unlawfully and forcibly" enters the home because it is presumed that the person intends to engage in violent behavior; thus, an individual is presumed to have a reasonable fear of harm.

Critical Thinking Exercise

Some state laws allow for individuals to "stand their ground" in public places if they feel threatened. These laws remove the "duty to retreat" requirement and enable individuals to use self-defense if they reasonably believe it is necessary to defend themselves against a threat of death or serious bodily harm, as long as they are in a place lawfully. This issue emerged during the Trayvon Martin case in 2012, in which Martin was shot by George Zimmerman during a nighttime altercation. Do you feel that "stand your ground" laws should exist? Why or why not? What are some problems that could occur when enforcing these laws? Before you consider these questions, see https://en.wikipedia.org/wiki/Shooting_of_Trayvon_Martin for more information about the case.

Excuses

Sometimes, individuals are not held criminally liable because they have a legal excuse. Insanity is an example of an excuse that is recognized in the criminal law (discussed later). Other examples include intoxication, age, and duress.

Intoxication can be an excuse from criminal liability in some circumstances. **Involuntary intoxication** is a defense in all criminal offenses due to the nature of the intoxication. Generally, the law recognizes three ways to become involuntarily intoxicated. First, an individual may not know that he or she had ingested the drug. Second, an individual may be forced to consume a drug under duress. Finally, the intoxicating substance that was ingested by an individual may have unforeseeable side effects. On the other hand, **voluntary intoxication** is rarely an excuse to criminal liability. Even if it is, it is usually not a complete defense; in other words, it can be used to mitigate an individual's behavior and perhaps get charges reduced. Despite this, some states have abolished the intoxication defense completely.

Another possible excuse from criminal liability is **age**. It has been argued that younger individuals (typically under the age of 14) are not capable of forming intent and, therefore, cannot appreciate the gravity of their actions. After the age of 14, however, youths are assumed to possess criminal intent. States have the option of handling a youthful offender in adult court if the prosecution can prove that the youth has the capacity to form intent. Otherwise, youths will be adjudicated in the juvenile justice system.

Duress is another excuse from criminal liability. In this situation, a person must be under threat of death or serious bodily injury that causes the individual to commit a crime. Additionally, it must be shown that a reasonable person would believe that committing the crime is the only course of action and that the individual was not responsible for the situation. Some legal theorists, however, posit that duress should not be fully recognized, as they believe that individuals should resist to the utmost when confronted with this situation. Without proof of such resistance, these theorists posit, an individual should not use duress as an excuse.

Mental Capacity

Although considered an excuse in criminal law, mental capacity deserves a section of its own. An individual can be relieved of criminal liability if his or her **mental capacity** is such that it renders the individual incapable of understanding the wrongness of his or her actions. Insanity is a common example. The term *insanity* is a legal one; it is not a medical diagnosis like schizophrenia or bipolar disorder. The term is defined differently from state to state, so there is not one clear-cut rule that establishes whether someone was insane at the time of the offense.

The first legal definition of insanity was known as the **M'Naghten Rule**. M'Naghten was an English citizen suffering from delusions of persecution who felt it was necessary to assassinate Sir Robert Peel, the founder of the British police system and the home secretary at the time. M'Naghten did not kill Peel, but instead killed Peel's secretary, whom M'Naghten mistakenly believed was Peel. M'Naghten's lawyers claimed that he was insane at the time of the crime and should not be found guilty. As a result of this case, the M'Naghten Rule was established and has become known as the "right versus wrong" rule. Under this rule, individuals must prove that they were in such a state of mind that they could not know what they were doing or that they did not know that what they were doing was wrong (see *M'Naghten's Case* [1843]).

Most states and the federal government adopted the M'Naghten Rule, but other states felt that the rule should be expanded to account for issues involving self-control. The substantial capacity test was proposed in 1962, and it states that an individual

> is not responsible for criminal conduct if at the time of such conduct, as a result of a mental disease or defect, a person lacks substantial capacity either to appreciate the wrongfulness of his conduct or to conform his conduct to the requirements of the law. (American Law Institute 1962)

It was thought that the M'Naghten Rule was too strict, and this test provided more leeway for individuals who knew right from wrong, but could not control their behavior. Today, some states and the federal government adhere to the M'Naghten Rule in some form, while other states apply the substantial capacity test (for more information about the insanity defense, both its history and new developments, see Reider 1998).

Web Activity

See www.pbs.org/wgbh/pages/frontline/shows/crime/trial/history.html for a timeline of the insanity defense as well as changes to the insanity defense after the trial of John Hinckley, who was found not guilty by reason of insanity for the shooting of President Ronald Reagan in 1981.

Web Activity

For a list of insanity defenses used in the states, see the textbook website (www.oup.com/he/lab6e).

VICTIM'S RIGHTS

An often overlooked component of the criminal justice system, victims are critically important in criminal law. Historically, victims and/or their families would exact justice for any sort of harm; today, the state is responsible bringing offenders to justice. It has been argued that victims have been cast aside now that the state has assumed this responsibility; as a result, there have been a number of programs that have been created to assist victims with their cases in court as well as their recovery from the crime itself. A number of states have adopted constitutional amendments to protect the rights of victims; however, the federal government has yet to adopt such a provision in its constitution.

RECENT TRENDS IN SUBSTANTIVE CRIMINAL LAW

Criminal law is always changing; government bodies propose changes to the law on a regular basis, so that laws that are in place today may not be in effect next year. One of the reasons that the law changes regularly is that certain events in society result in public support for new legislation.

The Internet and Substantive Criminal Law

An ongoing problem for the criminal justice system is the use of the internet to engage in criminal behavior. Since the first webpage was launched in 1991, the internet has undergone a world of changes, making it difficult for any agency to monitor. Today, the internet is home to a host of criminal behaviors; some of the better-known violations are downloading files illegally, identity theft, posting child pornography, spreading viruses, and sponsoring terrorism. Early regulation of the internet was the primary responsibility of the federal government through the use of civil law. Many early issues dealt with copyright law and trademark protection. However, as the internet has evolved, so has its abuses, leading to a host of criminal laws to deal with this behavior. Laws against cyberstalking, unauthorized access, and theft of wireless devices did not exist 30 years ago. Computer technology is rapidly changing and efforts to keep up with emerging technology is ongoing and expensive. State and federal government agencies, as well as private companies, are responsible for detection and control of cybercrime. In the federal system, efforts to update legislation on computer crime are constantly being proposed to deal with the changing nature of computer crime. Recently, proposals have been made to extend the RICO (Racketeering Influenced and Corrupt Organization) statute, originally enacted to deal with organized crime, to computer-related crime. In a recent proposal, the Department of Justice noted that

> the fight against organized crime is far from over; rather, much of the focus has moved online. RICO has been used for over forty years to prosecute organized criminals ranging from mob bosses to Hells Angels to insider traders, and its

legality has been consistently upheld by the courts. Just as it has proven to be an effective tool to prosecute the leaders of these organizations who may not have been directly involved in committing the underlying crimes and to dismantle whole organizations, so too can it be an effective tool to fight criminal organizations who use online means to commit their crimes. The Administration's proposal would simply make clear that malicious activities directed at the confidentiality, integrity, and availability of computers should be considered criminal activities under the RICO statute. (Downing 2011: 4)

Another problem with the internet and crime is that there are no traditional boundaries and jurisdictions. Laws vary from state to state and from country to country, but the internet is worldwide, resulting in difficulty in determining which state or country has the jurisdiction to handle internet crime. Because of this, interstate and international task forces are being created to help jurisdictions work together to deal with these issues. For example, in 2009, the US Secret Service unveiled the European Electronic Crime Task Force, which involves working with European Union countries to monitor and investigate computer crime across Europe (Clark 2009).

Despite this, recent hacking incidents have illustrated the difficulty in pursuing the individuals involved. Individuals operating in foreign countries are able to hack into computer systems of international corporations and expose sensitive material. For example, hackers into Apple's iCloud storage site exposed nude photos of various celebrities. It is believed the hack occurred in China. Also, hackers into Sony Pictures' system revealed information about actors' salaries, movie scripts, and other information. It is believed that North Korea was behind the hack. Relatedly, investigations into the hacking of emails, servers, voting machines and the spread of false information during the November 2016 election has been ongoing. It is alleged that Russian operatives, in connection with candidate Donald Trump's campaign, were able to obtain information about the campaign strategy of the Democrat party and use this information to influence the election and elect Donald Trump.

Web Activity

For information about Russian influence in the 2016 election, see the 2020 report issued by the Senate Intelligence Committee at https://www.intelligence.senate. gov/sites/default/files/documents/Report_Volume2.pdf

---

Web Activity

For more information about other hacking incidents, see https://www.csoonline. com/article/2130877/the-biggest-data-breaches-of-the-21st-century.html

Terrorism, Homeland Security, and Substantive Criminal Law

After the attacks on September 11, 2001, many states and the federal government implemented laws to combat acts of terrorism. One such act was the Homeland Security Act of 2002, establishing the Department of Homeland Security as a cabinet post in the executive branch. The department's mission is to "prevent terrorist attacks within the United States; reduce the vulnerability of the United States to terrorism; and minimize the damage, and assist in the recovery, from terrorist attacks that do occur within the United States" (see http://www.dhs. gov/xabout/laws/law_regulation_rule_0011.shtm). The department sponsors legislation that "combats terrorism and enhances security" (see http://www.dhs. gov/xabout/ourmission.shtm). Examples of recent legislation include regulations that allow the department to monitor and regulate high-risk chemical facilities (Department of Homeland Security Appropriations Act of 2010) and enhancing port security (Coast Guard Authorization Act of 2010).

States also implemented homeland security and/or emergency response departments similar to the federal Department of Homeland Security. These agencies are responsible for implementing laws passed by the state legislatures for combating domestic terrorism. The U.S.A. Patriot Act defines domestic terrorism as "activities that involve acts dangerous to human life that are a violation of the criminal laws of the United States or of any state; appear to be intended to intimidate or coerce a civilian population; to influence the policy of a government by mass destruction, assassination, or kidnapping; and occur primarily within the territorial jurisdiction of the United States" (see Section 802, https://www. congress.gov/107/plaws/publ56/PLAW-107publ56.pdf). Critics of this definition claim it is too broad and could net those who engage in ordinary street crime. In fact, a number of states have used their terrorism legislation to cover gang activity or any other activity that could fall within the wording of the statute.

Other events have highlighted breaches in security regarding sensitive data. For example, WikiLeaks is an online organization devoted to publishing news leaks and classified information. It has been implicated in the release of US State Department information about detainees at the Guantanamo Bay Naval Base after September 11, 2001. Julian Assange, the founder of WikiLeaks, is being investigated by the United States as possibly violating numerous federal laws, including the Espionage Act of 1917. Also, Edward Snowden, a former contractor for the National Security Agency, leaked classified information about global surveillance systems, endangering intelligence operations. Snowden escaped US custody and sought asylum in a number of countries; currently, he resides in Russia. The US government has filed charges against Snowden, including theft of government property and violation of the Espionage Act of 1917.

Web Activity

For more information about WikiLeaks, see http://www.huffingtonpost.com/news/wikileaks/.

Web Activity

For more information about Edward Snowden, see http://www.theguardian.com/us-news/edward-snowden.

COVID-19 and Substantive Criminal Law

The COVID-19 pandemic has uprooted the day-to-day lives of many around the world, resulting in job losses, school closings, business failures, and other issues. As a result, the federal, state, and local governments in the United States are passing legislation to combat the struggles faced by millions. In March 2020, the US Congress passed the CARES Act (Coronavirus Aid, Relief, and Economic Security Act), a $2.2 trillion relief package which is the largest economic stimulus package in US history. The Act provided funding for unemployment benefits, small business loans, and state and local governments to address the fallout from COVID-19. In addition, President Trump and state governors have issued numerous executive orders that have attempted to stop the spread of the virus. Examples of these orders involve the operation of schools, enforcement of quarantines, and testing and reporting strategies for the virus.

Web Activity

Direct access to the CARES Act can be found at http://frwebgate.access.gpo.gov/cgi-bin/getdoc.cgi?dbname=107_cong_public_laws&docid=f:publ056.107.pdf.

PROCEDURAL LAW

Thus far, this chapter has provided a general overview of many of the aspects of substantive criminal law. The following section focuses on an equally important component of the law—procedural law. As stated earlier, procedural law describes the procedures that government bodies must follow when carrying out the law. Most of the procedural law in the United States is rooted in the US Constitution, which has articulated policies that federal, state, and local governments must follow.

The federal Constitution is essentially composed of two parts: the body of the Constitution, which outlines the structure and function of the federal government, and the amendments, which involve changes to the original document. The body of the Constitution is largely a blueprint for the federal government. It defines the three branches of government and specifies the role and responsibilities of each. When the Constitution was being drafted in 1787, the Framers were divided over whether the document should contain provisions that protected the rights of citizens from a newly created federal government. This division was the result of some of the Framers not trusting the new government, since they felt that a stronger federal government would infringe on the rights of citizens. These individuals likened the new federal government to England's government, from which the United States had recently achieved independence. Prior to the American Revolution, the English government had infringed on the rights of the American colonists, abridging their freedom of speech and press, not allowing representation in the English government, and engaging in the practice of entering homes without cause to search for seditious material. Those skeptical of the new federal government wanted to ensure that it would not be another England and pushed for the Constitution to include these protections (see Schwartz 1992). As such, the body of the Constitution contains four protections of individual rights: a prohibition against ex post facto laws, a prohibition against bills of attainder, the right to habeas corpus (all found in Article I, Section 9), and the right to a trial by jury (found in Article III, Section 2).

The **ex post facto** provision prohibits retroactive laws; in effect, a law that is passed tomorrow cannot be applied to behavior that one engages in today. The provision against **bills of attainder** is in place to prohibit the imposition of punishment without trial. The right to **habeas corpus** allows an individual to challenge illegal confinement by the government. Finally, the right to a **trial by jury** guarantees that individuals are judged by a jury of their peers instead of one or two individuals who may not be neutral. These rights were considered important enough to be placed in the body of the Constitution. Despite this, some of the Framers insisted that these provisions did not go far enough and demanded that more rights be included. These rights were created and passed as the Bill of Rights in 1791.

The Bill of Rights is composed of the first 10 amendments to the Constitution, which were passed *en masse* in 1791. Since then, the Constitution has been amended 17 times, bringing the total number of amendments to 27. The Bill of Rights was passed to allay the fears of those skeptical of the new federal government, and the provisions found in the Bill of Rights encompass a wide range of protections (Schwartz 1992). See Box 2.3 for a list of the Bill of Rights and what they cover. For procedural criminal law purposes, this chapter will focus on four of these amendments: the Fourth, Fifth, Sixth, and Eighth. There will also be a focus on the Fourteenth Amendment, passed in 1868, but this will appear later in the chapter.

BOX 2.3

The Bill of Rights and the Fourteenth Amendment

First Amendment: Congress shall make no law respecting an establishment of religion, or prohibiting the free exercise thereof; or abridging the freedom of speech, or of the press; or the right of the people peaceably to assemble, and to petition the government for a redress of grievances.

Second Amendment: A well-regulated militia, being necessary to the security of a free state, the right of the people to keep and bear arms, shall not be infringed.

Third Amendment: No soldier shall, in time of peace be quartered in any house, without the consent of the owner, nor in time of war, but in a manner to be prescribed by law.

Fourth Amendment: The right of the people to be secure in their persons, houses, papers, and effects, against unreasonable searches and seizures, shall not be violated, and no warrants shall issue, but upon probable cause, supported by oath or affirmation, and particularly describing the place to be searched, and the person or things to be seized.

Fifth Amendment: No person shall be held to answer for a capital, or otherwise infamous crime, unless on a presentment or indictment of a grand jury, except in cases arising in the land or naval forces, or in the militia, when in actual service in time of war or public danger; nor shall any person be subject for the same offense to be twice put in jeopardy of life or limb; nor shall be compelled in any criminal case to be a witness against himself; nor be deprived of life, liberty, or property, without due process of law; nor shall private property be taken for public use, without just compensation.

Sixth Amendment: In all criminal prosecutions, the accused shall enjoy the right to a speedy and public trial, by an impartial jury of the state and district wherein the crime shall have been committed, which district shall have been previously ascertained by law, and to be informed of the nature and cause of the accusation; to be confronted with the witnesses against him; to have compulsory process for obtaining witnesses in his favor, and to have the assistance of counsel for his defense.

Seventh Amendment: In suits at common law, where the value in controversy shall exceed twenty dollars, the right of trial by jury shall be preserved, and no fact tried by a jury, shall be otherwise reexamined in any court of the United States, than according to the rules of the common law.

Eighth Amendment: Excessive bail shall not be required, nor excessive fines imposed, nor cruel and unusual punishments inflicted.

Ninth Amendment: The enumeration in the Constitution, of certain rights, shall not be construed to deny or disparage others retained by the people.

Tenth Amendment: The powers not delegated to the United States by the Constitution, nor prohibited by it to the states, are reserved to the states respectively, or to the people.

Fourteenth Amendment (Section 1 only): All persons born or naturalized in the United States, and subject to the jurisdiction thereof, are citizens of the United States and of the state wherein they reside. No state shall make or enforce any law which shall abridge the privileges or immunities of citizens of the United States; nor shall any state deprive any person of life, liberty, or property, without due process of law; nor deny to any person within its jurisdiction the equal protection of the laws.

SOURCE: US Constitution (1789).

Web Activity

For links to and interesting facts about the US Constitution, go to https://www
.archives.gov/founding-docs.

The *Fourth Amendment* is in place to protect against unreasonable searches and seizures by government entities. In colonial times, the colonists were growing increasingly weary of an overreaching English government. Colonists began to speak out and criticize the English government's implementation of strict policies, such as expansive taxation, and the English government itself. In response, the English government considered this criticism seditious libel and authorized the use of general warrants to break into homes and businesses, not only to search for evidence of seditious libel, but also to search for individuals who were disobeying English law, such as those who refused to pay taxes. These warrants permitted government officials to ransack homes and businesses without just cause, and this was the reason for the creation of the Fourth Amendment (Zalman and Siegel 1997).

The Fourth Amendment protects individuals from unreasonable searches and seizures by the government, but not all searches. If government officials wish to search an individual's home, they must secure permission to do so from a judge. This comes in the form of a warrant. The information contained in the warrant contains the name and address of the individual or home to be searched, as well as a specific description of the person or items to be seized. This information must be justified by a standard known as **probable cause**. This standard is difficult to define, but the US Supreme Court, in *Brinegar v. United States* (1949), provided a definition: probable cause exists when "the facts and circumstances . . . [and] . . . reasonably trustworthy information [are] sufficient in themselves to warrant a man of reasonable caution in the belief that an offense has been or is being committed" (p. 176). In effect, more evidence must exist than not that an individual has committed a crime. Once government officials have provided this information, they must get a warrant approved by a judge before a search may take place.

At times, government officials engage in unreasonable searches and seizures. For whatever reason, a warrant may not be secured if probable cause does not exist. As a result, the US Supreme Court ruled in *Mapp v. Ohio* (1961) that searches and seizures that violate Fourth Amendment provisions are subject to the **exclusionary rule**; that is, illegally seized evidence is excluded from a prosecution. The exclusionary rule helps to ensure that government officials conduct their procedures in a legal manner and provides a penalty when they do not.

Since its inception, the Fourth Amendment has been the subject of numerous court cases that have attempted to modify it to account for changing times and circumstances. The Amendment's provisions now go beyond someone's home and office to include such things as vehicles, drug tests, telephones, and computers—none of which existed at the time of the creation of the Fourth Amendment. In addition, there are circumstances that do not require the use of a warrant or the standard of probable cause. It would take an entire textbook to delve into the various permutations of the Fourth Amendment; as a result, this chapter only hopes to provide a general overview. For more information about the Fourth Amendment, see Hemmens, Worrall, and Thompson (2004).

The *Fifth Amendment* features an amalgam of provisions that include a broad range of procedural rights. One of the most important provisions is the due-process clause, which forces government officials to abide by fair procedures when an individual is subject to the criminal justice process. The due-process provision encompasses all other procedural rights, as they are simply specific forms of due process.

Perhaps the best-known provision of the Fifth Amendment is the **self-incrimination** clause. This specifies that an individual cannot be compelled to confess involvement (or noninvolvement) in criminal activity. Historically, the English government, dating back to the 1200s, used torture and psychological coercion to elicit confessions from accused individuals, many of whom were innocent. As a result, the self-incrimination clause of the Fifth Amendment was created to prohibit government officials from compelling individuals to confess to something they did or did not do.

Another important provision of the Fifth Amendment is the protection against **double jeopardy**. The double-jeopardy clause prohibits the government from prosecuting someone again after that individual has been acquitted or convicted. In essence, the government does not get "two bites at the apple" if it is not happy with a particular verdict.

A fourth provision of the Fifth Amendment is the right to a **grand jury** proceeding. A grand jury consists of a number of ordinary citizens who review the charges against an individual and decide if the charges warrant a trial. The grand jury requirement was deemed important by the Framers of the Bill of Rights because they felt that a prosecutor, who is a government official, would have too much power in making charging decisions (Zalman and Siegel 1997).

The *Sixth Amendment* is often called the "trial rights amendment" because of its provisions regarding aspects of the trial process. The first provision is the right to a **speedy trial**, which benefits both the defense and the prosecution. A speedy trial helps the defense by minimizing the amount of time that an accused individual must endure until his or her case is resolved. This is especially true if the accused is jailed prior to trial. A speedy trial assists the prosecutor because it ensures quick justice, provided the accused is guilty.

Critical Thinking Exercise

The idea of a speedy trial often appears to be violated when one reads about a case finally going to trial months or years after the crime was committed and the offender was caught. Look up the speedy trial guidelines for your state. Based on that information, how long can a trial be put off? Do you believe this is reasonable or justified?

The right to a **public trial** ensures that trials are open to the public. English courts were notorious for secret proceedings, and the Framers of the Bill of Rights wanted the public to act as a watchdog over government proceedings to ensure that illegal procedures were not being used against the accused.

An accused individual also has the right to an **impartial trial**. This means that judges and juries are to be unbiased and neutral when making decisions about an accused individual's case. To ensure this, juries are selected through a fairly rigorous process that hopes to draw out any biases that individual jury members may have.

Relatedly, the right to a trial by jury is included within the Sixth Amendment's protections. Although specifically listed in Article III, Section 2 of the Constitution, the right to a trial by jury has been interpreted as a Sixth Amendment right as well, since a jury trial is inferred by the other trial rights listed within the Sixth Amendment. This right seeks to safeguard the right to a jury of one's peers in place of a government trial.

In keeping with the abhorred practices in England, colonists who allegedly committed crimes were taken to England for trial, which hurt the accused because many English citizens were biased against colonists. The Sixth Amendment provides that an accused individual has the right to be prosecuted in the state and county where he or she allegedly committed the crime. In addition, accused individuals have the *right to know what they are being charged with* (in order to establish a defense against those charges), the *right to know who their accusers are* (to ensure that these witnesses are not fabricating the charges), and the *right to call witnesses to testify on their behalf.* Early English practice did not allow accused individuals to know the charges, to question witnesses, or even to put on a defense.

The final provision in the Sixth Amendment is the **right to counsel**. Most accused individuals do not know the intricacies of the law and need skilled attorneys to assist them. In addition, attorneys are able to offset any questionable governmental actions that could possibly harm the accused, such as trying to elicit confessions. Attorneys are present to ensure that due process is followed. Initially, this provision was interpreted to mean that if individuals could afford attorneys they could use them, but the poor were denied representation. This has since changed, and individuals who cannot afford attorneys can be provided them at the government's expense.

The *Eighth Amendment* is considered the "punishment amendment" because two of its three provisions deal with criminal punishment. The first provision, the right against **excessive bail**, was created to restrain the government from detaining individuals before they were found guilty. During a bail decision, a judge is prohibited from imposing a bail amount that is too high in relation to the accused individual's crime, flight risk, or threat to the community. The right against excessive bail does not guarantee that the bail amount must be affordable to the accused individual, nor does it guarantee the right to bail in general.

The right against **excessive fines** was created to prevent the government from imposing financial penalties that did not accord with an individual's charge. The **cruel and unusual punishment** clause has a varied history, with lawmakers and judges still trying to decide what the clause actually protects. Some US Supreme Court rulings declare that the clause prohibits not only barbarous modes of punishment, like the rack and thumb screws, but also any punishment that is grossly disproportionate to the crime at hand (see *O'Neil v. Vermont* [1892]). Recent US Supreme Court decisions, however, have backed away from the disproportionality argument. In *Harmelin v. Michigan* (1991), Justice Antonin Scalia declared that the cruel and unusual punishment clause says nothing about proportionality and, in effect, only protects against certain forms of punishment that are not regularly used. Despite this, some judges do consider proportionality to be an Eighth Amendment issue and will overturn a punishment if they feel the punishment is too severe for the offense charged.

Another issue involving the Eighth Amendment is the use of the death penalty. While the use of the death penalty per se is not unconstitutional (*Gregg v. Georgia* [1976]), the US Supreme Court has ruled that its use for certain offenders or offenses is unconstitutional. For instance, the Court ruled that the death penalty for rape was cruel and unusual (*Coker v. Georgia* [1977]), as was the use of the death penalty for those who are mentally retarded (*Atkins v. Virginia* [2002]) or who were under the age of 18 at the time of their offense (*Roper v. Simmons* [2005]). Although states have been carrying out executions every year, in 2020, the federal government executed its first inmate in 17 years.

Web Activity

For these and other US Supreme Court cases, search the Cornell Legal Information Institute's website at http://www.law.cornell.edu/supct/.

Web Activity

See the textbook website for an illustration of states and their use of the death penalty (www.oup.com/he/lab6e).

INCORPORATION

The previous discussion outlined the primary criminal procedure rights found within the US Constitution and the Bill of Rights. Since these are federal documents, these provisions protect individuals from violations of rights by the federal government. Protection against state and local encroachment on procedural rights was not guaranteed and individuals had to rely on state constitutions to provide these protections. Some state constitutions followed the federal lead and provided extensive procedural rights to their citizens, while others did not. This was problematic because it resulted in an unfair and unequal application of the laws (Zalman and Siegel 1997).

The ratification of the **Fourteenth Amendment** in 1868 was the catalyst for extending the reach of the US Constitution and the Bill of Rights to the states. The Fourteenth Amendment consists of five sections, but the first section is most relevant here. This section outlines a due-process clause that applies to states. As mentioned earlier, the Fifth Amendment contains a due-process clause as well; however, because it is in the Bill of Rights, it only applies to the federal government. The Fourteenth Amendment's due-process clause specifies that no state shall "deprive any person of life, liberty, and property without due process of law." Since 1868, the US Supreme Court has issued a number of decisions that have used this clause to justify forcing the states to adopt the procedures found in the US Constitution and the Bill of Rights. The US Supreme Court was given this authority in the cases *Marbury v. Madison* (1803) and *Fletcher v. Peck* (1810). In these cases, the practice of **judicial review** was established, in which the US Supreme Court has the power to review federal and state laws to ensure that they comply with the US Constitution.

Using its power of judicial review, the US Supreme Court has incorporated, or made applicable to the states, most of the procedural rights found in the US Constitution and the Bill of Rights. This process of **incorporation** was selective and time-consuming, as the Court had to wait for cases to come before it before the Court could issue a ruling. Initially, the Court only incorporated the procedural rights it thought were "fundamental" and "essential" (see *Palko v. Connecticut* [1937]), but, over time, the Court came to realize that all rights found within the US Constitution and the Bill of Rights were fundamental; if they were not, they would not be there. Today, all states and the federal government abide by the provisions in these documents. In fact, some states have gone beyond what these documents specify, providing more rights to their citizens than is required.

Despite the fact that federal and state governments must recognize these procedural rights, none of these rights is absolute. As stated earlier, there are scenarios involving searches and seizures that do not require a warrant or probable cause, as specified in the Fourth Amendment. The same is true for the other procedural rights articulated above. Over time, the provisions found in the US Constitution and the Bill of Rights have been modified to account for circumstances that simply did not exist when these documents were created. For example, the number of accused individuals who come into contact with the criminal justice system is much larger than the number in 1791. The system has had to accommodate these numbers without collapsing. As a result, accused individuals are asked to waive many of their rights, including their right to a speedy trial, their right to have an attorney, and their right against self-incrimination. Courts have also scaled back many of these procedural rights. For instance, only individuals who face more than six months' incarceration are given the right to trial by jury. For more information about the extent of procedural rights in this country, see Samaha (2012) and Zalman and Siegel (1997).

TRENDS IN PROCEDURAL CRIMINAL LAW

As noted above, courts have restricted many of the procedural rights found in the US Constitution and the Bill of Rights. In many cases, this restriction is the result of security issues that place public safety on a higher ground than individual rights. For instance, because of the potential danger of police work, courts have allowed police to engage in searches without a warrant and arrests without probable cause to ensure that police officers are not placed in precarious situations.

The Internet and Procedural Criminal Law

As mentioned earlier, the internet has exploded with new technologies and new ways to conduct criminal behavior. As a result, the criminal justice system has had to improve its investigation techniques to stay ahead of cybercriminals. When the US Constitution was written, the Framers had no idea about the possibilities of internet technology; as a result, the Constitution and the criminal justice system have had to adapt. Although laws are in place to protect the privacy of individuals from electronic surveillance (see, for example, the Electronic Communications Privacy Act of 1986), the realities of the internet have stretched the original purpose of many of these laws. The use of cellphones and email, as well as the participation in third-party sites such as Facebook and YouTube, has placed the Constitution in, "a complex, often convoluted area of law" (*United States v. Smith* [1998]). Lower courts have upheld searches of a suspect's cellphone text messages soon after arrest (*United States v. Finley* [2007]) as well as the seizure of subscriber information given to a third-party internet provider (*United States v. Perrine* [2008]).

National Security and Procedural Criminal Law

The U.S.A. Patriot Act, passed after September 11, 2011, has also allowed federal authorities to engage in more expansive wiretapping and other electronic surveillance. The act allows more expansive surveillance of telephone and internet service providers as well as voice mail and email communications. Any activity that federal authorities deem is related to even a remote threat to national security is subject to increased surveillance and fewer constitutional protections. This is something that many view as important for the safety of the nation. Others, however, feel the federal government has given itself too much authority to investigate such activity, since it alone defines what is a threat to national security. One controversial aspect of investigation is the use of global positioning systems (GPS) for surveillance. Lower courts have been divided about the warrantless use of GPS by police. However, the US Supreme Court recently ruled that warrantless use of GPS by police, placed on the suspect's car to monitor the suspect for almost a month, violated the suspect's reasonable expectation of privacy, thereby curtailing a practice increasingly used by police (*United States v. Jones* [2012]).

COVID-19 and Procedural Criminal Law

The COVID-19 pandemic has caused massive disruptions in the day-to-day life of millions around the world. In the United States, a disagreement has emerged about the use of quarantines and facial coverings to stem the spread of the virus. To some, state and local governments that mandate quarantines and facial coverings are a direct assault on individual rights, to the extent that protests and marches are taking place to advocate against these requirements. To others, these mandates are essential in a public health crisis and individuals must be willing to give up certain individual rights for the good of society as a whole. Balancing public health mandates and individual liberties is at a critical juncture and will remain until the COVID-19 pandemic is over.

Web Activity

Generally, state and local governments have broad powers to act in the best interests of public health during a pandemic; this includes restricting individual rights. See https://jamanetwork.com/journals/jama/fullarticle/2764283 for a discussion of these powers.

CONCLUSION

Both substantive law and procedural law are critical to the function of society and all entities that exist within it. This chapter provided a general overview of the numerous aspects of substantive and procedural law. Many authors devote entire textbooks to each of these aspects, but this text is simply unable to do so. What this chapter does contain, however, is the information needed to understand the presence of the law in the society, in particular, the criminal justice system. The criminal justice system exists because of the law; something or someone must be responsible for the enforcement of the law as written. The criminal justice system, moreover, does not exist in a vacuum; it must abide by the law just as individuals, groups, and corporations must.

As this chapter was not able to delve too deeply into the many permutations of the law, the reader is encouraged to consult the many sources of information provided throughout the chapter to gain a more thorough understanding of both substantive and procedural law.

KEY WORDS

actus reus	cruel and unusual	exclusionary rule
administrative law	punishment	Fourteenth Amendment
age	deadly force	grand jury
bills of attainder	direct cause	habeas corpus
case law	double jeopardy	harm
causation	duress	impartial trial
common law	ex post facto	incorporation
concurrent cause	excessive bail	involuntary intoxication
constitutional law	excessive fines	judicial review

justification
mala in se
mala prohibita
mens rea
mental capacity
M'Naghten Rule
precedent

principle of legality
probable cause
procedural law
proximate cause
public trial
right to counsel
self-incrimination

speedy trial
statutory law
strict liability
substantive law
trial by jury
voluntary intoxication

SUGGESTED READINGS

Bergman, P., and S. Bergman. (2020). *The criminal law handbook: Know your rights, survive the system*, 16th ed. Berkeley, CA: NOLO.

Epstein, L., K. McGuire, and T. Walker. (2020). *Constitutional law for a changing America*, 8th ed. Thousand Oaks, CA: Sage Publications.

Friedman, L. (1993). *Crime and punishment in American history*. New York: Basic Books.

Lippman, M. (2018). *Contemporary criminal law: Concepts, cases, and controversies*. Thousand Oaks, CA: Sage Publications.

Ross, D. (2018). *Civil liability in criminal justice*, 7th ed. Cincinnati: Anderson.

Scheb, J., and J. Scheb. (2011). *Criminal law and procedure*, 7th ed. Florence, KY: Cengage.

Singer, R., and J. LaFond. (2010). *Criminal law: Examples and explanations*, 5th ed. New York: Aspen Publishers.

Walker, S. (1980). *Popular justice: A history of American criminal justice*. New York: Oxford University Press.

CHAPTER 3

Policing and Law Enforcement

CHAPTER OUTLINE

After reading this chapter, you should be able to:

- Distinguish between the law enforcement, order maintenance, and service functions of police work
- Discuss community policing, pointing out key concepts
- Discuss the broken windows theory of policing
- Explain the difference between problem-oriented policing and community-oriented policing
- Identify and discuss what is meant by intelligence-led policing
- List and discuss different levels/types of police structure (e.g., local and county)
- Briefly discuss different federal law enforcement agencies and their mandates
- Point out various aspects to police organization
- Distinguish between single-entry and dual-entry tracks
- Identify different stages of the hiring process
- Discuss issues related to police subculture
- Define and discuss police corruption
- Outline the use of force continuum
- Point out various emerging issues for police

INTRODUCTION

We commonly speak of the police as the "gatekeepers" of the criminal justice system, because the vast majority of criminal cases brought before the courts result from decisions made by the police. Although the police are thought of as *law enforcers*, arresting criminals is only a small portion of police work. The police also foster **law compliance** and provide an array of services that are not *directly* linked to crime. Almost 80 percent of a patrol officer's time is devoted to activities other than law enforcement. However, the law enforcement image dominates the public face of the police.

As the law reflects the collective will of a people, the police are the "muscle" behind that society's law. Those who do not voluntarily obey the law will have it imposed upon them; the police are the primary means by which the law is imposed. Egon Bittner described the role of the police as "a mechanism for the distribution of non-negotiable coercive force employed in accordance with the dictates of an intuitive grasp of situational exigencies" (1970: 46). Though other occupations and social institutions have the right to use force in a limited set of circumstances (for instance, to restrain a patient who may hurt himself, or to discipline children), only the police have a general mandate to use force for the common good.

The police may use force to ensure that the law is obeyed and public order preserved. When the police actually use force is the essence of police **discretion** (Brown 1981). It is not possible to write a law, or a rule, that will cover every possible situation the police might encounter. Nor will the police necessarily know with certainty every factual matter that attends every call they answer. The police combine their knowledge with the array of verbal and nonverbal information that attends each unique situation, make an accurate judgment about what's going on (the "situational exigencies"), and decide on the proper response. However, the concept of "an intuitive grasp of situational exigencies" is now under considerable challenge due to technological advances like body-worn cameras and—perhaps more importantly—citizens' cell-phone cameras (see below).

Not every police action is a coercive one, of course. The right to use force on behalf of society lies behind many of the other things police do. In broad terms, there are three primary responsibilities of police work: **law enforcement**, **order maintenance**, and **service**. These aspects were first explored by James Q. Wilson in his 1968 book *Varieties of Police Behavior*.

Law Enforcement

"Enforcing the law" by apprehending criminals after crimes occur is an important part of police work, but it is only one element of the law enforcement mission. The entertainment media portray policing as an exciting career of hunting criminals, thwarting robberies in progress, engaging in high-speed car chases, making dynamic entries, and apprehending desperate criminals. In truth, these events happen infrequently. The police are far more likely to deal with crimes committed by people who are drunk, depressed, mentally ill, or simply overwhelmed by life stresses, than they are with so-called master criminals.

Tense confrontations, take-down moves, and an enticing array of high-tech weaponry and science seem to be the tools of the trade. While these are important, by far the greater tools are patience, good communication skills, and knowledge of human psychology. The ability to enforce the law by bringing criminals to justice rests in large part on the willingness of the public to cooperate with the police (Black 1981; Mastrofski, Snipes, and Supina 1996). The foundation for that is laid in the routine interaction between police and citizens in the course of everyday, nonemergency activities.

Crime prevention has been a prime function of police work, ensuring the safety of the community by denying criminals the opportunity to commit crime and by defusing volatile situations before they reach the point of violence (Lab 2016). Visible **patrol**—on foot, in motor vehicles, on bicycles, or on horseback—is seen as a means of preventing crime by **deterrence**. Active patrol raises the possibility that a criminal will be seen and apprehended. The impression that the police are always around and ever vigilant discourages criminals from committing crime: that is the essence of police deterrence. Often, the presence of authority, backed up by powers of arrest, will scatter potential troublemakers or quiet boisterous behavior.

Police foster crime prevention in other, less flashy ways as well. Officers help organize and support community-based self-help activities, like **Neighborhood Watch**, to observe and report suspicious activity in the neighborhood (Garofalo and McLeod 1988; Rosenbaum 1987). Community involvement may range from supplemental **citizen patrols** to initiating court action against landlords of properties where drug sales take place. A wide range of anticrime activities take place at the block level. Citizen patrols, **property marking** projects, **safe havens** for children, looking after each other's property when people are away, and block parties can all be organized under the umbrella of Neighborhood Watch.

Patrol officers, **school resource officers**, Police Activity League volunteers, and others participate in a wide variety of community-building activities, both on and off duty, to keep youngsters safe and to encourage law-abiding activities (Bond 2001; Newman et al. 2000). Gang intelligence helps defuse feuds that otherwise might turn violent, and skilled officers sometimes negotiate truces between rival gangs. Officers host self-defense workshops and conduct property surveys to help reduce individuals' risks of victimization and make numerous referrals to social service agencies across a wide spectrum of problems they encounter.

Order Maintenance

Crime is not the only thing in modern life that can cause concern. All sorts of conflicts can create alarm, concern, fear, or inconvenience. Loud and boisterous groups of teenagers; heated, chest-thumping bar arguments; and noisy arguments over finances between the husband and wife in the next apartment all disturb the peace and tranquility of neighbors. Those who call for police interventions do not necessarily expect the officers to make arrests, as long as they restore order. Though arrests are possible, most incidents are resolved through other means: mediation, referral, or the mere threat of arrest. In some cases, such as a dispute between a landlord and tenant over the payment of the rent, the police may have no legal authority in the matter (rent disputes are a matter of civil law), but they may serve as referees. Their presence and authority act as a safety valve: both parties can back down without losing face.

Service

Service, the third function of the police, takes a wide variety of forms depending upon the location. Directions, assistance to disabled motorists, funeral escorts, administration of various kinds of permits, emergency relays of blood, checking vacant residences or looking in on vulnerable adults, aiding with traffic control at road construction and emergency scenes, and many more services are provided by local police and sheriffs' deputies.

Because of this wide diversity of tasks, police officers are trained to be generalists. Most officers begin their careers doing uniformed patrol work. They will be called upon to answer an almost unimaginable array of different needs. These include assisting in childbirth, breaking up fights, talking down suicidal "jumpers," interviewing abused children, trading gunfire with desperate criminals, intervening in domestic arguments, assisting mentally ill and confused persons, and investigating corrupt police officers.

Police officers frequently describe their work as "long hours of sheer boredom, punctuated by moments of sheer terror." In contrast to Hollywood portrayals, the reality of police work is that exciting events happen infrequently and favorable results can be elusive. Those who expect exciting careers in law enforcement are likely to find that much of their time is devoted to social work, helping people cope with life, occasionally resolving low-level problems, and building interpersonal relationships with the community.

THE ROLE OF POLICE IN SOCIETY

Throughout history, the police in Anglo-American society have reflected the conditions and needs of the dominant society, even though periodically the police have been slow to recognize and adapt to legitimate social change. The police must operate in the tension between rapidly changing social conditions and a conservative, slow to change legal environment. Individual, organizational, and subcultural changes usually develop more slowly than the larger social ones, often creating visible tensions between the police and parts of the community. That was true of the **civil rights movement** of the 1950s and 1960s, and certain aspects of present conditions seem to be harbingers of a reprise of that era.

Web Activity

Students who are interested in the historical development of the English and American police, as well as a discussion of different American police eras, can find material on the textbook's website (www.oup.com/he/lab6e).

At the same time, the police today are far more professional than their generational predecessors of earlier eras, and in general much less "tools" to be wielded by local politicians. For instance, when the former occupant of the White House made offhand remarks to the effect that arrestees should be roughed up, the police themselves were generally outspoken. Many police chiefs and departments made public statements to the effect that such behavior was neither legal nor ethical, and that the standards of behavior expected under the law would continue to be observed (Berman 2017).

That is not to say that police do not have to respond to the direction of local officials: far from it. In the wake of the shooting death of Michael Brown in Ferguson, MO, in August 2014, an investigative report revealed that police enforcement of minor violations was seen as a revenue-generating device by the city authorities. Those enforcement activities were focused overwhelmingly on lower-income residents with fewer resources to respond legally (US Department of Justice 2015).

As America moves toward the third decade of the 21st century, a number of social tensions have burst into the public view, and directly or indirectly involve the police. One movement demands the removal of Confederate statues which, in the minds of its proponents, indirectly glorify slavery and treason. In doing so, it gives rise to the resurgence of a resistance movement that insists the statues commemorate states' rights, honorable soldiers who fought for what they believed in, and an honorable history. While those two opinions have clashed in public space, they have provided a vehicle for far-right groups like the Nazi Party and its various analogs to assert white supremacy, among other beliefs noxious to most Americans. They, in turn, have provoked the rise of equivalent groups on the far left, such as the AntiFa movement (AntiFascist). Both sides wear masks, brandish and sometimes use weapons, and engage in provocational activities just short of—and sometimes boiling over into—outright violence. The police are caught in the middle, obliged to defend the right of all sides to free expression, but also charged with protection of target from assailant, regardless of political beliefs.

The politically fired debate over immigration controls also have impact on the police, as well as on jails and holding facilities under police control. Long-standing precedents have created set requirements for the detention and conditions of release of detained person. Attempts to add federal-level immigration charges on detained persons must conform to legal strictures as well, and state prisoners cannot be detained for federal convenience without authorizing paperwork. Such paperwork is often slow to materialize. In response, the federal government has moved to try to create incentives for such activities. A November 20, 2017, press release from the Office of Justice Programs Office of Community Oriented Policing Services (OJP OCOPS) noted that:

> In September, the Justice Department announced additional priority consideration criteria for FY2017 COPS Office grants. Applicants were notified that their application would receive additional points in the application scoring process by certifying their willingness to cooperate with federal immigration authorities within their detention facilities. Cooperation may include providing access to detention facilities for an interview of aliens in the jurisdiction's custody and providing advance notice of an alien's release from custody upon request.

Eighty percent of the awarded agencies received additional points based on their certifications of willingness to cooperate with federal immigration authorities (https://www.justice.gov/opa/pr/attorney-general-sessions-announces-98-million-hire-community-policing-officers).

"Willingness to cooperate" does not mean "defy the requirements of law" in practical terms. The limitations of federal agencies such as ICE and the Border Patrol can lead to a gap between willingness and actual practice. At the street level, as well, the impression that local police are the agents of federal immigration authorities can mean a loss of valuable trust and cooperation from whole communities of those who are here legally, either as naturalized citizens or on visas. The police can ill-afford to be viewed as targeting the loved ones of their citizens, particularly against the backdrop of unsettled law. In recent years, ICE and the Customs and Border Protection components have come under political pressure to void their previous cautionary practices in favor of fast-tracking the anti-immigrant policies of former President Trump. Issues like the summary repatriation of asylum seekers and the separation of children from their parents have caused major revulsion among the American people. In such instances, though, it is possible to discern the enforcement agents as the "tools" of a political henchman.

Shifting social conditions are not the only focus of police activity, of course. The predominant part of police work remains the enforcement of the criminal law and the maintenance of social order, as it has been for decades. The various initiatives of previous decades, such as **broken windows**, **problem-oriented**, and **community-oriented policing** (see the web material) have coalesced under the current heading of "intelligence-based policing." However, the rapid expansion of cyber-crime and internet-based criminal activities have created a new demand for police services unknown to previous generations.

Web Activity

Explore influences on the development of community policing on the textbook website (www.oup.com/he/lab6e).

Intelligence-Led Policing

Drawing upon the example of "intelligence-based medicine," the police of the modern era are basing decisions more and more upon crime analysis and other data systems. With roots in the **Kansas City Preventive Patrol Experiment**, the **Minneapolis Domestic Violence Experiment**, and the other evaluative projects of the 1970s and 1980s, crime analysis has become more than the mere production of year-end statistics. New York's **CompStat** process was the first contemporary use of integrated statistics in real time. Advances in computer technologies now make it possible to do far more. Mapping tools and analytic software manage not only crime data but also incorporate trend data from other functions that might affect police operations, such as land use, economic development, and demographic trends.

The expansion of criminal enterprises in a global economy has created demands for better information about conditions beyond local boundaries. The war on terror has led to the creation of fusion centers to collect, assess, and coordinate information about possible terrorist activities. The centers are also tracking the connections among other criminal enterprises as well: guns, drugs, gangs, human trafficking, child pornography, and many others. Police professional associations also update their members across jurisdictional lines on topics such as tactics, new threats, new technologies, and legal developments in the various federal districts.

Web Activity

There is a Society of Police Futurists, an offshoot of the World Futures Society. You can read more about their work at http://www.policefuturists.org.

STRUCTURE

Police agencies have different mandates depending on their level of political authority, region of the country, and specific charter. Government police agencies are authorized at the local, tribal, county, state, and federal levels. In addition, various special police forces may be authorized. Based on 2016 data (the most recent available) more than 15,300 police and law enforcement agencies exist in the United States, employing more than 701,000 full-time police officers and agents. In addition, just under 350,000 civilian employees augment the work done by sworn personnel (Hyland 2018).

Local

The blue uniforms and patrol cars of the nation's municipal police forces are the image most associated with the police. Their legal jurisdiction is usually limited to the borders of the town or city that hires them, though there are exceptions. Fresh pursuit of a suspect, **mutual aid** compacts among municipalities, and being sworn in as special officers or deputies for other agencies all may extend police officers' local authority.

Most municipal police agencies are small. Uniformed generalist patrol work is a universal entry point, and many officers spend most of their careers doing patrol work. In larger departments, increased specialization in the form of detectives, juvenile officers, SWAT (Special Weapons and Tactics) team members, and the like is possible in later career steps, as are promotions to supervisory positions.

Sheriff

The county **sheriff** is one of the oldest police offices and in many states is authorized by the state constitution. Unique among law enforcement personnel, sheriffs serve all three branches of criminal justice: policing, courts (sheriffs provide security to courtrooms and serve civil and criminal writs), and corrections (sheriffs run most county jails). Deputy sheriffs often start their careers in jails as correctional officers and work their way up to uniformed patrol and investigations.

Sheriffs are elected officials in 48 of the 50 states, but the duties of sheriffs' departments vary regionally. In the South and West, they are the primary law enforcement services for many rural and unincorporated areas. In the urban centers of the Northeast, sheriffs tend to be court officers but provide only limited law enforcement because most of their jurisdictions have full-time municipal police.

County Police

In some densely populated urban areas, county police departments have taken over the law enforcement duties of the sheriff. Organized like large municipal departments, county departments are responsible to the county executive or county council rather than to an elected sheriff. County police may have concurrent jurisdiction with municipal police agencies located within the county. In such instances, like the sheriffs' offices and state police, the county police tend to concentrate on areas without other police resources, cooperating with the municipal departments when the need arises.

Constables

In many parts of the country, the old office of **constable** has been abolished or restricted to minor court and service duties. In Texas, the office of constable is comparable in many ways to the sheriff or the county police, generally serving court writs but also providing patrol services in some areas.

Special Police

State laws authorize police forces for special limited purposes, such as railroads (which run through multiple jurisdictions), college campuses, school districts, mass-transit systems, parks and woodlands, and the like. The best known is the Port Authority of New York and New Jersey Police, which lost many officers in the September 11, 2001, attack on the World Trade Center.

A variation on the "special police" concept are the part-time officers (variously called "reserves," "special officers," or "auxiliary officers," among other titles) who work for municipal, county, and sheriffs' departments in addition to their regular jobs. They may work on either an hourly paid basis or as volunteers, depending upon the agency and the state's authorizing statutes. With proper training, they may perform full police duties, especially in rural areas. Otherwise, they supplement regular police in support roles: directing traffic, providing crowd control at major events like concerts and fairs, and assisting in a variety of roles. Many sheriffs' departments have "sheriffs' posses" who can be called upon for additional staffing of special events and search-and-rescue operations. Their powers usually are less than those of full-time officers, but they provide valuable resources and expertise.

State

State police functions take one of two forms. **State police** have standard law enforcement duties and general jurisdiction throughout the state. **State patrols** or highway patrols primarily enforce traffic laws on state highways; they have police powers and training but no general police jurisdiction. States with highway patrols may also have an independent bureau of criminal investigation that provides criminal investigation and crime lab services across the state. Other elements of state government may employ investigators and officers with special police powers, such as the welfare, motor vehicle, revenue, alcoholic beverage control, and natural resources departments. Some jurisdictions grant police powers to corrections employees, especially probation and parole officers.

Federal

Federal agencies have specific powers and jurisdiction under federal law and do not enforce state or local laws. There are more than 90 federal law enforcement agencies, including the Border Patrol, Customs Service, Federal Protective Services, US Mint Police, and smaller police forces for various parts of the federal government (the Capitol, Supreme Court, Environmental Protection Agency, and so forth). In many cases, federal and state jurisdictions overlap as drugs, firearms, explosives, and bank robberies may all be part of an interstate or even international criminal enterprise. For these and emerging problems, such as human trafficking and international internet fraud, federal and state agencies coordinate their investigations through **Multi-Jurisdictional Task Forces**, usually under the direction of the regional US District Attorney. Although almost every federal agency has some kind of investigative service specific to its mandate, federal criminal justice agencies are grouped in three cabinet-level departments: Justice, Homeland Security, and Treasury.

Web Activity

Visit http://www.justice.gov/agencies to explore information on the wide range of federal agencies that are involved in enforcing the law.

Many agencies were incorporated into the new Department of Homeland Security (DHS) in the wake of the September 11 attacks against American targets. To coordinate the nation's defenses and deal more effectively with the threat of international terrorism, agencies with relevant missions were brought under the direction of a single agency. The creation of the DHS at the cabinet level combined many smaller federal enforcement functions under a single office.

Among the components of the new DHS are the Secret Service; the Border Patrol, renamed Customs and Border Protection; the Immigration and Naturalization Service, renamed Immigration and Customs Enforcement (ICE); the US Coast Guard; the Federal Law Enforcement Training Centers (FLETC), which train the agents for all but two of the federal enforcement agencies; and the Transportation Safety Administration. Other components relating to nuclear detection, threat assessment, intelligence, animal research, and similar functions were brought under the DHS umbrella selectively from their former homes in other federal agencies.

Web Activity

Investigate the different components of the DHS at http://www.dhs.gov/department-components.

Created in 1908, the FBI has a mandate to investigate approximately 200 federal crimes, including bank robbery and kidnapping, unless Congress specifically designates jurisdiction to another agency. Criminal acts and conspiracies that cross state lines usually fall to the FBI, the enforcement arm of the Justice Department. The FBI crime lab provides forensic support for investigators throughout the nation, and the National Academy provides advanced training for state and local officers. Recognizing the emerging needs created by globalization, the FBI has established offices in foreign countries and has been involved in the training of police forces in emerging nations and the countries of the former Soviet bloc. In 2005, the FBI began training all new agents to be intelligence-gathering officers, both in antiterror investigations and in the investigation of transnational enterprise crime.

The Drug Enforcement Administration (DEA) was established in 1973, combining several existing antidrug offices under the Justice Department. The DEA has primary responsibility for coordinating national drug enforcement efforts and is the sole agency authorized to pursue overseas drug investigations.

The Alcohol, Tobacco, Firearms, and Explosives Bureau (still referred to as the ATF or BATF) is an enforcement arm of the Treasury Department. Created in 1972 when it was split from the Internal Revenue Service, ATF has powers based in the tax laws and other federal laws and regulations relating to alcohol, tobacco products, firearms, explosives, and arson. Another Treasury function, the Secret Service, was created in 1865 to investigate money counterfeiting. Protection of the president of the United States was added after the 1901 assassination of President McKinley. Fraud in commerce and fictitious securities documents also lie within its investigative mandate.

The US Marshals Service is the oldest federal law enforcement agency, created by the Judiciary Act of 1789. Marshals protect the federal judiciary, transport federal prisoners, and protect endangered federal witnesses (the Witness Protection Program). In addition, marshals manage assets seized from criminal enterprises and may even run businesses until their sale under the asset forfeiture laws.

Tribal

The US Constitution recognizes Indian tribes as sovereign entities, and tribal lands may have their own police forces. The Navajo nation is representative of the more developed agencies. The Federal Bureau of Indian Affairs also has a separate police force for tribal lands, whose territorial dimensions may cross municipal, county, and even state lines. Like their municipal and state counterparts, tribal police have jurisdiction over anyone on tribal land, whether Native American or not. Tribal jurisdiction over its own members may include traditional methods of dispute resolution (community circles, banishment, property exchanges) as well as the contemporary criminal and civil courts.

Critical Thinking Exercise

What advantages would there be to having a national police force with centralized, universal training standards, and common equipment, salaries, and benefits?

Private Police

Over the last several decades, the United States has seen a growth in special **private police** forces. Most are not "police" in the same sense as state or municipal officers because they do not have the authorization of law or general police powers that come with a sworn position. However, a small but growing number of private police forces now have state-authorized jurisdiction in some privately controlled places such as vacation resorts. They are uniformed and equipped in much the same way as their municipal counterparts, and many have completed preservice police training.

Private police forces are an augmented form of private security, with powers derived from the property rights of the corporate and incorporated entities that employ their services. They are **first responders** for alarms (intrusion, fire, and health emergencies), exercise a qualified set of access-control powers to limit visitors to the properties under contract, and sometimes handle disputes in much the same way that police patrol officers would. Professional organizations make a point of coordinating and interacting well with local police agencies, though there are fly-by-night, disreputable agencies as well.

Private police provide a more systematic patrol presence for those who can afford their services. In addition, they relieve the pressure on local agencies to answer alarm calls, the vast majority of which are false alarms (accidental activations or equipment malfunctions). The modern equivalents of the ancient night watchman and the store detective, their level of training and range of duties are considerably greater than those of their predecessors, reflecting the more complex requirements of asset protection and personal security in the modern age.

The former sharp distinctions between public and private policing have blurred in recent years. The new electronic commerce has created new challenges and opportunities. The need for the physical security of locked doors has not disappeared, but it has been augmented by demands for protection of the electronic infrastructure (data), intellectual property (trade secrets), and goods in transit. Corporations now address the issues of asset protection, including electronic surveillance, personnel background checks, process integrity, data protection and verification, and the personal protection of corporate personnel.

Critical Thinking Exercise

Is the cause of justice served by having private police to protect the wealthy? What conflicts are possible when private police and public police jurisdictions overlap?

In addition, private security forces now often work under contract for public police agencies, providing security at crime scenes, guarding prisoners in hospitals, and even conducting background checks on potential new employees. Their relationship to the formal police authority is similar to that of private security contractors in military zones overseas.

Critical Thinking Exercise

What are some of the positive and negative consequences of having American law enforcement fragmented among so many different jurisdictions?

ORGANIZATION

Sworn officers in American police and law enforcement agencies are organized in a hierarchical form, with a **chain of command** conveying information from the front line to the administrative decision-makers and conveying orders and information back down. In larger departments, patrol officers report to shift supervisors (sergeants), who report to shift commanders (lieutenants), who report to precinct commanders (captains). Precinct and unit commanders report to divisional heads (deputy chiefs). Police work is organized by task requirements (sworn or civilian) as well as by geography and by time.

Sworn Versus Civilian

For many years, almost every position in a police department was held by a uniformed police officer or a plainclothes detective. Women held only secretarial jobs and "matron" positions in jails. Support positions could be places to which officers were assigned as a punitive measure or "plum jobs" that offered a daytime Monday-to-Friday refuge from rotating shift work.

In modern times, many departments employ civilians (also called nonsworn or contract employees) to perform tasks that do not require the extensive training and experience of a sworn officer. Records, dispatching, fleet maintenance, personnel and budget, and even crime-scene investigations may be staffed by non-sworn personnel. They are trained only for their special function, do not have police powers or carry weapons, and generally are paid less than sworn officers. Some agencies practice "outsourcing," contracting with private security agencies to perform many services formerly done by uniformed police officers: guard crime scenes, transport prisoners, and guard prisoners while they are in medical facilities.

Specialization

Patrol officers have general duties attending to a wide variety of calls and situations. In order for police departments to function efficiently, however, a number of specialist positions must be filled. Best known are the detectives or investigators, who do not answer calls. Their time is spent interviewing witnesses and following up on leads in unsolved crime cases. Detectives may specialize in a certain type of crime (homicide, burglary, robbery, sex crimes, and so forth) or conduct all kinds of criminal investigation. Crime analysis, gang intelligence and intervention, school resource officers, training coordinator, **HAZMAT** (hazardous material), and high-risk warrant service, among others, are task-specific functions for sworn officers. Supervision is also a specialty job: as a rule, once promoted to sergeant or above, police officers do not handle calls unless circumstances force them to take police actions. Their primary responsibilities are to observe and assist patrol officers or investigators and to coordinate efforts. The farther up the hierarchy one rises, the more the duties are managerial and administrative in nature, except in small agencies where everyone is a generalist.

Geography

In the smallest local departments, officers are responsible for covering the entire town or village. Elsewhere, officers patrol specific parts of town called **beats**. They are responsible for answering all calls within that beat, as well as for preventing crimes and resolving problems.

Larger agencies are organized into **precincts** containing several beats. There are, for instance, 76 precincts in New York City; 6 in Austin, Texas; and 4 in Minneapolis, Minnesota. It is easier to manage smaller areas within a large city, enabling the precinct commander to be more responsive to citizens' concerns.

Sheriffs' departments may also be divided into different districts or may operate out of a central office. In addition, sheriffs' offices may assign deputies to local municipalities, known as **contract cities**, for a specified number of hours according to a contract negotiated between the city and the sheriff. Contracts guarantee basic police services while relieving smaller cities of part of the expense of maintaining their own departments.

The phrase **beat integrity** refers to a policy of keeping officers assigned to one specific beat consistently in order to develop knowledge about the players and build relationships with the community. This represents a significant change from the pre-1960s policies that moved officers frequently to different areas of the city in an effort to thwart corruption. However, officers may cross beat boundaries to assist other officers if necessary, and to cover high-priority calls if the beat officer is tied up on a previous call.

State police agencies must cover entire states and organize into **troops** for the same reasons that police departments organize into precincts. In rural areas, troopers may operate out of their homes (such as the Connecticut Resident Trooper program) but are responsible to a troop-level administration.

Federal agencies responsible for national coverage organize into administrative regions and generally maintain offices in major cities. Federal agencies also work cooperatively with local and state agencies through **regional task forces** for various purposes, recognizing that crime does not confine itself to jurisdictional boundaries. Short-term task forces may devote their efforts to tracking down a serial rapist or a prolific bank robber. Long-term resources are devoted to organized crime such as racketeering, insurance fraud, illegal drug importation and distribution, human trafficking, and smuggling.

Time

Because crime and public emergencies occur around the clock, dispatch services and police coverage must be available 24 hours a day, seven days a week. Police agencies tend to staff their shifts differently according to the volume of activity expected for various parts of the day. There are many different shift schedules ranging from the standard 40-hour workweek of five eight-hour days to the popular 4–10 and 3–12 shifts (four 10-hour or three 12-hour days). The two basic models are **rotating shifts**, in which officers periodically change from days to evenings to nights, and **steady shifts**, in which work hours are determined by a seniority system or a bid lottery.

Overlapping shifts and **power shifts** provide extra police presence during the active evening hours and on weekends. More officers are available to handle the call load and provide backup in dangerous situations. Depending upon the nature of union contracts or other work rules, the power shifts may be staffed by officers who volunteer to work the evening hours on a regular basis, without rotating to day and midnight assignments.

Smaller agencies may provide nighttime coverage by an "on-call" arrangement. Officers work their shifts and return home to sleep but can be called out again for an accident or some criminal incident. Another agency such as the sheriffs' office or state police also may provide after-hours coverage.

Investigators and crime-scene technicians generally work day and evening shifts, with either minimum staffing or on-call status for the overnight hours. Other support positions such as records, planning and research, personnel, and purchase and supply usually do not work around the clock or on weekends. They tend to be Monday-to-Friday jobs because their work entails interaction with other public- and private-sector offices on the standard work schedule.

POLICE WORK AND CAREER PATHS

Municipal policing remains a single-point-of-entry career. Officers working in municipal departments begin in patrol, doing shift work and answering a wide variety of calls. The diversity of patrol activities provides a learning base of experience. After that, three basic career paths are possible: officers may remain in patrol for their entire careers; they may move from patrol into some specialty role, most typically as investigators or detectives; or they may follow a mixed career of supervisory promotions and specialty assignments that lead to administrative posts.

Sheriffs' departments may have single- or dual-entry tracks. **Single-entry tracks** mean that deputies begin their careers working in the jails, unarmed, supervising prisoners. When a patrol position becomes available, jail deputies have the first opportunity for the slot, subject to seniority and testing rules. The emerging professional movement in corrections has led some sheriffs to create **dual-entry tracks**. Deputies hired for corrections functions are hired with an understanding that they will be working only in jails, and those seeking law enforcement positions apply directly for patrol positions. Jail deputies may apply for patrol slots later if they wish, but they do so on a level playing field, with no seniority advantages or "inside track" compared to outsiders.

Federal agencies have different requirements, depending upon their needs and mandates. Some have uniformed branches as well as investigators; others tend to be exclusively investigative in nature. The FBI is one of the investigative agencies, and because of the sensitive nature of its work, generally does not hire persons right out of college. The Bureau looks for candidates who have established a solid work record and credit history, among other qualifications, so many aspiring FBI agents work in uniformed police service until they meet the eligibility requirements. By contrast, the Border Patrol has expanded rapidly to meet the demands to secure the nation's borders; many college students have stepped directly into Border Patrol slots upon graduation.

The Hiring Process

The older police career model, which endures in many areas, began with candidates being hired by an agency. At that point, the town or city sent them to a **police academy** for training and state certification as a police officer. As police training and education requirements expanded, other options developed. Today, persons seeking a police career may pay for their own **preservice training** before being hired, which may give them a competitive edge in the job market.

In some states, candidates can pay to go to a regular police academy. In others, alternative police certification processes are integrated into academic programs at two-year, community, and vocational colleges. Students graduate with an associate's degree and state certification as a police officer, although they have no police powers until an agency hires them. It is not a guarantee that they will be hired, and certifications often expire after a specified period of time if the graduate has not obtained work in an authorized agency. Nevertheless, preservice certification represents a savings for the municipality, which can put the officer to work immediately without having to pay for training.

Police recruits must pass a battery of tests to be hired, even with preservice certification. Written, psychological, and physical tests, as well as **background checks** for character and conduct, are standard in most areas. Some agencies require polygraph exams; still others put candidates through assessment centers to test their skills and instinctive reactions in various situations.

No preservice training options exist for those seeking federal law enforcement jobs. The FBI and DEA maintain their own specialized academies in Quantico, Virginia. All other federal agencies train their agents and officers at the FLETC in Georgia or Arizona.

There are two primary models for police training academies. **Stress-based academies** are run similar to military boot camps: they are residential and isolated from other groups; they tend to concentrate heavily on physical fitness as both a goal and a form of punishment for minor infractions or errors; they incorporate military trappings such as marching in formation; and they interweave classroom instruction with practical, hands-on exercises. **Campus-based academies** are run in two-year and technical college campuses, and the police academy curriculum is often part of an accredited associate's degree. Classroom instruction is augmented by practical exercises similar to those in stress academies, including mandatory state certification in firearms use and defensive/pursuit driving. Because of the setting, where trainees intermingle with students from numerous other academic disciplines, the boot-camp trappings are generally absent. Each model has strong proponents, primarily based in philosophical preferences rather than scientific evaluation of the effectiveness of the model.

The "boot camp" stress academy is currently under criticism for a perceived overemphasis on use of force to the exclusion of de-escalation tactics, recognition of mental illness as a driver of irrational behavior, and the like. A rash of deaths of Black and other minority-group citizens at the hands of police officers has spurred the Black Lives Matter movement among others: the deaths of Michael Brown, George Floyd, and Breonna Taylor have generated national headlines, and promoted calls for a broader and more mature range of police responses to challenged individuals.

Critical Thinking Exercise

What are the relative merits of the stress academy model of training and the campus academy model? How might each be changed to provide even better preparation for street duty?

Field Training

Most departments have a full-time **Field Training Officer (FTO)** program that provides the bridge between academy learning and autonomous authority in the field. Officers-in-training ride with experienced officers who have a mandate to expose the rookies to as many situations as possible, evaluating and critiquing the trainees' responses as part of the field learning process. Once the FTO program is complete, rookies may work independently, but most undergo an additional period as probationary employees. If their performance is poor, they can be released without any further action. If they pass their probationary period, they become full-fledged members of the agency, accorded all civil service and bargaining unit protections where applicable.

Promotion

The requirements for being promoted to supervisory rank or to specialty positions vary widely. At the low end, seniority is still found in some departments. The person who has been in the department the longest gets the next open position, regardless of his or her training, education, or general fitness for the job. At the other end of the spectrum are batteries of written tests, oral interviews, and assessment center tests. A few departments also incorporate a "promotability score" based upon past performance and supervisors' assessments of the individual's skills that will be necessary for the new job. Unlike rookie officers, however, the newly promoted individual goes through no formal "field training," but learns their new job by doing it, though often with word-of-mouth assistance of others in related positions.

Criminal investigation often requires a long-term commitment to cases, interviewing people, following up leads, assessing physical evidence, and preparing affidavits for warrants and cases for court. It is difficult to conduct investigations if one is always being called off to answer another call for service, so most police agencies have an investigative specialist position, usually called **detective**. In some agencies, detective is a rank and is considered a promotion above patrol officer. In others, it is considered an assignment and holds the same rank within the organization as a patrol officer.

Because of its high profile and clarity of focus, criminal investigation, or detective work, is a prized assignment for many police officers. In smaller organizations, detectives are investigative generalists. In larger agencies, detectives are specialized, devoting their time to a single category of crime. They may work in several different investigative units over the course of their careers.

Undercover assignments are a special type of investigation, where the officers pretend to be criminals or "fringe players" in order to gather intelligence on criminal networks or to buy drugs and stolen merchandise. Undercover officers differ from plainclothes officers, whose police status is known or acknowledged; an undercover officer's police identity is secret. Occasionally undercover police run **sting operations** where officers pose as criminal fences or drug dealers;

john details are a variation used against street prostitution and cruising activities. Police officers (usually women, though similar operations are conducted in gay male cruising areas) pose as prostitutes in order to arrest "johns" who solicit them for sex.

Internal Affairs, now often called the Office of Professional Responsibility or a similar title, is the most specialized investigative function. It has the responsibility for investigating allegations of crime and misconduct by other police officers in the organization. Juvenile investigations is both an investigative unit specializing in juvenile crime and a support unit that works with social service agencies to get juvenile offenders back on the straight and narrow.

Other specialties exist. Only a few cities have full-time SWAT or SRT (Special Response Team, a more contemporary appellation) squads, but many have trained personnel who can be mobilized into a team at need; smaller cities and towns often participate in regional SWAT or SRT teams. Hostage negotiations and barricaded persons situations are typical situations for SWAT/SRT. HAZMAT is a similar specialty, requiring additional training and equipment for dealing with incidents like toxic waste or chemical spills, volatile chemicals in clandestine drug labs, or accidents in legitimate business and manufacturing sites. Agencies near large bodies of water often have marine units for monitoring water traffic and for rescue; many densely populated urban areas have police helicopter units for surveillance, search, and rapid deployment across wide-flung areas.

Training is a vital element of any agency for preparing new recruits, updating veterans on changes in law and procedure, and introducing new techniques and technologies to all members of the agency. School resource officers are similar to juvenile officers but work exclusively in the schools, providing a combination of security, investigation, and public relations. They may deal exclusively with students or may have responsibilities for both student and staff conduct. Drug Abuse Resistance Education (D.A.R.E.) is a special form of school liaison, a national antidrug curriculum taught by uniformed police officers. In some departments, crime-scene technicians are sworn officers; in others they are civilians.

Police officers are often supervisors for civilianized support units, such as Dispatch or Records. In addition to knowledge of the various police jobs that the unit supports, they have the legal authority to handle difficult questions and requests and can provide technical knowledge of the criminal and procedural laws when needed.

ENDURING ELEMENTS AND ISSUES

Across the multiple types and approaches to policing, there are certain themes common to the American police. Many of them center on what scholars call the **police subculture**, the views of the world shared by many police officers. Police discretion, the **use of force**, corruption, handling of special constituencies, and relations with the community, particularly minority citizens, are all intertwined with this hard-to-define concept.

Police Subculture

The idea of a police subculture at odds with mainstream society stemmed from the politically charged era of the 1960s. Two schools of thought emerged to explain the adversarial relationships of the day. Police opponents viewed the overwhelmingly Caucasian, almost entirely male police as racist, ignorant, authoritarian, and thuggish, completely out of touch with a changing society. In this viewpoint, police work attracted mean-spirited bullies.

The other school of thought held that people were drawn to police work out of a sense of altruism, but the nature of police work transformed them. The major scholars of the police of the 1960s drew a picture of police whose "working personality" was marked by concepts of danger, authority, and cynicism (Niederhoffer 1967; Skolnick 1966). The nature of their work meant dealing with people at their worst, handling problems of abuse and death on a regular basis, being personally reviled, and having their motives questioned. These combined to harden police officers, bringing about a defense mechanism. Those scholars also noted that the police were given to the use of stereotypes as a "perceptual shorthand" to discern and minimize danger.

The wider admission of women and minorities to policing has had some impact on police culture, but certain common themes are still recognized. Police officers work within a moral framework as much as a legal one, assessing situations on the basis of their assessment of the persons they interact with. A feeling of "us against them" predominates in many areas, though **community policing** has broken down that attitude in many others. Crank (1998) summarized many of the themes of police culture: the necessity and righteousness of force; reliance upon an undefined "common sense" and personal bravery in the face of sudden and potential danger; and a moral division of the world into "good" and "bad" people, with the police as a "thin blue line" between civilization and chaos. Others include solidarity in the face of opposition, individualism and personal autonomy, unpredictability, and survival. In the present day, however, icons such as the "thin blue line" have been co-opted by some with white supremacist views, even to the extent of joining the Ku Klux Klan and similar right-wing groups.

Because most officers are socially and politically conservative, the police culture adapts slowly and sometimes grudgingly to changes in the social and legal environment. Guyot (1979) likened the process of creating change in police organizations to "bending granite." This resistance often puts the police at odds with large segments of the public, as it did in the 1960s, and gives rise to a series of concerns about police behavior. Common to all of the concerns is the manner in which police exercise their discretion.

Police Corruption

Corruption is the use of the police position for personal gain. While it is common to refer to police powers as those of arrest and the right to use force, police discretion also gives the police the power *not* to arrest, and indeed not to take action at all. In the 19th and early 20th centuries, with police salaries as low as the hiring standards, police were susceptible to bribes to "look the other way," "lose" evidence, or focus their enforcement efforts on criminals' or politicians' business competitors. During Prohibition, bootleggers bribed police in cities on a widespread basis. In modern times, higher standards and better salaries have improved the police as a whole, but pockets of corruption are revealed periodically.

More problematic than the bribing of police by organized crime are cases when the police themselves become criminals. The classic case in modern times was "The Pad" in New York City, revealed by Frank Serpico to the Knapp Commission in the early 1970s. Systematic police corruption shook down merchants for protection money like the racketeers of earlier periods. Police shaking down drug dealers, confiscating their drugs, and selling the drugs themselves has been a problem in several cities, as uncovered by the Mollen Commission's investigation of NYPD corruption in the 1980s and the Los Angeles Rampart Division CRASH scandal of the late 1990s. More contemporary research by Stinson has revealed fewer instances of organized police crime but has brought to light a far larger number of individual cases.

Harassment

The clear-cut moral division of the world focuses police attention on those they deem "bad." Anyone whose appearance or behavior signals "trouble" is likely to be subjected to scrutiny, usually in a field interrogation contact to determine who they are and what they are up to. Constant police pressure on violent street gangs and drug dealers is considered a good thing, serving law-abiding citizens by reducing the opportunity for criminals to act out. When the net is widened to include law-abiding citizens whose demeanor is without reproach and who bear only a superficial resemblance to the criminals, the police affront the autonomy and personal dignity of citizens. If that happens on a regular basis, the perception grows that the police are merely **harassing** people they do not like for reasons with little or no relation to the police mission.

Racial profiling remains a continuing concern, arising from police efforts to intercept bulk drugs before they can be marketed in the cities but also extending to weapons crimes. Cases in New Jersey and Maryland documented that state police stopped and searched minority motorists' cars in numbers far greater than their proportion of highway users. The underlying assumption equating race with criminality—the belief that African Americans and Hispanics are more involved with drug trafficking than whites—was not borne out by the search results: drugs were found at equal rates in minority and white motorists' cars. Other jurisdictions have found similar patterns of racial disparities in stops, though in less dramatic numbers. The fundamental objection is to the use of race rather than behavior as a reason for initiating a police inquiry. Other objections arise from the manner in which minority motorists are treated during contact.

Web Activity

The city of East Haven, Connecticut, came under scrutiny for its police department's treatment of Hispanic citizens. You can read about this at http://www.nytimes.com/2012/01/25/nyregion/connecticut-police-officers-accused-of-mistreating-latinos.html?pagewanted=all. More recently, the NYPD's "Stop and Frisk" program was discontinued after it came under intense criticism for targeting young African American and Latino males.

Improper Use of Force and Police Brutality

The power to use "non-negotiable coercive force" in defense of the law and social order is vital to the police role. In the vast majority of police–citizen interactions, police use force properly, if at all—most incidents are resolved without force. Like any other power, however, it can be subject to abuse. There are two primary categories of abuse. *Wrongful* use involves using force for the wrong reason, such as to retaliate against a person for "disrespect" to the officer. *Disproportionate* use occurs when the level of force far exceeds the level of resistance or aggression of the subject. The police are also required to protect the life and safety of those they use force against once the situation is brought under control.

Web Activity

You can find one presentation on the use of force continuum at the National Institute of Justice website: http://www.nij.gov/topics/law-enforcement/officer-safety/use-of-force/Pages/continuum.aspx.

Legitimate force may be used to bring resisting subjects into compliance. This usually means submitting to arrest, although people may also be forced out of areas where they are trespassing. Police are trained and equipped to employ force in accordance with the **force continuum**, which links the level of police force to the aggressiveness and resistance of the citizen (see Figure 3.1).

The force continuum begins with the authoritative presence of the officer, moves through commanding voice and directions to the first actual application of physical force, a guiding push or firm grip to steer a person away from a particular point. Physical resistance from a citizen is required for higher levels of force, including pain compliance holds (wristlocks and other pressure-point techniques), devices like pepper spray and electrical shocks from stun guns, and the use of impact weapons like nightsticks. Deadly force is the final step, reserved for a narrowly defined set of circumstances.

Federal funding has promoted the development of less lethal weaponry to assist the police in their mission while minimizing the risk of harm to officers,

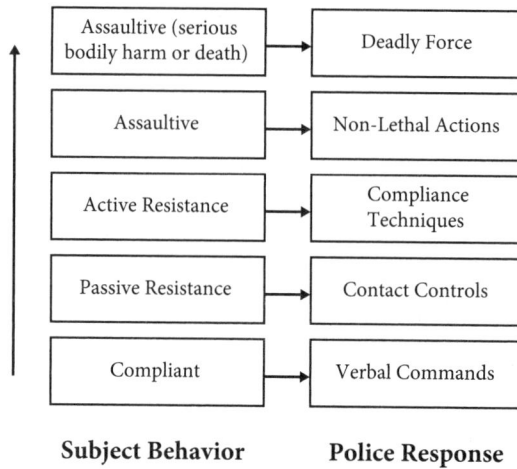

Subject Behavior		Police Response
Assaultive (serious bodily harm or death)	→	Deadly Force
Assaultive	→	Non-Lethal Actions
Active Resistance	→	Compliance Techniques
Passive Resistance	→	Contact Controls
Compliant	→	Verbal Commands

Figure 3.1 Use of Force Continuum
SOURCE: Constructed by authors.

suspects, and bystanders. Incapacitating chemical agents like pepper spray, beanbag rounds that knock a person down but do not penetrate the skin, capture nets fired from shotguns, sticky foam, disorienting lights and stun grenades, and other weapons still in the development stage all seek to provide safer alternatives to gunfire.

Police have the power to use deadly force only to save their own lives or those of a third party. A common-law "fleeing felon" rule allowed the use of lethal force to apprehend any accused felon. In 1985, the US Supreme Court in *Tennessee v. Garner* restricted the use of lethal force to situations of imminent and articulable danger. While police sidearms are the most obvious instruments of lethal force, blunt objects such as a baton or nightstick are also capable of inflicting deadly harm if used improperly or against the wrong target, such as a blow to the head.

Periodically, the issue of the use of force is brought to the public's attention by a high-profile case. In late 2014, a series of use-of-force events leading to the deaths of civilians occurred over a compressed period of time: many of those incidents were captured on video, either through bystanders' cellphone recordings or officers' dashboard or body-worn video cameras.

The shooting death of Michael Brown in Ferguson, Missouri, is widely acknowledged as the starting point for the Black Lives Matter movement protesting police shootings in particular, any use of force in general. "Hands up! Don't shoot" was one slogan of the protests, arising from early claims that Michael Brown had his hands in the air in surrender as he was shot. Unlike some of the later incidents, no video evidence or the encounter emerged. A grand jury heard substantial conflicting eyewitness testimony: some reported the "hand up" story, but other substantiated the officer's claim that Brown had attacked him, had tried to take the officer's sidearm, and was charging at the officer when he was shot.

Forensic evidence supported the officer's account of the incident, and the grand jury returned "no bill" on the charge of murder against the officer.

A seemingly rapid series of similar events followed, adding fuel to the flame. The wrongly named "chokehold" death of Eric Garner in New York City led to "I can't breathe" as another slogan, as Eric Garner's last words were recorded on a bystander's cellphone video during his arrest. The shooting deaths of Tamir Rice in Cleveland and John Crawford in Beavercreek, Ohio; of Laquan McDonald in Chicago; of Breonna Taylor in Louisville; and a drug raid on the wrong house in Atlanta that led to the shooting death of a 92-year-old woman all followed a series of contested shootings, including several in Albuquerque, New Mexico.

The outcry led to protests against police across the country and was directly responsible for the assassination of two New York City police officers by a mentally disturbed Maryland man who set out to "put wings on pigs" by killing two officers for every citizen who died as a result of police action.

Web Activity

Additional examples of events involving the use of force can be found on the textbook website (www.oup.com/he/lab6e).

A number of secondary issues attend the public debate about the police use of deadly force. Police and their conservative supporters assert that shootings are more likely to occur because of the violence in high-crime areas (the residents of which are disproportionately minority); criminologists who have investigated the claims find no substantiation for it across the range of shootings, although individual incidents do fall under that heading. Defenders claim that white and Blacks shot by the police tend to be roughly equal in number, including both armed and unarmed suspects; critics of the police note that while the raw numbers are approximately the same, Blacks are a distinct minority in the population, and the "equal" numbers actually represent a disproportionate number of Black victims. Very few police officers are held criminally liable, even in highly questionable shootings, because judges and juries are reluctant to second-guess the potential for danger. Even when officers are fired for misconduct, appeals boards often require their reinstatement.

Critical Thinking Exercise

What can be done to mend relations that are damaged by a good-faith erroneous shooting? If a member of your family, a close friend, or even someone you knew casually were shot and killed by police officers under comparable circumstances, what would you expect to happen?

The Blue Wall of Silence

The cultural theme of feeling unappreciated and under fire combines with themes of danger and solidarity to create the **blue wall of silence**. Some police officers who know of wrongdoing by other police will not take action against them or provide information against them to investigators because of two things. First, police mistrust their superiors and fear being given disproportionately harsh punishment to set an example or to alleviate political pressure on their administrators. Second, they fear alienating their brother and sister officers, upon whom they depend for backup assistance in dangerous situations. Unions also fear that employee rights will be abrogated under political pressure, so they intervene as advocates and lawyers for officers accused of wrongdoing. To the public, it appears that "the police protect their own," even against legitimate grievances and complaints of the community. The blue wall is no longer as strong as it was once thought to be, as professional and community-oriented officers realize that the police must clean their own house for legitimacy and that a rogue officer is as much a danger to them as are criminals. Nevertheless, it is entrenched in some agencies still, and the issues that give rise to it remain salient.

Policing the Police

The periodic scandals that arise from police misconduct are followed by public cries for police reform. In the past, most reforms were promises of better internal management by the police agency. In effect, clear rules would be written, better training would be devised, and supervision would be stricter. Police agencies asserted that the illegal behavior featured in the headlines was solely confined to "bad apples" who were not representative of the majority of police officers, who were honest, fair, and devoted to the public good.

More recently, the cyclical nature of police scandals has led people to question the ability of the police themselves. Because criminal convictions of police officers are difficult to obtain, aggrieved citizens and advocacy groups have pursued lawsuits against police agencies, asserting a pattern and practice of denial of civil rights. In addition, the federal Justice Department has moved against some police departments, using lawsuits to craft **consent decrees** that articulate specific changes the departments must make. Typically, those changes are monitored by outside entities that report to the federal court; the issue of racial profiling by the New Jersey State Police resulted in one such consent decree.

Federal intervention depends upon the willingness of the current administration to intervene. Lawsuits can also take years to settle. At the local level, residents concerned with police misconduct have begun to call for **civilian review** of police. Allegations of police misconduct are heard by boards composed entirely of residents or a mixture of residents and police officials. Conduct is judged based upon community expectations rather than just police practice. In the best models, police experts identify the acceptable standards and types of training that support police policy. The judgments made are then based on whether or not the officers' conduct was in accordance with law, with policy, and with community expectations of conduct. If discipline is recommended, typically the police chief is responsible for its administration.

Critical Thinking Exercise

Should citizens have the power to judge the actions of a police officer via civilian review boards or other mechanisms? Or is it necessary to have been a police officer in order to determine that a police officer's decision in any matter was correct or incorrect? Is it necessary to be a doctor in order to judge medical malpractice?

Special Constituencies

Police often face issues regarding communities with special needs. The mentally ill are much more prominent on the streets of the nation in the wake of the deinstitutionalization movement in the 1950s that closed asylums and hospitals. Their behavior may be frightening to citizens, and some are potentially dangerous. Immigrant communities bring new languages, different social customs and expectations, and often antagonism toward the police based upon their experiences with extremely corrupt and brutal police in their homelands. Police often lack the language skills and social understanding to make contact with the communities, thus hindering service. In both cases, individuals are also vulnerable targets for criminals who take advantage of their inability or reluctance to communicate with the police. In addition, community policing attempts to establish positive relations with immigrants are often in conflict with the federal laws and enforcement mandates to deport those illegally in the country. Some local agencies do not cooperate with the ICE because cooperation would inhibit their ability to protect the legitimate immigrant community. Other agencies complain that when they do apprehend illegal immigrants, the understaffed ICE cannot take them into custody and the police are forced to release them. The elderly are also emerging as a new concern for police, who have to deal with issues such as Alzheimer's disease, dementia, isolation, and loneliness.

FUTURE ISSUES

At the time of this writing, challenges facing the American police include a combination of older and emerging issues. Terrorist attacks emanating from al Qaeda and other Middle East terrorist organizations have provoked calls for racial profiling of Arabs, despite the continuing problems of African American and Hispanic profiling domestically. Immigration rules are in a state of flux, but the same problems remain for police who must deal with local immigrant communities. Civil liberties are perceived to be threatened in exchange for what is believed to be greater security against terror.

Critical Thinking Exercise

How do you think the recent national attention to terrorism will affect law enforcement practices in the United States? How will it affect the daily activities of local police agencies and officers?

Technology also poses many new challenges for the police. Computer fraud and identity theft are new forms of theft for which most police agencies are not prepared. They lack the necessary state-of-the-art equipment, and only a handful of officers have the necessary skills to track cyberspace looters, hackers, and other electronic predators. The very notion of jurisdiction changes in cyberspace, and American laws may conflict with laws of the European Union, China, and others.

Invasive technologies may soon be widely available, threatening traditional expectations of privacy. The case of *Kyllo v. United States* (2001) required the police to observe privacy as it existed in 1789 when the Constitution was adopted, banning police use of any new technologies that revealed intimate details of a house (such as thermal imagers, which were used in the *Kyllo* case). That technology may soon be widely available to the public and to the criminal element, however, requiring both new investigative skills and new countermeasures to protect police resources. Implanted chips, cloning, live human–computer interface, augmented reality systems, and many other issues will raise long-term and potentially profound changes that the police will have to face. The most recent development is the widespread availability of quadcopters, known colloquially as drones. Drones raise considerable concerns over privacy, as legitimate uses clash with potential illegal activities: the same flyover cameras that permit monitoring of crops, remote facilities, and potential hazards can also be used to surreptitiously record private citizens' activities, both outside and inside the home. Despite a relatively low weight-bearing capacity at the present time, drones have a proven capacity to transport uncut drugs across borders, and to carry contraband of various types (including cellphones and guns) over prison walls. The recent discovery of a crashed drone on the grounds of the White House has raised alarms about the delivery of improvised explosive devices (IEDs) or biological weapons packages. Other robotic constructs could use the ground or even underground tunnels for similar types of deliveries.

GPS technology is developing rapidly, and is already a feature in newer automobiles. That greatly increases the ability of the police to track known or suspected criminals, and to recover stolen vehicles and other goods. However, the courts still require the police to obtain a warrant before placing a GPS device on a target's vehicle, or to piggy-back on corporately maintained vehicle-monitoring services such as OnStar. The same is true for accessing information on individuals' cell phones and other portable devices: the Supreme Court unanimously ruled in *Riley v. California* (573 US 373, 2014) that the search of cellphones seized incidental to arrest required a separate warrant, to protect the personal privacy of the information they contain on a basis comparable to personal papers and effects.

While body-worn cameras are increasingly sought by the police and demanded by their critics, comparable privacy issues attend their use. When the cameras are turned on, particularly on calls in private dwellings, and how long recordings are maintained (and also the conditions for their editing and disposal), as well as to what uses their content may be put for analysis work, are all considerations that are being worked out. At the same time, however, body-worn cameras and social media technologies are bringing changes to the notion of "intuitive grasp of situational exigencies": the 1989 Supreme court decision in *Graham v. Connor* (490 US 386) replaced the governing standard of "substantive due process" with the Fourth Amendment's requirement of "'objective reasonableness' in light of the facts and circumstances confronting them, without regard to their underlying intent or motivation."

Though the Court rejected the idea of 20-20 hindsight as being useful in any way, today such "hindsight" is inevitable, as officers' descriptions of the situational exigencies have been contradicted in many cases by visual and audio evidence from dashboard cameras, body-worn cameras of the arresting officers or backup units, and bystander cellphone video recordings of the event. The issue has not yet been fully defined or resolved, but the days when an officer's post-event report description was the sole means of assessing situational exigencies are long past.

Nanotechnology is developing at a rapid pace, with positive implications for medicine already demonstrated, but negative possibilities abound. The public is most familiar with the 3D printer, rapid layering of plastics to form solid objects. A 3D printed firearm has already been claimed, and widespread manufacture of cheap, anonymous, one-use firearms represents a potential threat to the public. As nanotechnology develops further, computer codes for constructing designer drugs, poisons, and explosives through molecular assembly are a different threat.

Economic issues at the state level are undermining the incapacitation model that has held sway over correctional policies for several decades. Faced with rising prison costs and court mandates against overcrowding, legislatures have changed their mandate to the euphemistic "community control," releasing thousands of prisoners well before their sentences have been completed. Without corresponding resources devoted to probation and parole, prisoner reentry is largely unmonitored except by the police. At the same time, the knowledge that conviction will lead to either less time in "the joint" or perhaps even no time at all undermines whatever efficacy remained in the concept of deterrence. While the long-term impacts are not yet recognized, it is a reasonable expectation that the main burden of community control will fall to the already overstretched police.

Social expectations are also changing. The nation's punitive drug laws are under attack as too harsh, wrongly applied, and the wrong approach to the problems of drug abuse. While the trend toward decriminalizing marijuana—and even legalizing it at the state level—is no longer viewed as dangerous as it once was, the opioid epidemic sweeping the nation has created new demands on the police. Families encourage the use of Narcan and other naloxone treatments, which reverse the effects of potentially fatal drug overdoses, in order to give addicted loved ones a second chance. On the other side of the debate, experiences of law enforcement and EMS personnel suggest that for many addicts, the "second chance" is simply to get high again. They report giving repeated doses to the same individuals, sometimes only hours after a revival, and openly question the wisdom of providing a "fail-safe" to continued self-destructive behavior.

The addition of fentanyl, and now carfentanyl, to the opioid crisis is also changing police procedures. At least two officers have died as a result of inadvertent contact exposure to the drug while trying to revive an overdose victim or searching a crime scene. Gloving and double-gloving are increasingly the rule for officers in such cases, and many agencies no longer do field testing of suspected drugs. Instead, they treat them as potentially toxic substances, and refer them to crime laboratories as such.

The nature of privacy in public spaces is being redefined by closed-circuit TV, social media, GPS tracking, and other technologies. The line dividing federal and state rights is being redefined in the states' favor by the Supreme Court at the same time that many state crimes are being "federalized" in hopes of securing harsher penalties. The impact of globalization upon the economy, laws, and social expectations of the nation—indeed, in a longer view, even upon the concept of the nation-state and sovereignty—has not fully been realized. Globalization is a long-term force with short-term ripples. The "war on terror" may be a short-term problem, but it has long-term implications for civil rights and civil liberties. Technology has implications for both and presents an even more uncertain future as the definition of what it is to be human is determined. All of these present the possibility of another period of radical change for the police, adjusting to new factors in the human and social condition.

CONCLUSION

The police represent a constantly evolving network of agencies and individuals who are empowered to use force but are also expected to use knowledge, insight, and understanding to solve a wide variety of problems that afflict American society. Because of their power to arrest, the police are the gatekeepers of the rest of the criminal justice system, but the greater impact of police work lies in situations that are resolved without arrest. Changes in police work are driven by changes in law, evolutionary changes in social attitudes, and emerging technologies. New challenges such as the impact of globalization and the intersection of American law with foreign law will be added to the ongoing challenges of proper selection, training, inculcation of values, and guidance.

KEY WORDS

background checks	beats	broken windows
beat integrity	blue wall of silence	campus-based academies

chain of command
citizen patrols
civil rights movement
civilian review
community-oriented
  policing
community policing
CompStat
consent decrees
constable
contract cities
corruption
crime prevention
detective
deterrence
discretion
dual-entry tracks
Field Training Officer
  (FTO)
first responders
force continuum

harassment
HAZMAT
Internal Affairs
john details
Kansas City Preventive
  Patrol Experiment
law compliance
law enforcement
Minneapolis Domestic
  Violence Experiment
multijurisdictional task
  forces
mutual aid
Neighborhood Watch
order maintenance
patrol
police academy
police subculture
power shifts
precincts
preservice training

private police
problem-oriented
  policing
property marking
racial profiling
regional task forces
rotating shifts
safe havens
school resource officer
service
sheriff
single-entry tracks
state patrols
state police
steady shifts
sting operations
stress-based academies
troops
use of force

SUGGESTED READINGS

Police Culture
Crank, J. P., and M. A. Caldero. (2000). *Police ethics: The corruption of noble cause.* Cincinnati: Anderson.
Muir, W. K. Jr. (1977). *Police: Streetcorner politicians.* Chicago: University of Chicago Press.

Community-Oriented and Problem-Oriented Policing
Goldstein, H. (1979). *Improving policing: A problem-oriented approach. Crime and Delinquency,* 25, 236–258.
Greene, J. R., and S. D. Mastrofski (eds.). (1988). *Community policing: Rhetoric or reality.* New York: Praeger.
Sparrow, M., M. H. Moore, and D. Kennedy. (1990). *Beyond 911: A new era for policing.* New York: Basic Books.
Trojanowicz, R., and B. Bucqueroux. (1990). *Community policing: A contemporary perspective.* Cincinnati: Anderson.

Modern Reform: Initial Studies
Klockars, C. (1985). *The idea of police.* Beverly Hills, CA: Sage Publications.
Reiss, A. J. Jr. (1971). *The police and the public.* New Haven, CT: Yale University Press.

CHAPTER 4

The Court System

CHAPTER OUTLINE

After reading this chapter, you should be able to:

- Explain what is meant by a dual court system
- Discuss the adversarial nature of the court
- Point out key points in the history of federal courts
- Discuss the US Courts of Appeal
- Discuss the history and types of state courts
- Compare and contrast trial courts of limited and general jurisdictions
- List and define the various actors in the courtroom, including the distinctions between federal and state
- Outline the typical movement of cases through the court system
- Discuss the selection of jurors
- Explain the difference between indeterminate and determinate sentences
- Discuss the appeals process
- Identify and define different types of specialized courts
- Give examples of how courts have increased victim involvement

INTRODUCTION

The court system is often referred to as the link between police and the correctional system, although this is something of a misnomer. While it may be true that the court system is, in effect, the second primary aspect of the criminal justice system, its role spans the entire system. In many cases, the court system is involved in criminal cases before police make an arrest and after a person has been subject to some form of correctional sanction. Generally, the court system has two basic functions: to adjudicate defendants charged with crimes and to ensure the entire criminal justice system is engaging in fair procedures as the law is enforced. This is a large undertaking, which is why the court system is viewed as a complex, and often misunderstood, component of the criminal justice system.

BASIC TENETS OF THE COURT SYSTEM

Federal and state governments have their own laws and court systems. Although these systems may vary from state to state and between states and the federal government, all court systems have the same basic guidelines regarding the administration of laws in their respective jurisdictions.

First, the United States has what is called a **dual court system**, which simply means that the federal government has its own court system and the states have their own court systems. This may seem obvious, but when it comes to the enforcement of the law, having 51 different court systems can become quite complex.

The federal court system is responsible for violations of federal law and state court systems are responsible for violations of the laws in their respective states. It becomes complicated, however, when state and federal laws conflict with one another and the court system must get involved. An example of this is seen with the use of marijuana or medical marijuana. Currently, 33 states allow for the medical use of marijuana, while 11 states allow for the recreational use of marijuana (ProCon.org 2020). Federal law, however, prohibits the use of medical and recreational marijuana. Thus, an individual in California, which authorizes the use of medical and recreational marijuana, could be held liable in federal court for use of the drug, even though it is allowed under state law. Because of this conflict between laws, the court system has to get involved to resolve the issue. Numerous individuals have challenged the federal law prohibiting the use of the drug for medical purposes, and perhaps as many have challenged state laws allowing for its use. As a result, state and federal courts have both become involved in these cases, illustrating the complex nature of a dual court system.

Web Activity

For more information on the dual court system, see http://www.uscourts.gov/about-federal-courts/court-role-and-structure/comparing-federal-state-courts.

Another issue involving both federal and state court systems is jurisdiction. The term *jurisdiction* in the court system does not refer to a specific geographic area, but to the authority of courts to hear certain types of cases. For instance, the federal court system only has jurisdiction to rule on cases involving federal law; it does not have the ability to rule on cases involving state law, unless the state law conflicts with federal law or the US Constitution. Appellate courts do not have the jurisdiction to conduct trials; this is the jurisdiction of lower state and federal trial courts. Finally, juvenile courts do not have jurisdiction to hear issues involving divorce or custody issues. In effect, each court, whether at the state or federal level, is limited in the types of cases it is allowed to rule upon. A defendant cannot simply go to any court he or she wishes in order to be heard; he or she must go to the court that specializes in the particular issue at hand.

Another tenet of state and federal court systems is the **adversarial system of justice**. An adversarial system relies on two opposing parties; in criminal cases, this involves a defendant versus the state (in the form of a prosecutor). In addition, this system involves a neutral body, in the form of the judge or jury, that decides the outcome of the case. Generally, it is the responsibility of the state to prove its case against the defendant. This reflects the presumption of innocence; in effect, a defendant is presumed innocent until proven guilty by the state. On the other hand, a defendant must challenge a state's case and question the evidence that the state brings forward. It should be known that a defendant is not responsible for proving his or her innocence at trial; the state must prove guilt.

When adjudicating cases, the court system often must balance the needs of the state versus the rights of the defendant. This is sometimes referred to as the crime-control versus due-process model of justice. Packer (1968) developed models to illustrate how the criminal justice system must try to accomplish its goals while ensuring the fair and equal application of the law. The crime-control model, as its name implies, focuses on the reduction of criminal behavior. It stresses the swiftness and certainty of case outcomes, suggesting that any delay in the adjudication of criminal cases undermines the ability of the system to reduce crime. The crime-control model posits that many defendants who are arrested are factually guilty, so the court system should waste no time in convicting and sentencing them. On the other hand, the due-process model emphasizes the protection of rights of defendants. This model is concerned about the violation of rights in the name of crime control and works to ensure that the criminal justice system does not violate the law in order to enforce the law. It views swiftness in the administration of justice as a concern, as it increases the likelihood of mistakes being made and innocent people being punished. The criminal justice system has tried to strike a balance between these two competing models although, at times, one or the other predominates. The court system is the primary component of the system that is charged with ensuring that the law is enforced in a fair and equal manner.

Critical Thinking Exercise

How well has the court system balanced the crime-control and due-process models? Which model do you believe is dominant in criminal courts? Is this appropriate? Should it be changed? How? Why?

HISTORY OF THE COURTS

Chapter 2 discussed the origins of criminal law in this country, and the court system has largely been responsible for ensuring that the law is enforced fairly and equally. However, the term *court system* is a very general one and encompasses a number of courts at both the federal and state levels. As such, it is important to understand the history of both the federal and state court systems in order to appreciate the role of the courts today.

History of Federal Courts

As the US Constitution was being drafted, many of the drafters felt it was necessary to create a national court system. During the Constitutional Convention in 1787, two competing plans were proposed to establish the federal court system. The New Jersey Plan called for the establishment of one federal court: a Supreme Court. This plan called for the state court systems to play an active role in adjudicating federal matters. In effect, proponents of the New Jersey Plan were skeptical of a strong, centralized federal judiciary and wanted the states to maintain some control over federal court matters. Under this plan, state courts would conduct trials and other lower-level federal court proceedings, and the process of appeal would take the case to the one federal Supreme Court.

An alternative, the Virginia Plan, proposed a broader and more centralized federal court system with the establishment of a Supreme Court and various lower federal courts. This plan argued that states should not be involved in federal court matters and that the federal government should have a judiciary system just as states do. A compromise between these two competing plans was reached, and the result is found in Article III of the US Constitution: "The judicial power of the United States, shall be vested in one supreme court, and in such inferior courts as the Congress may from time to time ordain and establish." In essence, this created the one Supreme Court that both plans advocated, but allowed Congress to create lower federal courts when necessary. At first, this compromise seemed to benefit the proponents of the New Jersey Plan, as no vast federal court system was created. However, over time, the compromise greatly favored the proponents of the Virginia Plan, who eventually saw the creation of a centralized federal court system.

Since the US Constitution allowed Congress to establish lower federal courts, it was only a matter of time before these courts were created. One of the first concerns of the first Congress was the creation of the lower federal court system. In the Judiciary Act of 1789, the lower federal court system was finally established. This act further defined the role and makeup of the Supreme Court and established two levels of lower federal courts: trial courts and appellate courts.

US Supreme Court

The Judiciary Act of 1789 stated that the Supreme Court was to consist of one chief justice and five associate justices. In its first decade of existence, the Court floundered, not really knowing or understanding its role in a federal system of government. According to Carp and Stidham (1990), the Court did not rule on a case in its first three years of existence and decided only around 50 cases during its first decade. This situation was greatly altered, however, with the appointment of John Marshall as the third chief justice in 1801. Marshall is credited with giving the Supreme Court its vision and establishing rules and guidelines that governed the Court's procedures. One of these guidelines was the issuance of a single opinion of the Court. Until this point, each individual justice issued his own ruling with his own rationale; this made it quite difficult for those responsible for enforcing the rulings to know what to do. Marshall created the practice of allowing one opinion of the Court (now called the ruling of the Court or the majority opinion) in order for the Court to present an air of unification around a particular ruling. During Marshall's tenure, the Court was involved in a number of rulings that are considered some of the most important decisions in judicial history (Box 4.1).

BOX 4.1

Key US Supreme Court Rulings During John Marshall's Tenure as Chief Justice

Marbury v. Madison **(1803)**. This case established the Court's practice of judicial review. In this case, President John Adams, during his lame-duck presidency, created numerous federal judgeships. The judgeships were approved by the Senate but, when President Thomas Jefferson took office, four of the judicial appointees had not received their commissions. The secretary of state, James Madison, refused to deliver the commissions, as he and the new president disapproved of the newly created judgeships. The four judicial appointees asked the US Supreme Court to force Madison to deliver the commissions, relying on a writ of mandamus, a federal provision that allows a court to compel a public official to perform a duty. The US Supreme Court refused to intervene, finding that the federal provision gave the Court a power that the US Constitution did not give it; that is, unless the US Constitution states that the Court can or must enforce a writ of mandamus, any law that says otherwise is unconstitutional. Thus, the US Supreme Court struck down the federal provision as unconstitutional and established the practice of judicial review—the ability to declare laws unconstitutional.

    McCulloch v. Maryland **(1819)**. This case dealt with the powers of the federal government over those of the states. In 1791, Secretary of the Treasury Alexander Hamilton wanted Congress to charter a national bank called the Bank of the United States. Thomas Jefferson, who was secretary of state at the time, opposed the national bank, claiming that the US Constitution did not give Congress the power to charter one. Hamilton disagreed, claiming that the "necessary and proper" clause in Article I gave Congress the authority to enact policies for the good of the nation. The bank was created and given a 20-year charter. When the charter expired in 1811, it was not renewed. After the War of 1812, it was evident that a national bank was needed to handle the business of the nation. As a result, the second Bank of the United States was chartered in 1816. State and local banks did not agree with the creation of the national bank, so state legislatures looked to restrict the bank's business. In Maryland, a tax was imposed on bank operations. James McCulloch, a cashier at the Baltimore branch of the Bank of the United States, refused to pay the tax and the case went to court. Ultimately, the US Supreme Court ruled that the national bank was constitutional and that the federal government has broad powers to enact laws for the good of the nation. In effect, this case allows the federal government to trump state governments on issues in which the governments conflict.

    Barron v. Baltimore **(1833)**. This case involved the power of the US Supreme Court to become involved in cases in which state governments violate the rights of their citizens. In Baltimore, Barron owned a profitable wharf. The city of Baltimore wished to repave the streets near the wharf, and when the streets were excavated, the debris slid into Barron's wharf, rendering it useless. Barron objected, claiming that since the city of Baltimore had ruined his business, he should be compensated. He claimed that the just-compensation clause of the Fifth Amendment required the government to pay for any damages. Initially, Barron won his case in lower court, but the US Supreme Court ruled against Barron, deciding that the just-compensation clause of the Fifth Amendment applied only to the federal government. In effect, the US Supreme Court refused to apply the just-compensation clause to Barron's case, finding that if state or local governments violate one's rights, one must look to the state or local courts for a remedy, not the federal courts. This ruling set the stage for a century of cases in which the US Supreme Court refused to apply the protections of the Bill of Rights to state actions. Ultimately, the US Supreme Court applied, or incorporated, these rights to the states and, now, states must offer the protections found in the federal Bill of Rights.

Web Activity

For access to full opinions by the US Supreme Court, visit its website at www.supremecourt.gov/opinions/opinions.aspx

The US Supreme Court is considered the final arbiter for issues involving federal law and the US Constitution. Once the US Supreme Court has made a decision in a case, that decision is final and cannot be reviewed by any other court. Although the Court has primarily appellate jurisdiction, it does have original jurisdiction in some cases. For example, the Court is the first and only court to hear cases involving disputes between two states, such as boundary disputes.

Today, the US Supreme Court is composed of one chief justice and eight associate justices. When deciding to hear cases, the US Supreme Court has a large amount of discretion, unlike the courts of appeal. The Court hears oral arguments in only a fraction of cases petitioned for review each year. In fact, out of approximately 7,000 cases on the Court's docket each year, only about 100 are selected for oral arguments.

Web Activity

For more information about the US Supreme Court's caseload, see https://www.fjc.gov/history/exhibits/graphs-and-maps/supreme-court-caseloads-1880-2015.

The US Supreme Court only hears cases that involve what it considers to be the most important policy issues. Cases that come to the Court come from the US Courts of Appeal (for cases involving federal law) and state supreme courts (for cases involving conflicts with federal law or state violations of the US Constitution).

Web Activity

For more information about the history of the US Supreme Court, visit www.supremecourthistory.org.

US Courts of Appeal

The Judiciary Act of 1789 also established the **appellate courts** of the federal system. The country was divided into federal court circuits—southern, middle, and eastern—and an appellate court was established for each. The courts were staffed by two US Supreme Court justices and a lower federal court judge (called a "district judge," which will be examined later). The lower court judge was responsible for establishing the court's caseload, and the Supreme Court justices traveled to each circuit to hear cases at the appellate level, a practice known as "circuit riding." This practice was grueling for the justices and the caseload of the appellate courts increased, especially after the Civil War, making the existing system ill equipped to handle a mounting workload. This system of hearing appellate cases continued until 1891, when Congress passed the Evarts Act. This act created nine federal appellate courts, one for each judicial circuit at the time, that were to hear appeals from the lower federal trial courts. Each appellate court, called a "circuit court," was staffed by newly created circuit court judges, thereby relieving the US Supreme Court justices of their circuit-riding duties. This created a more uniform system of hearing appeals.

The US Courts of Appeal have **appellate jurisdiction**, which means that cases do not originate there and these courts only hear cases that are brought up on appeal, after a lower court has decided an outcome. When federal appellate courts were established in 1789, the country was divided into three appellate circuits. Today, there are 11 appellate circuits, and each circuit consists of multiple states.

There is one US Court of Appeals in each of these circuits, and these courts are identified by their circuit—for example, the US Court of Appeals for the Eighth Circuit. There are two other federal appellate courts. One represents the D.C. Circuit (Washington DC) and one represents the Federal Circuit, which handles cases involving international trade and federal administrative law.

Web Activity

For an illustration of the boundaries of the federal courts, see the textbook website (www.oup.com/he/lab6e).

According to the Administrative Office of the US Courts (2019), approximately 48,000 cases were filed in the courts of appeal in 2019. Of these, only about 20 percent involve federal criminal law issues. Although decisions by the US Courts of Appeal may be petitioned for review by the US Supreme Court, these federal appellate courts are often the "court of last resort" for federal law because the US Supreme Court rarely reviews decisions made by these courts.

Most of the cases heard by the courts of appeal come from the federal district courts. Defendants must appeal their cases in the courts that cover their states. The federal courts of appeals have no control over the cases they hear; that is, there is no discretionary authority to reject appeals. When deciding cases, the courts of appeal usually utilize three-judge panels, which rotate membership periodically. A majority of the panel is sufficient for a ruling. In rare instances, all of the judges in a circuit may sit to hear a case. This is called an *en banc* proceeding.

US District Courts

The trial courts of the federal system, 13 **district courts**, were established by the Judiciary Act of 1789. The 11 states in the union at the time and the territories of Maine and Kentucky were considered districts, so the organization of the federal trial courts was entirely state-contained; that is, no federal district crossed state lines. Each district court was staffed by one district court judge who, as mentioned earlier, also had a role in hearing appellate cases. As new states entered the union, more district courts were created.

After the creation of the lower federal courts in 1789, each state was considered a district with one district court. Today, some states are divided into multiple districts because they are simply too populated to have just one district court. There is at least one district court in every state. There are currently 90 district courts in the 50 states and the District of Columbia and four others in Guam, Puerto Rico, the US Virgin Islands, and the Northern Mariana Islands.

As mentioned above, district courts are the trial courts of the federal system. According to the Administrative Office of the US Courts (2020), 90,000 criminal cases were filed in district courts in 2019, mostly for immigration, firearm/explosive, and drug violations. Despite this, civil cases compose the bulk of cases that move through the district courts. US District Courts have **original jurisdiction**, which means that these courts have the authority to hear cases for the first time and decide an outcome.

History of State Courts

The federal court system is probably better known to the public, but state court systems were in existence before the federal court system was established. In colonial times, local courts, often called justice of the peace courts or magistrate courts, handled lower-level court matters. County courts were the trial courts of the colonies and appeals were handled by the royal governor (Carp and Stidham 1990). After the revolution, state court structure was largely the same as that of the colonial courts, although the royal governor was no longer present.

The various states had largely been left to their own devices when it came to the creation and administration of their court systems. Most states had systems for handling various levels of court procedures, such as trials and appeals, but encountered problems as industrialization and population increased after the Civil War. Local courts began to struggle with increased caseloads and different types of cases, which involved newly created laws dealing with issues such as business and child labor. As a result, state courts were forced to find innovative ways to deal with these issues, including creating more courts and specialized courts, although some states are still facing some of the same problems today.

State Supreme Courts

These courts are the courts of last resort for issues involving state law. Most states call these courts "supreme courts," but a few designate them as "courts of appeals" or other names. The number of judges who serve on state supreme courts varies depending upon the state, but the judges hear cases *en banc*. These courts have original jurisdiction in some matters, but largely have appellate jurisdiction. Like the US Supreme Court, state supreme courts exercise a fair amount of discretion in deciding which cases to hear. As a result, appeals involving state law typically will end at the intermediate appellate court level.

State Courts of Appeal

These courts are often called "intermediate courts of appeal" because they compose the middle level of the court system between trial courts and the state supreme courts. Despite this, 11 states do not have intermediate courts of appeal; the appeal load is so low that this level of court is not needed. In these situations, the state supreme court is the only state appellate court. State courts of appeal primarily have appellate jurisdiction.

State courts of appeal do not exercise the same amount of discretion as the state supreme courts; they must hear all appeals that are filed with the court in order to provide a resolution to each. Because of this, the state supreme court is able to exercise much discretion because many appeals are resolved at the intermediate level. In those states that do not employ intermediate appellate courts, state supreme courts must hear all appeals and provide resolutions.

The number of judges serving on state courts of appeal varies depending upon the state. Like the federal courts of appeal, cases at this level are typically heard by three-judge panels. As stated earlier, most appeals end at this stage because the state supreme court is highly discretionary when selecting appeals to hear.

Trial Courts of General Jurisdiction

Trial courts of general jurisdiction are considered the major trial courts at the state level. These courts handle the more serious criminal and civil cases that arise in state courts. The actual names of these courts vary depending upon the state, but most trial courts of general jurisdiction are called "district," "circuit," or "superior" courts.

Generally, each state is divided into districts, usually counties, and each district employs one major trial court. In rural areas, these districts may encompass several counties and judges will travel to each county in the district to hear cases. In other areas, judges are assigned to specific courthouses and cases come to them. According to the Courts Statistics Project (2020), approximately 15 million criminal cases are filed each year in these courts, vastly outnumbering the number of cases filed in federal trial courts. Criminal cases comprise approximately 22 percent of these cases, while civil cases comprise approximately 35 percent.

Trial Courts of Limited Jurisdiction

These courts compose the lowest level of courts in the state court system. These courts go by a variety of names, including "magistrate," "municipal," "city," and "justice of the peace" courts. They have limited jurisdiction because they are restricted to handling only certain types of matters: in effect, minor matters. In criminal cases, these minor matters include misdemeanors, but they also include the early stages of felony cases, such as first appearances, bail hearings, and appointment of counsel. These courts also handle cases involving traffic and small claims issues.

Although **trial courts of limited jurisdiction** are restricted in the types of matters they can handle, they constitute the bulk of court systems in the country—about 85 percent of all judicial bodies. The number of cases that are handled by these courts is approximately 55 million cases per year (Court Statistics Project 2020), most of which are traffic offenses (34 million). This has resulted in overcrowding problems, when courts do not have the resources to handle the increasing numbers of cases coming into the system. The number of each of these courts varies from state to state, and more populated areas have numerous courts of limited jurisdiction in certain counties.

State courts vary in organization and structure. Additionally, state courts have different names for their courts. Box 4.2 illustrates three different court systems. California has a streamlined and organized court system; throughout the state, all courts of limited and general jurisdiction are called "superior courts." California's intermediate appellate courts are called "courts of appeal" and its court of last resort is called the "supreme court."

Ohio has four types of limited-jurisdiction courts, each handling similar cases. Counties and cities in Ohio vary as to which type of limited-jurisdiction court they will use. For example, municipal courts are found in 129 municipalities (cities) in Ohio, but there are only 35 county courts statewide. Generally, a particular county will have only one or the other operating within the county. Additionally, Ohio's trial courts of general jurisdiction are called "courts of common pleas," which is a unique name for this type of court. This name is a holdover from British common-law courts in existence in England until the 1800s. Most states call these courts "superior courts," "district courts," "circuit courts," and the like. Ohio's court of last resort is called the "supreme court."

Finally, New York provides a good illustration of a state court structure in need of organization. New York has eight limited-jurisdiction courts; again, the county or city will determine which court it will use. Additionally, New York has two trial courts of general jurisdiction—called a "supreme court" and a "county court"—with county courts operating outside of New York City. New York also has two intermediate appellate courts; counties in New York are combined into "departments" and each department has an appellate court that serves those counties. The first intermediate appellate court, the "Appellate Divisions

BOX 4.2

Illustration of Three Different Court Systems

California

Supreme Court	COLR A S
CSP Case Types: • Appeal by permission criminal, civil, limited administrative agency. Appeal by permission writ –other, habeas corpus/post-conviction relief (non-death penalty). • Exclusive death penalty . • Original proceeding writ application. Exclusive bar/judiciary, certified question .	link

↑

Courts of Appeal	IAC A S
CSP Case Types: • Appeal by right criminal, civil, administrative agency . • Appeal by permission criminal, civil, administrative agency. Interlocutory appeals in criminal, civil, administrative agency. • Original proceeding writ application, certified question, advisor opinion, original proceedings–other.	link

↑

Superior Court *Jury trials except in appeals, domestic relations, and juvenile cases*	GJC A S
CSP Case Types: • Tort, contract, real property ($25,000- no maximum), limited civil ($0 - $25,000) miscellaneous civil. Exclusive small claims (up to $10,000), probate/estate, mental health, civil appeals. • Appeal by right misdemean or, civil (up to $25,000). • Exclusive domestic relations. • Exclusive criminal. • Exclusive juvenile. • Exclusive traffic/other violations. • Original proceeding writ.	link

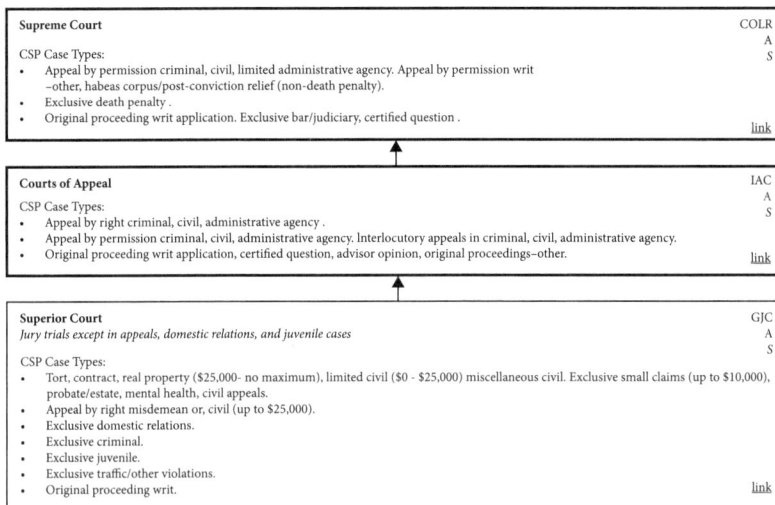

SOURCE: http://www.courtstatistics.org/state_court_structure_charts/california.

Ohio

Supreme Court	COLR A S
CSP Case Types: • Appeal by right felony (death penalty), administrative agency, writ, appeal by right – other. • Appeal by permission criminal, civil, administrative agency, administrative agency, writ, appeal by permission – other. Interlocutory appeals in criminal, civil, administrative agency, writ • Exclusive death penalty • Original proceeding application for writ. Exclusive bar/ judicical, certified question, original proceedings – other.	link

↑

Court of Appeals	IAC A S
CSP Case Types: • Appeal by right criminal, civil, administrative agency, writ, Interlocutory appeals in criminal, civil, administrative agency, writ. • Original proceeding application for writ, original proceedings–other.	link

↑

Court of Common Pleas *Jury trials in most cases*	GJC A M
CSP Case Types: • Tort, contract, real property ($15,000–no maximum), administrative agency appeals, miscellaneous civil. Exclusive mental health, probate/estate. • Exclusive domestic relations. • Felony, misdemeanor. • Exclusive juvenile. • Traffic/other violations (juvenile only).	link

Municipal Court *Jury trials in most cases*	LJC M	**Countty Court** *Jury trials in most cases*	LJC M
CSP Case Types: • Tort, contract, real propery ($0–$15,000), small claims (up to $5,000), miscellaneous civil. • Criminal. • Traffic infractions, ordinance violations. link		CSP Case Types: • Tort, contract, real propery ($0–$15,000), small claims (up to $5,000), miscellaneous civil. • Criminal. • Traffic infractions, ordinance violations. link	

Court of Claims *Jury trials in some cases*	LJC S	**Mayors Court** *No jury trials*	LJC L
CSP Case Types: • Limited civil. link		CSP Case Types: • Misdemeanors. • Traffic/other violations. link	

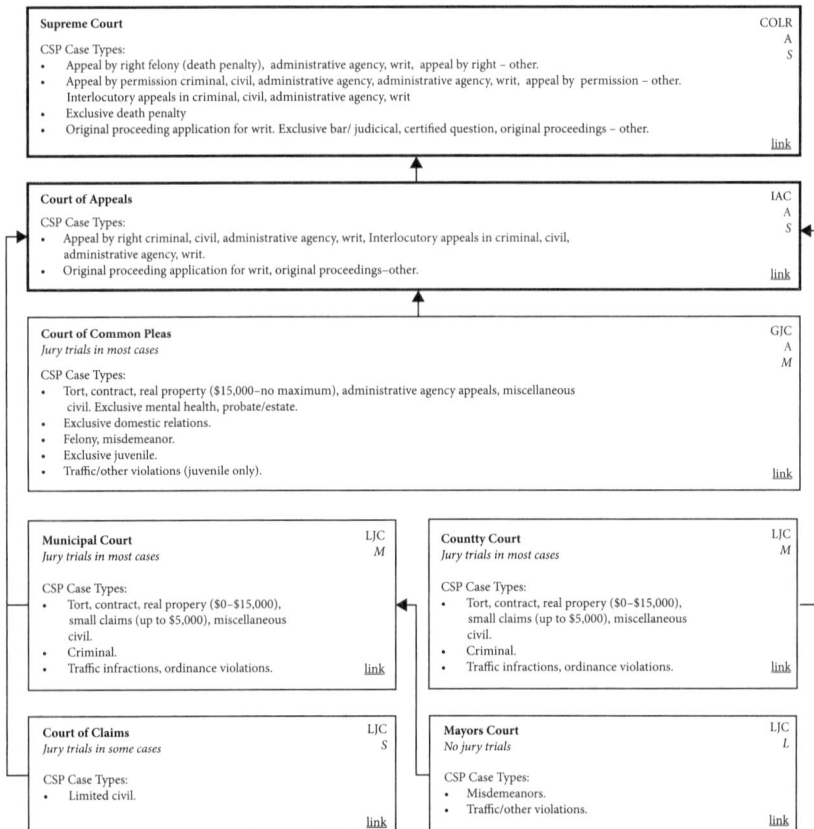

SOURCE: http://www.courtstatistics.org/state_court_structure_charts/ohio.

New York

Court of Appeals — COLR / S

CSP Case Types:
- Appeal by right limited criminal limited civil, limited administrative agency, appeal by right–other. Interiocutory appeals by right in limited criminal, limited civil, limited administrative agency.
- Appeal by permission criminal, civil, administrative agency, Interlocutory appeals in criminal, civil, administrative agency. Appeal by permission-other.
- Original proceeding bar admission, lawyer discipline/eligibility, judicical discipline/qualification, certified question, original proceedings -other.   link

Appellate Divisions of Supreme Court — IAC / A / S

CSP Case Types:
- Appeal by right(matters originating in Supreme and Country courts) criminal, civil, administrative agency, writ. Interlocutory appeals in criminal, civil, administrative agency, writ.
- Appeal by permission (matters originating in other cours) criminal, civil, administrative agency, writ. Interlocutory appeals in criminal, civil, administrative agency, writ
- Original proceedings application for writ, bar/judiciary, original proceedings- other.   link

Appellate terms of Supreme Court — IAC / S

CSP Case Types:
- Appeal by right criminal, civil, administrative agency, writ, appeal by right–other. Interlocutory appeals in criminal, civil, administrative agency, writ.
- Appeal by permission criminal, civil, administrative agency, writ, appeal by permission–other. Interlocutory appeals in criminal, civil, administrative agency, writ

Supreme Court — GJC / A / S
Jury trials

CSP Case Types:
- Tort, contract real property, miscellaneous civil.
- Exclusive marriage dissolution.
- Felony, misdemeanor.   link

County Court — GJC / S
Jury trials

CSP Case Types:
- Tort, contract real property ($0 - $25,000), civil appeals, miscellaneous civil.
- Criminal.   link

Court of Claims — LJC / S
No jury trials

CSP Case Types:
- Tort, contract, real property   link

District Court — LJC / S
Jury trials except in traffic
CSP Case Types:
- Tort, contract, real property ($0–$15,000), small claims (up to $5,000)
- Felony, preliminary hearings, misdemeanor.
- Traffic infractions, ordinance violations.   link

CityCourt — LJC / S
Jury trials for highest level misdemeanor
CSP Case Types:
- Tort, contract, real propery ($0–$15,000), small claims (up to $5,000)
- Felony, preliminary hearings, misdemeanor.
- Traffic infractions, ordinance violations.   link

Family Court — LJC / S
No jury trials
CSP Case Types:
- Guardianship
- Support, paternity, adoption.
- Exclusive domestic violence.
- Exclusive juvenile.   link

Civil Court of the City of New York — LJC / S
Jury trials

CSP Case Types:
- Tort, contract, real property ($0–$25,000), small claims, (up to $5,000),
- miscellaneous civil.   link

Criminal Court of the City of New York — LJC / S
Jury trials for highest level misdemeanor

CSP Case Types:
- Preliminary hearings, misdemeanor.
- Traffic infractions, ordinance violations.   link

Town and Village Justice Court — LJC / M
Jury trials in most cases

CSP Case Types:
- Tort, contract, real property ($0–$3,000), small claims (up to $3,000)
- Preliminary hearings, misdemeanor
- Traffic/other violations.   link

Surrogates' Court — LJC / S
Jury trials in probate/estate

CSP Case Types:
- Probate/estate.
- Adoption.   link

Legend

☐ = Appellate level
☐ = Trial Level
↑ =Route of appeal

COLR = Court of Last Reort
IAC = Intermediate Appellate Court
GJC = General Jurisdiction Court
LJC = Limited Jurisdiction Court

A = Appeal from Admin. Agency
S = State funded
L = Locally funded
M = Mixed: state and locally funded

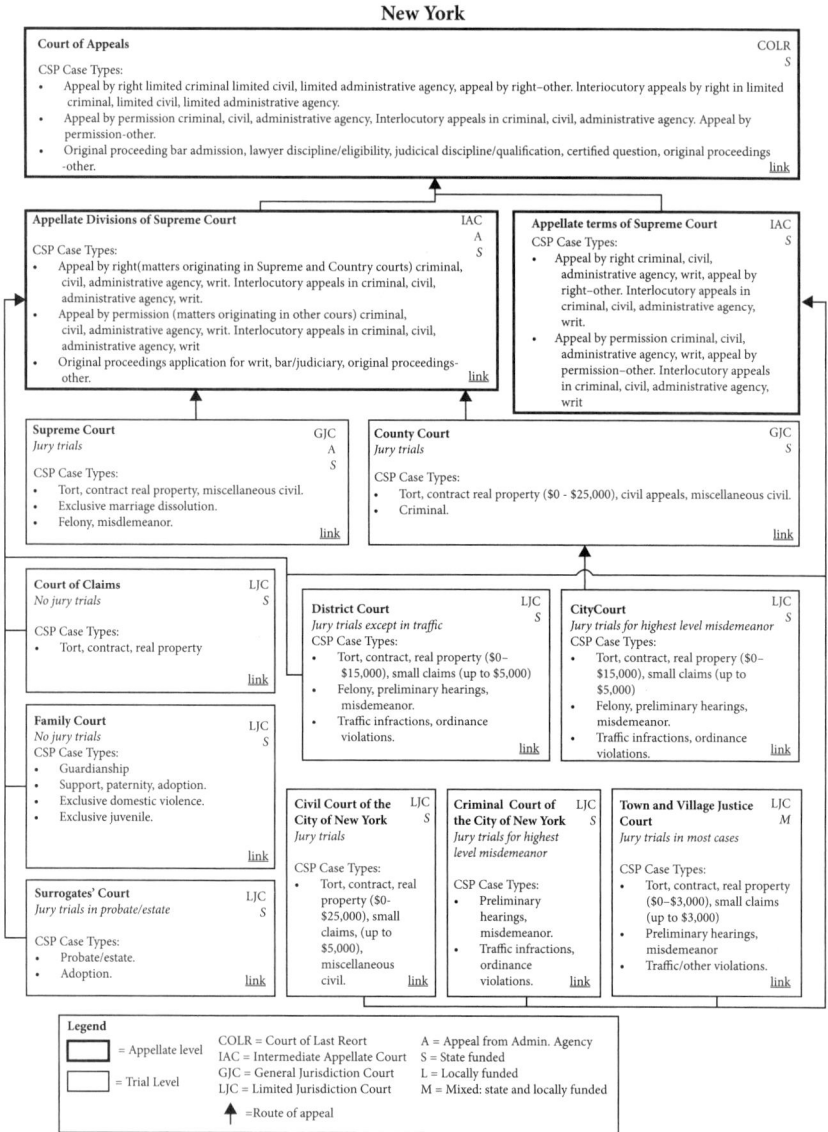

SOURCE: http://www.courtstatistics.org/state_court_structure_charts/new-york.

of Supreme Court," serves departments outside of New York City. The second appellate court is called the "Appellate Terms of Supreme Court" and this court handles appeals from departments representing the counties encompassing New York City. Finally, New York's court of last resort is called the "court of appeals." As can be seen, states differ widely in the way they structure their courts.

ACTORS IN THE COURT SYSTEM

Each level of the court system in state and federal courts consists of individuals who are responsible for processing defendants through the system. This chapter has already mentioned judges with regard to their presence at the various levels of the court system, and the judge is perhaps the most visible actor in court. There are two other prominent actors, the prosecutor and the defense attorney, who occupy equally important positions. The judge, prosecutor, and defense attorney compose the courtroom workgroup, a concept used to illustrate how each individual actor works with the other actors to move cases through the court system. Although the criminal justice system is considered an adversarial system, there are no true adversaries in practice. Generally, prosecutors and defense attorneys work together to create mutually beneficial case outcomes, and judges are on hand to assist in the negotiations. This process is typically seen in overcrowded court systems, when all participants are eager to move cases off of their dockets and out of the system quickly through the use of practices such as guilty pleas or dismissals. In addition to the major actors in the court system, there are other actors such as clerks of court, court administrators, bailiffs, probation officers, and others who serve important functions in the court system.

Judges

As mentioned, **judges** are perhaps the most visible actors in the court system. They are also considered the most powerful, since they make many important decisions at all levels of the court system. They also exercise a large amount of discretion, as evidenced by the many roles that judges undertake. In lower courts, judges conduct bail hearings, assign counsel, accept guilty pleas, conduct misdemeanor trials, sentence defendants, conduct preliminary hearings, issue warrants, and rule on the admissibility of evidence. In trial courts, judges preside over felony trials and sentence defendants. At the appellate level, judges review decisions of lower courts and issue rulings based on the merits of the case. Judges are present at every level of the court system and issue important rulings on every aspect of a case.

Federal Judges

The path to becoming a judge in the federal court system is fairly straightforward. Federal judges are called "Article III" judges because their appointment is outlined in Article III of the US Constitution. The president nominates a person for a federal judgeship, and that person must be confirmed by the Senate. Federal judges serve no specified terms of office; instead, they have life tenure and leave the federal bench through retirement, death, or impeachment. There are no formal qualifications for becoming a federal judge, such as a minimum age requirement or minimum experience practicing law. There are, however, informal qualifications that can determine whether an individual is appointed to the federal bench. Typically, nominees have distinguished law careers or have actively supported the political party in office. As such, federal judges are considered political appointees and must endure a highly political process to be confirmed by the Senate.

An advantage of judicial appointment is that it leaves the decision to individuals who are able to judge the qualifications of a particular candidate. It also allows judges to make their decisions a little more freely, in that they are not subject to the will of the public and election cycles. A disadvantage is that the appointment is quite political, with ideology overshadowing qualifications in some cases. In addition, federal judges who make unpopular decisions cannot be removed from the bench easily. Life tenure enables judges to stay on the bench for an extended period of time.

Web Activity

For more information about federal judges, visit the website of the Federal Judicial Center at http://www.fjc.gov/.

State Judges

There are varying routes to becoming a state judge. Over half of the states utilize an election process, where voters decide who will be the next judge in their community. One type of election is called a **partisan election**, in which candidates declare a political affiliation. Other states utilize the **nonpartisan election**, in which the candidates' political affiliations are not specified. Despite this, a judicial candidate's party affiliation usually becomes known because the state's political parties contribute money to their candidates' campaigns. Elected judges usually serve a term of office and must be reelected after the term is complete.

An advantage of judicial elections is that the public can choose judges it feels are best qualified to serve. Also, judges can be held accountable for their rulings and voted out of office if the public feels they are not performing well. A disadvantage of judicial elections is that they are often not as publicized as other elections, and the public may not educate itself on the qualifications of a particular candidate, voting instead on criteria that have little to do with a judge's ability to serve.

Another selection method found in some states is called **merit selection**. This method involves a group of lawyers and citizens who make recommendations to the governor about qualified nominees. The governor ultimately appoints the judge, who serves a short term of office, perhaps a year, and then is placed on the ballot for a "retention election." This retention election asks voters if they wish to retain the judge for a full term of office. The vast majority of judges are retained by voters.

An advantage of merit selection is that it takes partisan politics out of the process: lawyers and citizens hold the cards in the selection. Also, merit selection gives voters a chance to see a judge in action before he or she is retained: voters do not have to wait for a full judicial term (usually six years) to vote someone out of office. A disadvantage is that although power is taken away from political parties, it gives more power to the legal profession, which may reward its own.

A final selection method for state judges is gubernatorial or legislative appointment. Only a handful of states allow either the governor or legislature to appoint judges. In this system, the governor or the state legislature has the sole authority to appoint judges; there is usually no other entity (such as the Senate in federal cases) to approve the choice of the governor or legislature. The governor or legislature is also responsible for reappointment after the term of office is complete.

As with the federal system, politics comes into play with gubernatorial and legislative selection. Governors may give appointments to those who have supported their campaigns or those who could help them politically. According to Carp and Stidham (1990), legislatures often appoint former lawmakers to the post; in fact, the authors claim that legislatures appoint their former members as judges in 80 percent of cases.

Web Activity

For more information about the selection of judges in various states, see the website of the American Judicature Society at http://www.judicialselection.us/judicial_selection/methods/selection_of_judges.cfm?state.

Prosecutors

While judges are considered the most visible actors in the court system, **prosecutors** often work behind closed doors. Much of what prosecutors do is not readily visible to the public; as a result, the role of the prosecutor is cloaked in mystery. Prosecutors are most often seen by the public in courtrooms arguing cases on behalf of the state, but this constitutes only a small portion of their time. In the early stages of a case, prosecutors make bail recommendations to judges, file charges against defendants, conduct preliminary hearings and grand jury proceedings, file motions with judges, engage in plea agreements, represent the state at trial, and make sentencing recommendations.

Critical Thinking Exercise

Similar to the earlier issue of lifetime appointments, political appointments to the bench are not without controversy. Do you believe this is an appropriate means for seating judges? Does this process guarantee quality judges, or does it open the door for less-than-qualified judges? If the latter, what problems can this create? What changes (if any) should be made in this system?

Federal Prosecutors

Prosecutors in the federal court system work for the US Department of Justice. As head of this department, the US attorney general is nominated by the president, is confirmed by the Senate, and serves as a member of the president's cabinet. The position of attorney general is largely an administrative one, directing the work of those who work for the department. As such, he or she is not involved in everyday federal court matters. This responsibility is given to US attorneys and their assistants.

As mentioned earlier, the country is divided into federal court districts, and each district is assigned a US attorney and multiple assistant US attorneys. US attorneys are nominated by the president and confirmed by the Senate, and assistant US attorneys are appointed by the attorney general. These individuals have the responsibility of prosecuting cases in federal court and defending the United States when it is sued in civil court. US attorneys are able to exercise tremendous discretion in their jobs; there is no real formal oversight of US attorneys in their respective districts.

State and Local Prosecutors

The role of prosecutors at the state and local levels is not that much different than their role at the federal level, although the route to becoming a prosecutor at the state level differs. Like the federal system, states have attorneys general, who are usually selected by voters in statewide elections. The role of the state attorney general differs from state to state, but one main characteristic is the lack of authority over local prosecutors. In effect, the state attorney general does not have much authority to get involved in matters at the local level, limiting his or her role to providing legal advice and defending the state when it is sued in civil court. In recent years, state attorneys general have become increasingly involved in civil matters, especially matters that involve consumer protection.

The individuals responsible for prosecuting violations of criminal laws are the local prosecutors. Local prosecutors are usually elected at the county level, and they represent the county in which they are elected. These prosecutors are called by a number of titles; the most common are "district attorney," "chief prosecutor," and "county attorney." The chief prosecutor's job in a county is both administrative and prosecutorial, in that he or she organizes and directs the responsibilities of assistants as well as going to court and prosecuting criminal defendants in higher-profile felony cases. The assistants, often called assistant district attorneys or assistant prosecutors, are largely responsible for the early stages of a criminal case and minor criminal offenses. These assistants are typically hired by the chief prosecutor and are not subject to election by voters. It has been noted by Neubauer and Fradella (2014) that assistant district attorneys are usually hired right out of law school, work only a few years at a prosecutor's office, and use the office as a stepping-stone into private practice or upper-level positions in the criminal justice system (such as judge).

Web Activity

The American Bar Association lists the functions and duties of a prosecutor. This report can be found here: https://www.americanbar.org/groups/criminal_justice/standards/ProsecutionFunctionFourthEdition/.

Defense Attorneys

Defense attorneys have the (largely) thankless job of defending the accused against prosecution by the government. Although defendants in the criminal justice system have the right to be represented by an attorney, many cannot afford their services.

As a result, the US Supreme Court has ruled in a number of decisions that poor individuals have the right to an appointed attorney in certain cases. The various forms of defense attorneys are discussed below.

Private Attorneys

Private attorneys, or retained counsel, are hired by defendants, who pay for the attorneys' legal services. Defendants who can afford them may have their attorneys represent them in any type and at any stage of a criminal case. In these instances, defendants literally get what they pay for and are able to have continuous representation if they can afford it. However, the bulk of criminal defendants cannot afford to pay for their own attorneys and must use attorneys provided by the government. In fact, in some areas, up to 90 percent of felony defendants are considered too poor to hire an attorney (Buckwalter-Poza 2016).

Appointed Attorneys

As mentioned earlier, a number of US Supreme Court rulings have insisted that defendants can have appointed attorneys represent them if they cannot afford one. In *Gideon v. Wainwright* (1963), the Court ruled that poor defendants charged with felonies have the right to court-appointed counsel. In the subsequent cases *Argersinger v. Hamlin* (1972) and *Scott v. Illinois* (1979), the Court extended the right to court-appointed counsel to defendants who face imprisonment. Although this seems like a victory for poor defendants, in reality, defendants do not have the right to court-appointed attorneys if they do not face imprisonment; thus, defendants who are subject only to probation or fines are not entitled to court-appointed counsel. In addition, although private attorneys can represent their clients at any stage of a criminal case, court-appointed counsel is generally not guaranteed at stages that are not deemed "critical," such as lineups, grand jury proceedings, and some appeals.

At both the state and federal levels, the methods of providing and appointing counsel vary. At the federal level, Congress is responsible for organizing and appropriating funds to the various districts for provision of counsel. In the states, most methods are organized and financed by the state and/or county. In general, there are three methods of providing counsel to poor defendants: assigned counsel, public defenders, and contract systems.

One of the appointed counsel systems involves the appointment of private attorneys who volunteer their services to the court. This **assigned counsel** system is primarily utilized in areas with smaller caseloads, since it is more economically feasible to provide counsel on a case-by-case basis. Typically, a judge maintains a list of eligible attorneys and chooses one when a case arises. These attorneys are usually paid on an hourly or per-case basis, but the rate of compensation is generally low, so low that critics question their ability to provide effective representation. In fact, North Carolina reports that assigned counsel makes only $55 per hour, which was reduced from $75 per hour in 2011. In addition, when assigned counsel submits billable hours to the judge in order to be compensated, judges reduce the amount in 15 percent of cases, resulting in many attorneys not being paid for the work they engage in to represent their clients (Gressens 2019). These leads to many attorneys cutting corners are not engaging in as thorough an investigation because they simply will not be compensated for it. Many attorneys leave the job due to this.

A second type of appointed counsel system is the **public defender**. The public defender system is usually a state- or county-administered organization that specializes in defending the poor. A public defender's office is usually staffed by numerous attorneys who are paid a yearly salary for their services. This system is typically found in medium- and large-sized urban areas that have considerable caseloads. Some proponents of a public defender system claim that the attorneys are able to provide expert criminal defense, because it is the only thing they do. Despite this, public defender systems have long been criticized for providing inadequate representation due to the numbers of cases they must contend with. In effect, although they may be experts in their field, public defenders may not have the time to concentrate on cases the way they should. In fact, in 2016, at least six states were sued because of their public defender system. In New Orleans, for example, after years of budget cuts, the chief district public defender stated that his budget was slashed from $9 million to about $6 million, with just eight investigators for 21,000 cases per year (Laird 2017).

Web Activity

The Brennan Center for Justice discusses how to achieve resource parity in indigent defense here: https://www.brennancenter.org/sites/default/files/2019-09/Report_ A%20Fair%20Fight.pdf.

A third type of appointed counsel system is called the contract system, which is relatively new compared to the other two. In this type of system, private attorneys bid to represent poor defendants for a fixed fee and a specified period of time. This method is seen as a way to save money on indigent defense because the state or county will likely choose the attorney who puts in the lowest bid. A downside is that the quality of representation may be low, because the attorney has only a set amount of money to use when defending clients.

Although not considered a formal, government-sponsored method of providing indigent defense, **legal aid** societies are being formed in many larger cities to work in conjunction with the established method in that area. Legal aid societies are usually supported by private contributions, which provide payment for the services performed by the attorneys who work for the organization. In addition, some attorneys work **pro bono**, donating their services out of what they see as a professional obligation. Finally, criminal defendants are allowed to represent themselves (called **pro se**), provided they meet certain requirements established by the judge in a particular case.

Regardless of the type of criminal defense, all attorneys are required to provide effective assistance of counsel, according to the US Supreme Court's ruling in *McMann v. Richardson* (1970). Since this ruling, the US Supreme Court has established guidelines for defendants to meet if they claim that their attorney provided ineffective assistance of counsel. In general, defendants must prove that the outcome of their case would have been different if their attorney had been effective, which is extremely difficult to prove (see *Strickland v. Washington* [1984]).

Critical Thinking Exercise

Debate over the quality of legal representation often involves the relative merits of hired versus appointed counsel. Many critics claim that those who can afford to hire their own counsel fare better in court. Do you believe that this is true? Investigate this claim. What evidence is there to support this position? What evidence is there that this position is false?

Other Court Actors

Many individuals work in the courtroom besides the various types of attorneys discussed above. **Bailiffs** are responsible for maintaining order in the courtroom, and law enforcement officers—usually deputies—transport detained defendants between the courthouse and jail. Probation officers work with the court to monitor those individuals who are sentenced to probation. In addition, probation officers are often responsible for completing a presentence investigation of a defendant. This involves providing the sentencing judge with detailed information about the defendant and the crime so that the judge may consider a number of issues before imposing a sentence.

There are numerous individuals who are responsible for the administrative aspects of the court. Clerks of court are the record-keepers of the case files that come before the court every day. Court reporters create a transcribed record of proceedings as they occur. Court administrators are responsible for supervising court staff and working with the judge on issues such as budgets and personnel.

Besides formal court personnel, there are others who appear in court from time to time. Victims and witnesses often come to court for official proceedings or to inquire about the state of their cases. Victims may also utilize victim advocates, who assist victims when their cases are processed by the criminal justice system.

In addition to victims and witnesses, jurors play a pivotal role in the court system. Although trials are uncommon in the court system, they enable defendants to have an adversarial process when formally charged with a crime. Jurors are responsible for assessing the evidence against the accused and determining if the state, in the form of the prosecutor, met the burden of proof in establishing guilt. The process of selecting jurors is discussed later.

MOVEMENT OF CASES THROUGH THE COURT SYSTEM

Most criminal cases follow a general trajectory as they move through the court system. As mentioned earlier, the court is involved in many cases before official arrests have been made, so the court's role is not relegated to dealing with cases after the police have completed their tasks. See Figure 4.1 for an example of a criminal case's progression through the courts in North Carolina.

Initial Stages to Formal Charging

One of the constitutional requirements of police work is to secure a warrant prior to making an arrest. Despite this, the US Supreme Court has authorized many types of arrest without a warrant; these are typically reserved for circumstances in which it is not feasible to take the time to secure a warrant. In other circumstances, police must secure a warrant from a judge in order to make an arrest. Police must go to a judge in a limited-jurisdiction court and support the information in the warrant (e.g., probable cause, evidence). Once the judge approves the warrant, the police may make a formal arrest. Police may also ask a lower-court judge to approve a search warrant in order to search a specific place for evidence.

After an arrest has been made, suspects are brought before a lower-court judge for their **initial appearance**. At this stage, defendants are informed of the charges against them, a bail decision is made, representation by a defense attorney is arranged (if applicable), and a date is set for the next stage in the case. In most misdemeanor cases, defendants plead guilty to the charges against them

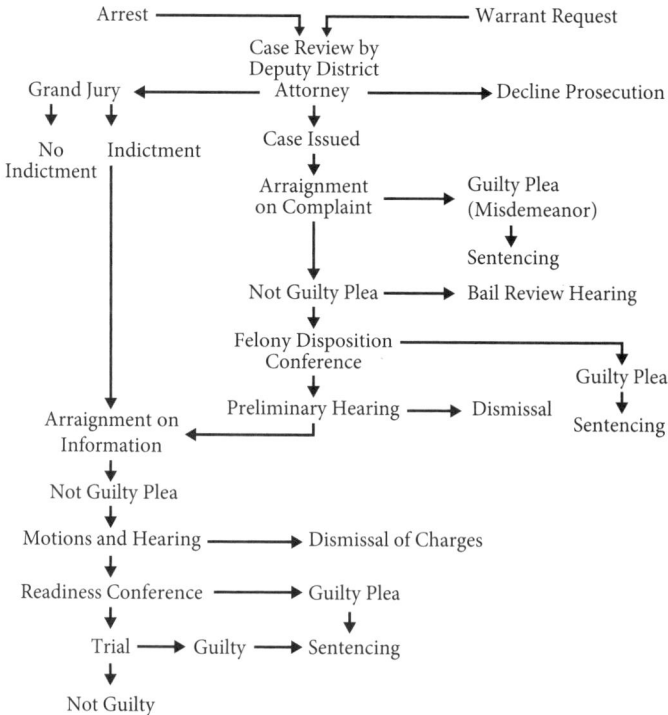

Figure 4.1 Movement of Cases Through the Court System
SOURCE: San Diego County District Attorney, https://www.sdcda.org/office/criminal-justice-system.html.

and are sentenced immediately. In many states, those charged with felonies are not allowed to plead guilty at this stage; instead, they plead not guilty and await the next stage of their case.

When a **bail** decision is made, the judge examines a number of variables to determine if a defendant is to be released into the community pending the resolution of his or her case. The primary variables are seriousness of the offense, prior record, and flight risk. Generally, the more serious the offense, the more extensive the prior record, and the higher the flight risk, the greater the likelihood that bail will be high or will be denied altogether. For some offenses, such as first-degree murder, bail is denied outright; a defendant has no chance to secure his or her release. In addition, the US Supreme Court has upheld the denial of bail for purposes of preventive detention (*U.S. v. Salerno* [1987]).

Regardless of the offense, prior record, or flight risk, if a defendant is deemed by the judge to be too dangerous to be released into the community, bail is denied. For most offenses, bail is granted; if a defendant pays the amount (called a bond), he or she is released and must return to court when his or her next court date is scheduled. Upon return, the bond is refunded to the defendant. If the defendant does not return to court, the bond is forfeited. Some courts will accept only a cash bond, while others will accept a collateral bond as well. In these cases, the defendants put up assets such as cars or property as collateral in return for release. In most cases, however, defendants are unable to pay the bail amount, so they use the services of bail bondsmen. Bail bondsmen usually require that the defendants pay a fee of 10 percent of the bail amount to the bondsmen; in return, the bondsmen pay the rest of the bond to the court, usually in the form of insurance, and guarantee the court that the defendants will appear for the next scheduled court date. The bondsmen keep the 10 percent of the bail amount as payment of services and can utilize any legal means at their disposal to ensure that the defendants appear for court.

The next stage of a case is usually a **preliminary hearing**. This occurs when a lower-court judge (not the judge at the initial appearance) views the evidence against the defendant to determine if there is enough probable cause to proceed to trial. In many states, the preliminary hearing is the only chance for a judge to view the evidence before a trial. In these cases, a prosecutor will issue an "information" to indicate that probable cause has been met and the defendant is formally charged with a crime.

In other states, a grand jury hearing takes place after the judge has ruled in a preliminary hearing that a case will proceed. A grand jury hearing is required in all federal prosecutions, but not state prosecutions, although 19 states require the procedure in felony cases. A grand jury is composed of citizens who serve for a set period of time during which they consider numerous cases. The prosecutor alone provides evidence of the crime—the defendant has no right to present a case—and the grand jury must find that there is probable cause to proceed to trial, usually by majority vote. If probable cause has been met, the grand jury issues a "true bill of indictment," the equivalent of a prosecutor's "information." If probable cause has not been met, then a "no true bill" is issued. The idea behind a grand jury is that the public is allowed to provide a check on the power of the prosecutor and judge—in effect, to be a watchdog over the courts to prevent malicious prosecutions. However, most states do not utilize a grand jury, since it has not been required by the US Supreme Court, and the vast majority of cases brought before grand juries end with indictments.

After formal charges have been filed, the next stage of a case is the **arraignment**. At this stage, the defendant is required to enter a plea to the formal charges against him or her. Defendants who have not yet pleaded guilty are likely to do so at this stage, since formal charges send a message that the criminal justice system has a strong case against the defendant. If a defendant pleads guilty, a sentence is then imposed. For those pleading not guilty, a trial date is set.

Plea Agreements

It is necessary to discuss plea agreements in a separate section due to the frequency of the practice in the court system. It has been estimated that 94 percent of convictions in state courts are the result of plea agreements, with a 97 percent plea agreement number in federal courts (Yoffe 2017). Plea agreements are often viewed as a necessary evil in a system that is ill equipped to take every case to trial. Plea agreements are a method of disposing of a court's caseload while trying to dispense justice at the same time.

A defendant can engage in a plea agreement at most stages of a criminal case. With few exceptions, such as felony defendants at first appearance, a defendant can decide to plead guilty if he or she feels it is warranted. As mentioned earlier, most misdemeanor defendants plead guilty and are sentenced at their initial appearance. Other defendants may plead not guilty and wait and see how their case progresses. There is always a chance (however slim) that the case will be dismissed later. Regardless of when the plea agreement occurs, most charged defendants plead guilty before a trial commences.

Plea agreements typically involve some sort of leniency on the part of the prosecutor and judge. Thus, a **plea bargain** occurs when the defendant makes a deal with the court to plead guilty in exchange for a charge or count reduction or a sentence reduction. In a charge or count bargain, a prosecutor may agree to reduce the charge from a felony to a misdemeanor or reduce the number of counts a defendant is charged with. In a sentence bargain, the prosecutor may agree to argue for a more lenient punishment at sentencing provided the defendant pleads guilty as charged. Some plea agreements involve no bargain at all, and defendants plead guilty as charged and are sentenced without any promised leniency.

Some argue that plea agreements, particularly plea bargains, allow defendants to "get off the hook" because their punishments do not fit their crimes. In fact, some communities have proposed or enacted bans on plea bargaining because of the sense that it allows criminals to escape harsher punishment. Critics also argue that plea agreements negate the adversarial process that is the cornerstone of the criminal justice system. In effect, plea agreements are orchestrated by the courtroom workgroup because the agreements are beneficial to everyone involved. Supporters argue that plea agreements are needed to help dispose of cases in crowded courts and that they result in sure convictions and punishment for defendants whom everyone knows are guilty. Regardless of the views on the practice, the use of plea agreements is something that will continue in the court system for a long time.

Web Activity

The state of New Jersey has placed its plea agreement form online. To view it, visit https://www.judiciary.state.nj.us/forms/10079_main_plea_form.pdf.

Assembly-Line Justice and Case Attrition

In the early stages of a criminal case, the court system is often accused of engaging in **assembly-line justice**, a term used to illustrate the movement of cases through the courts. In areas with large caseloads, it may not be possible for the courtroom workgroup to spend much time on cases, so each case is handled in a quick and efficient manner in order to move on to the next. This is especially seen in the lower courts, where initial appearances and plea agreements are handled much like a manufacturing assembly line. As mentioned earlier, in these crowded courthouses, it is not possible to devote a large amount of time to ordinary, run-of-the-mill cases, so they are handled in this fashion in order to concentrate on other, more serious cases, such as those that go to trial.

The handling of cases in such a manner is one of the reasons for **case attrition**, or the filtering out of cases from the court system. Case attrition is likened to a funnel, such that as cases progress through the criminal justice process, the number of cases decreases. Although case attrition is most visible in the court system, police also engage in the practice. For instance, police may choose not to arrest or file charges against a suspect; as a result, these cases are filtered out of the courts even before they enter it. Largely, however, case attrition occurs during the court process. Prosecutors may choose not to formally charge a suspect with a crime, due to lack of evidence or witness problems. Additionally, plea agreements contribute to attrition when cases are settled at the initial appearance. As a case progresses, defendants may choose to plead guilty at a later stage, such as at arraignment, or a prosecutor may dismiss the charges. In effect, attrition for whatever reason is necessary because the court system is simply not equipped to take every case to trial.

Critical Thinking Exercise

Due to the increasing number of cases coming into the criminal justice system, the court system has become overcrowded and assembly-line justice has resulted. To remedy this, some have called for the decriminalization of certain offenses, particularly drug crimes, because they are considered victimless. What are the advantages and disadvantages of such a strategy? Can you think of other mechanisms for reducing the influx of cases into the system?

Trial

After formal charges have been filed, a defendant enters a plea to those charges. If a defendant pleads not guilty, a trial date is set. According to the US Constitution, a defendant has a right to a jury trial, but this right is limited to defendants who are charged with "serious" offenses—those that authorize a punishment of six months' or more incarceration. In addition, those defendants who are eligible for jury trials may opt for bench trials instead. A **bench trial** occurs when a judge alone hears the evidence against a defendant and renders a verdict. According to Neubauer and Fradella (2014), a defendant may prefer a bench trial when the trial involves complex issues or when the case is emotionally charged.

If a jury trial is on the docket, the first step is to conduct jury selection. A **master jury list** is composed to identify potential jurors who are eligible to serve on a jury, usually people who are registered voters or who possess valid driver's licenses. Once the master jury list is created, a sample of potential jurors is selected from the list. This list is called the **venire**, or jury pool, and these individuals are notified by mail to report for jury duty. Once at the courthouse, the jury pool is questioned during a process called **voir dire**, in which the prosecutor and defense attorney (and some-times the judge) question the individuals on their knowledge about the case or potential biases they may possess. If the prosecutor or defense attorney wishes to exclude an individual from jury duty, he or she may dismiss the juror using one of two methods. The first method, called a **challenge for cause**, allows attorneys to dismiss an unlimited number of jurors for legal reasons specified in state and fed-eral statutes. An example of a challenge for cause would be that a potential juror is related to someone involved in the case.

A second method of dismissing jurors is called a **peremptory challenge**, in which lawyers may dismiss a limited number of jurors based on reasons that do not need to be specified to the court. A lawyer may not feel that an individual juror "looks right" and may dismiss the juror based on a mere hunch. The use of peremp-tory challenges has long been challenged in the courts, as it provides opportunities for both the prosecution and defense to "stack the jury" in their favor. Historically, the use of these challenges allowed both sides to engage in discriminatory practices by removing jurors based on race or gender (see *Batson v. Kentucky* [1986]). Courts therefore have imposed a limited number of peremptory challenges, making it more difficult for either side in a case to stack the jury.

Once jury selection is over, the trial begins. The trial starts with opening state-ments by the prosecutor and defense attorney, each telling the jury what he or she hopes to show with regard to the evidence. The prosecution presents its case first and the defense has an opportunity to cross-examine the prosecution's witnesses. In a trial, the prosecution has the burden of proving the defendant is guilty beyond a reasonable doubt. This is called the **burden of proof**. The defense, on the other hand, only has to question the prosecution's case enough to instill doubt in a juror's mind—the defense does not have to prove a defendant innocent. In fact, the de-fense does not have to present any evidence at trial if it believes that the prosecution has not met the burden of proof. In reality, defense attorneys usually provide some sort of defense, calling witnesses who can support its case or call into question any evidence the prosecution presents. Like the defense during the prosecution's case, the prosecutor is able to cross-examine defense witnesses at this time. Both sides then have another chance to refute any evidence given by the other side, a process called **rebuttal**.

During the trial process, both the prosecution and the defense present **evidence**. For the prosecutor, this evidence points to the guilt of the defendant. **Direct evidence** is the strongest form of evidence; examples include a confession by the defendant, eyewitness testimony, or the defendant's fingerprints at the crime scene. **Circumstantial evidence** is indirect evidence; this type of evidence implies or infers guilt on the part of the defendant. An example of circumstantial evidence would be a defendant being in the vicinity of a crime when it took place. In other words, there is no direct evidence that the defendant committed a crime; however, the defendant's presence in the area implies that the defendant is involved in the crime. For the defense, the evidence presented can accomplish two things. First, it can discredit evidence provided by the prosecutor. For example, if a defendant has confessed to the crime, the defense can argue that the defendant was coerced or threatened by police into confessing. Second, defense evidence can refute evidence provided by the prosecutor. For example, if an eyewitness testifies that he or she saw the defendant at the crime scene, the defense can counter that the defendant was nowhere near the crime scene at the time, providing an **alibi** for the defendant.

Once both sides have presented their cases, they are allowed to make closing statements to the jury. The prosecution emphasizes the evidence against the defendant and tries to convince the jury of the defendant's guilt. The defense also emphasizes its evidence, but stresses that the prosecutor must meet the burden of proof. After closing arguments, the judge provides instructions to the jury that outline the legal issues in the case (e.g., burden of proof, elements of the crime, possible verdicts). After instructions, the jury begins to deliberate the case. A unanimous vote is required for a verdict of guilty or not guilty. If the vote is not unanimous, there is no verdict and a **hung jury** is declared by the judge. If this occurs, the defendant may be prosecuted again on the same charge.

Sentencing

If a defendant has been found guilty by a judge or jury, the next stage is sentencing. Although the judge has formal sentencing responsibility, punishments for offenses are created by state legislatures and Congress (for federal cases). The various legislatures have adopted a number of sentencing schemes to achieve the goals that they consider important, whether they are retribution, deterrence, incapacitation, or rehabilitation. These schemes are addressed below.

Indeterminate Sentencing Schemes

In the past 100 years of punishment, **indeterminate sentencing** was the primary method utilized in the states. Indeterminate sentencing is usually associated with the goals of rehabilitation and incapacitation, tailoring sentences to the needs of individual offenders. In this scheme, a judge sentences a defendant to a minimum and maximum range of time; some states utilize indeterminate sentencing for incarceration sentences only, while others use it for incarceration and community supervision. The exact amount of time that is actually served by the offender is not specified at sentencing; instead, the parole board determines when and if an offender is eligible for release after the minimum term has been served.

Determinate Sentencing Schemes

In the late 20th century, there was a shift away from indeterminate sentencing schemes due to an increased "law-and-order" approach to crime. In this scheme, a judge sentences an offender to a punishment for a specific period of time. Also referred to as "flat" or "fixed" sentences, **determinate sentencing** results in a defendant knowing how long his or her sentence will be when a judge imposes it. In effect, a judge declares at sentencing that a defendant will serve X number of months or years of incarceration, probation, and so forth. In some states, prisoners can earn good-time credits for good behavior that decrease the amount of time spent in prison. Other states have abolished these credits, in hopes that defendants will serve their full sentences. Determinate sentencing schemes came about because many became skeptical of the rehabilitative aspects of indeterminate sentencing, feeling that defendants were not being punished for the crimes they committed.

Sentencing Guidelines

Regardless of the type of sentencing scheme, many states and the federal government have implemented **sentencing guidelines** to help curb what was considered to be inconsistent decision-making on the part of judges and parole boards. In many areas, guidelines were established by a sentencing commission or a legislative body to assist judges and others in providing appropriate sanctions for similar defendants. The varying guidelines range between "suggested" sentences and mandated, specific sentences with little to no variation. Usually, the guidelines consider the seriousness of the offense and prior record, but some guidelines may take into account a defendant's legal status at the time of the crime—for instance, if the defendant was on probation or parole—and victim injury. Some guidelines allow limited judicial discretion by allowing a judge to impose less or more severe punishment on a defendant if circumstances warrant it.

More recent additions to sentence guidelines include habitual offender and mandatory minimum punishments. With **habitual offender** punishments, states allow judges to sentence offenders to a more severe punishment if the offender has prior felony convictions. An example of a habitual offender punishment would be a three-strikes punishment. This occurs when a defendant has received a third felony conviction (with two previous felony convictions) and the sentence for the third conviction is increased to reflect the habitual offender status. In California, this punishment states that "the requirements for sentencing a defendant as a third strike offender . . . require . . . the new felony to be a *serious or violent felony* with two or more prior strikes to qualify for the 25 year-to-life sentence as a third strike offender" (emphasis in original) (see California's Three Strikes Sentencing Law at http://www.courts.ca.gov/20142.htm). With

mandatory minimum punishments, judges *must* sentence a defendant to a minimum amount of punishment for certain types of offenses. Georgia's "Seven Deadly Sins" law is an example of a mandatory minimum punishment. This law specifies that for a first offense of kidnapping, armed robbery, rape, aggravated sodomy, aggravated sexual battery, or aggravated child molestation, the minimum punishment is 10 years in prison, with no chance of parole. The minimum punishment for a first offense of murder is life with a possibility of parole after 25 years. A second offense for any of these seven offenses is life without the possibility of parole (see Truth in Sentencing in Georgia at http://www.dcor.state.ga.us/sites/all/files/pdf/Research/Standing/Truth_in_sentencing.pdf).

Critical Thinking Exercise

The use of sentencing guidelines in some states has reduced the discretion exercised by judges with regard to imposing punishments for crimes. As a result, sentences have become offense based rather than offender based. Do you think that a judge should be able to consider the circumstances of the offender when imposing a sentence? In effect, should an offender's lack of education, home life, history of abuse, and so forth play a role in punishment? Explain.

Available Sanctions

State legislatures and Congress have authorized a number of sanctions that may be imposed by judges. Although prison is often the first punishment that comes to mind, it is not the most common punishment used for law violators. Jail, probation, fines, and other sanctions are far more common than prison. **Prison** is reserved for the more serious (i.e., felony) offenders. The United States has the highest incarceration rate in the world, housing approximately 1.3 million inmates in state and federal prisons (Sawyer and Wagner 2020). In recent years, legislatures have authorized longer and mandatory prison sentences for some offenses, including drug-related offenses. This has resulted in a dramatic increase in the incarceration rate Prisons are typically state controlled, but private prisons have been constructed in some states in hopes of defraying some of the costs it takes to operate state prisons. One sanction that is reserved for the most serious offenders is the **death penalty**, which is utilized in 25 states and in the federal system. The death penalty is rarely imposed, as it is restricted to individuals who have committed the highest form of murder, variously called first-degree, aggravated, or felony murder. At the federal level, the death penalty may also be imposed on those convicted of treason and drug kingpins.

Jail is a form of incarceration for individuals who have been convicted of misdemeanors. Approximately 630,000 people are housed in jails (Sawyer and Wagner 2020), which also house those who are awaiting trial; this is known as pretrial detention. In the states, jails are typically operated at the county level; the federal government operates its own jails.

The primary alternative to incarceration is probation. Approximately 4.5 million offenders are on probation at the federal and state level (Jones 2018). The justification for probation is that incarceration is simply too much punishment for some offenders, but they simply cannot be released back into the community unpunished. Lower-level felony offenders and upper-level misdemeanor offenders are those typically placed on probation. Probation allows an offender to remain in the community as long as he or she abides by certain conditions, such as finding or maintaining employment, avoiding alcohol, submitting to drug tests, and meeting with a probation officer for a specified period of time.

For some offenders, probation is not a severe enough punishment, but incarceration is considered too harsh. A remedy to this is the use of **intermediate sanctions**, so named because they lie somewhere between prison and probation. Various intermediate sanctions include intensive supervision probation, electronic monitoring, house arrest, and boot camps. Intermediate sanctions tend to be used less frequently than regular probation, although the exact number of offenders serving intermediate sanctions is not known.

Fines are one of the oldest types of sanctions used and are typically reserved for traffic offenses or in conjunction with other types of punishment, usually probation. Fines are not utilized as extensively in the United States as in other countries, simply because most offenders in the US criminal justice system cannot afford to pay them.

Regardless of the types of sentencing schemes and available sanctions, there has been a trend of increased legislative involvement in the sentencing of offenders. This involvement has led to reduced discretion on the part of judges, who were often viewed by legislators and the public as being too lenient in their sentencing practices. This law-and-order approach to crime and justice has led to increased supervision of more offenders by the criminal justice system, something that has cost considerable sums of money.

Appeals

After an offender has been convicted and sentenced, he or she has the right to one **appeal**. This means that the offender has the opportunity to have his or her case reviewed by an appellate court in order to fix any problems that may have occurred during the case. These problems typically involve issues such as improper jury selection, defects in jury instructions, or admission of illegally seized evidence. Prosecutors, on the other hand, cannot appeal a finding of not guilty.

The right to one appeal carries with it certain constitutional requirements by which the state or federal government must abide. Offenders who appeal have the right to free transcripts of their trials and the right to appointed counsel. Despite this, many offenders do not appeal their convictions or sentences, simply because they view it as a waste of time and energy, especially when they will have completed their sentences before their appeals get through the appellate stage. In addition, appeals are rarely successful; in fact, Neubauer and Fradella (2014) estimate that less than 10 percent of defendants win on appeal. Most of these victories are minor, however. Convictions are typically upheld and sentences may be modified only slightly, or offenders are subjected to retrial only to be reconvicted the second time around.

After the first appeal is finished, offenders have the opportunity to file other appeals if they wish. Called **postconviction review** or a **collateral attack**, prisoners can challenge their convictions or sentences in a different proceeding. Collateral attacks are typically filed in federal court and are civil matters, not criminal appeals. They raise constitutional questions only, not errors in interpretation or application of the law, which are seen mostly in the first appeal of right. Offenders are not given free trial transcripts and are not provided with appointed counsel in these appeals. As a result, few offenders take advantage of the opportunity to file a collateral attack. A common type of collateral attack is habeas corpus, in which prisoners claim that they are being detained illegally. In recent years, Congress and the US Supreme Court have greatly restricted the filing of habeas corpus appeals in a number of ways. Now, offenders have a one-year deadline to file an appeal and are limited in the number of appeals that can be filed, among other things (see Antiterrorism and Effective Death Penalty Act 1996).

TRENDS IN THE COURT SYSTEM

Specialized Courts

Due to increasing numbers of individuals coming into the criminal justice system, the court systems in many areas have devised ways to handle these individuals, especially those with special needs. Special-needs offenders are those who are repeatedly seen in the system due to issues such as drug and alcohol abuse and mental illness. Court systems have created specialty courts that deal exclusively with certain types of offenders.

Foreign Intelligence Surveillance Court

Known as the **FISA Court**, this federal court was created by Congress in the Foreign Intelligence Surveillance Act of 1978. This court has jurisdiction over electronic surveillance of foreign agents. The Chief Justice of the United States appoints justices to hear warrant requests submitted by the Department of Justice. Despite this, the Protect America Act of 2007 allows the government to bypass the FISA Court if obtaining a warrant would take too long to gather timely information or if national security is at risk.

Drug Courts

Due to the increased enforcement and punishment of drug offenses in the past 20 years, court systems have become bogged down with large numbers of relatively minor drug offenders. As a result, many court systems created drug courts to process these cases efficiently without taking up the time and resources of the lower courts. Drug courts have been in existence since the mid-1980s and are in operation or are being planned in every state. Despite this, drug courts are not utilized statewide, either because particular areas have no need for them or because states simply cannot afford to operate them.

Drug courts emphasize treatment of lower-level drug offenders. A lower court typically identifies these offenders and transfers the cases to a drug court. The drug court then establishes a treatment program that entails drug treatment, counseling, and employment and life-skills training. The offenders are usually released into the community and must meet with judges periodically. This is similar to probation, but it is not a probation sentence. The offenders are monitored by judges, not probation officers, and the judges ensure that the offenders are progressing through the treatment program. The success of drug courts has been mixed. The research that has been conducted has found that offenders who were processed through drug courts and successfully completed their treatment programs had lower recidivism rates than offenders who were not processed through drug courts. This success is tempered, however, by the fact that being processed through drug courts and undergoing treatment is largely voluntary on the part of offenders. In effect, the success of drug courts could be explained by the possibility that offenders who volunteer to go through the drug court process want help for their problems and are willing to go through treatment (see Arnold et al. 2000).

Web Activity

For more information about drug courts, visit the website of the National Association of Drug Court Professionals at https://www.nadcp.org/.

Mental-Health Courts

It has been estimated that 5 to 15 percent of incarcerated offenders suffer from some form of mental illness. Many jails and prisons do not provide adequate treatment of mental illness while offenders are incarcerated, and fewer establish procedures for aftercare once the offenders are released. As a result, the mental illness, which may have contributed to the offenders' criminal behavior, remains untreated and the offenders are in no better position than they were before incarceration. This has led to the creation of mental-health courts in some areas. These courts establish guidelines for mental-health treatment in lieu of other punishments. Typically, **mental-health courts** place restrictions on the types of offenders that they process; for instance, these courts may prohibit eligibility for violent offenders.

Mental-health courts work with community treatment programs to establish appropriate procedures for both the treatment of the offenders and the safety of the community. Offenders are closely monitored throughout their treatment programs, which usually consist of not only mental-health treatment, but also life-skills and vocational training. If an offender successfully completes the program, some courts authorize removal of the original criminal charges from the offender's record (see Slate 2000).

Research on the effectiveness of mental-health courts has produced mixed results. One of the main issues is that mental illness is a lifelong disease, which means that offenders' needs must be managed for the remainder of their lives, which can prove difficult. However, some research has found that mental health courts help keep minor offenders from being incarcerated (Lucas and Hanrahan, 2016).

Web Activity

For a list of resources on mental health courts, visit https://www.ncsc.org/Topics/ Alternative-Dockets/Problem-Solving-Courts/Mental-Health-Courts/Resource-Guide.aspx

---

Veterans' Courts

The first veterans' court was established in Buffalo, NY, in 1998 with the goal of assisting veterans involved in the criminal justice system. Modeled on drug courts and mental health courts, veterans' courts serve the unique and complex needs of veterans; these include mental illness, substance abuse, and psychological trauma related to their service (Lucas and Hanrahan 2016). The goal of these courts is to rehabilitate veterans into productive members of society and research indicates that these courts are successful. Knudsen and Wingenfeld (2015) found that these courts improve the psychological well-being of participants, which leads to reductions of recidivism.

Web Activity

For a list of resources on veterans courts, see https://cdm16501.contentdm.oclc.org/ digital/collection/spcts/id/371

Domestic Violence Courts

Due to the increasing number of domestic violence cases in the criminal justice system (including repeat offenders and victims), **domestic violence courts** have been created to address a number of problems faced by the courts. For example, many domestic violence cases involve divorce proceedings and/or child custody issues, which can result in numerous cases being brought before different judges. The domestic violence courts would combine these cases in one court, with a judge overseeing all aspects of the case. The court also advocates early intervention and the use of community agencies in order to coordinate services for both victims and offenders.

Research on the effectiveness of domestic violence courts is mixed. Although Casey and Rottman (2005) argued that the courts increase the satisfaction of victims and offenders, Scott and Kunselman (2007) state that while the motives of these courts are noble, providing the needed services and reducing recidivism has not been successful.

Web Activity

For a list of resources on domestic violence courts, see http://www.ncsc.org/Topics/ Children-Families-and-Elders/Domestic-Violence/Resource-Guide.aspx

---

Increased Victim Involvement

In addition to special-needs offenders, courts are increasingly allowing victims to become involved in the resolution of their cases. Traditionally, the court system has excluded victims from case processing; in effect, once the victim has reported a crime, the criminal justice system takes over and represents his or her interests. The criminal justice system views crime as an offense against the state or federal government, not against an individual victim. Because of this, victims have felt excluded from the criminal justice process, feeling that their interests are not taken into account during the course of the case. As a result, the court system has become more sensitive to the needs of victims and has devised new methods of taking victims into account.

Restorative Justice

This philosophy posits that the criminal justice system needs to address the real victims of crime—not only the actual victims themselves, but also offenders, family members, and the community. The idea is that crime affects more than the government entity whose laws have been broken and that the system must, in effect, restore the injured parties to where they were before the crime occurred. **Restorative justice** enables offenders to understand the harms they have caused and gives them the chance to try to make things right. Victims are able to provide input and participate in the process, meeting with criminal justice personnel and community leaders to outline the best course of action for a particular victim. One common requirement in restorative justice is victim restitution, which involves the offender offering monetary compensation for the harm caused. In addition, the criminal justice system works with community programs to address offenders' needs for the purposes of integrating them back into the community and reducing future criminal conduct.

Alternative Dispute Resolution

Though most common in civil cases, **alternative dispute resolution** (ADR) is also used in criminal cases, usually misdemeanors. As the name suggests, ADR seeks to settle disputes in ways besides the formal court process. One common form of ADR is mediation, which involves a neutral individual (not a judge) who works with the parties involved to come to a mutual agreement as to a resolution. For example, in civil cases, lawsuits may be settled through mediation without ever having to go to court. In criminal cases, mediation resembles aspects of restorative justice, in that the victim and offender can work out their issues to the benefit of both. Usually, some sort of victim restitution is the aim of mediation. Some would argue that ADR is a form of restorative justice; however, offender reintegration does not occupy as predominant a position in ADR as it does in a true restorative justice program.

Use of Court Technology

Many courts are using new and updated technology to assist with court operations. One of the uses of this technology is to create a more efficient case management process through an increased use of computerized files, in essence creating an "e-court." Case files move among many individuals and offices within a court, so the use of case management technology is essential to keep the flow of cases moving. Although the court system is a long way from becoming paperless, case management technology allows all individuals involved in a case (e.g., the judge, prosecutor, clerk of court, defense attorney, probation officer) 24-hour access to case files. Thus, there is no longer the need to wait for a file as in a traditional paperwork scheme. Additionally, courts can measure their performance with the use of Courtools, an online measure instituted by the National Center for State Courts. These tools include such measures as access to the courts, fairness, length of case, and reliability of case files, among others. These tools allow courts to measure their performance and enact changes, if necessary.

Use of Jury Consultants
In general, the jury selection process involves the prosecutor and defense attorney choosing a jury that would favor their side. In doing so, they will choose or dismiss jurors based on their evaluation of a juror's perceived bias toward their case. To better assist in the jury selection process, jury consultants have been utilized to assess the characteristics of offenders, victims, cases, and jurors that are associated with a particular outcome. With the use of mock trials, jury consultants are able to determine what factors will influence a juror's vote. For instance, a jury consultant may determine that those with a higher income are more likely to vote to convict a lower-income defendant. With these conclusions, the jury consultant will advise attorneys on the juror characteristics that will be favorable to their side. Jury consultants are mostly hired by defense attorneys as opposed to prosecutors and are being increasingly used throughout courtrooms today.

Web Activity

For more information about trends in state courts, visit the website of the National Center for State Courts at https://www.ncsc.org/trends/annual-publication.

COVID-19 and the Courts
The court system is not immune to the struggles involved with COVID-19. Due to the fact that many court processes occur in-person and among groups of people, court systems throughout the country have modified their actions. According to the National Center for State Courts (2020), the five main ways that courts have done this are ending or postponing jury trials, suspending in-person proceedings, restricting access to courthouses, extending deadlines for filing paperwork or paying fines and court costs, and engaging in teleconferencing for meetings and hearings. The state and federal courts are different in terms of how they are addressing COVID-19 and the fallout from this remains to be seen.

Web Activity

For more information on how courts are dealing with COVID-19, see https://www.ncsc.org/newsroom/public-health-emergency.

CONCLUSION

As evidenced above, the court system is involved in many aspects of the criminal justice system. Courts can become involved in cases before an arrest is made and after an offender has served a sentence. The courts are primarily responsible for ensuring that the laws are followed properly, both by citizens and government entities, and seeing to it that law violators are punished. Although many cases never formally enter the criminal justice system, the number of cases that courts have to process has increased in recent years due to law-and-order policies that have increased the numbers and types of offenders who come to the attention of the system. State and federal legislatures have also reduced the discretion of judges by authorizing longer and mandatory prison sentences, which have dramatically increased the incarceration rate. Courts are trying to find a balance between the demands of politicians and the public that offenders should be punished and caseload issues that pressure the courtroom workgroup to get cases out of the system quickly and efficiently, often with punishments that do not fit the crime. This can be an incredibly difficult task, so actors in the court system must measure the ideological goals of retribution and deterrence against the practical goals of not allowing the courts to fall apart as caseloads mount.

KEY WORDS

adversarial system of justice
alternative dispute resolution
appeal
appellate courts
appellate jurisdiction
arraignment
assembly-line justice
assigned counsel
bail
bailiffs
bench trial
burden of proof

case attrition
challenge for cause
collateral attack
death penalty
defense attorneys
determinate sentencing
district courts
domestic violence courts
drug courts
dual court system
fines
FISA court
hung jury
indeterminate sentencing

initial appearance
intermediate sanctions
jail
judges
legal aid
master jury list
mental-health courts
merit selection
nonpartisan election
original jurisdiction
partisan election
peremptory challenge
plea bargain
postconviction review

preliminary hearing
prison
pro bono
pro se
prosecutors
public defender

rebuttal
restorative justice
sentencing guidelines
trial courts of general
  jurisdiction

trial courts of limited
  jurisdiction
venire
voir dire

SUGGESTED READINGS

Abadinsky, H. (2021). *Law, courts, and justice in America*, 8th edition. Long Grove, IL: Waveland Press.

Carp, R., R. Stidham, K. Manning, and L. Holmes. (2017) *Judicial process in America*. Thousand Oaks, CA: CQ Press.

Hemmens, C., D. Brody, and C. Spohn. (2020. *Criminal courts: A contemporary perspective*, 4th ed. Thousand Oaks, CA: Sage Publications.

Hume, R. (2018). *Judicial behavior and policy-making*. Lanham, MD: Rowman & Littlefield.

Spohn, C., and C. Hemmens. (2012). *Courts: A text/reader*. Thousand Oaks, CA: Sage Publications.

CHAPTER 5

✦

Institutional Corrections

CHAPTER OUTLINE

Inmates and Infectious Diseases
Inmates and Substance Use
Inmates and Mental Illness
Aging and Elderly Inmates
Future Directions for Institutional Corrections
Conclusion
Key Words
Suggested Readings

After reading this chapter, you should be able to:

- Identify different eras of punishment and point out highlights of each
- Discuss the recent trends in the philosophy of corrections
- Report on the populations size, disparities, and costs of imprisonment
- Define jails and detention centers and relate their features
- Compare and contrast different types of prisons
- Discuss issues related to privately operated prisons
- Compare and contrast the deprivation and importation models of prison
- List different special offender populations
- Discuss the problem of infectious diseases in prisons and jails
- Discuss the problem of handling inmates with co-occurring disorders of substance use and mental illness
- Point out issues and responses to an aging prison population
- Note milestone cases in the rights of prison inmates
- Illustrate the problems inherent in prison overcrowding
- Discuss future concerns and directions for institutional corrections

---

INTRODUCTION

Institutional correctional facilities have been used for centuries, ever since the Roman Catholic Church made use of confinement at the abbey during the Middle Ages. Even though there were precursors to the modern jails and prisons, corporal punishments such as flogging, branding, and other forms of torture were widespread across the world. The American colonists followed suit with these punishments over the centuries but soon came to realize that such sanctions were inhumane and inappropriate for some behaviors. Soon thereafter, the penitentiary became the primary method by which convicted offenders would be punished.

HISTORY OF PUNISHMENT

Punishment for the violation of group norms, rules, and laws is a common element across human history and societies. Whether the response is informally handed out by the head of a household or reflects the official commands of a modern-day court, social life imposes various restrictions on behavior and violations carry the possibility of a negative response. Punishment may be justified for a variety of social, political, moral, or religious reasons. In ancient times, punishment for a violation of a social norm or law was often handled locally, by either the family, clan, or head of the community. Larger and more organized societies typically used more formal procedures for investigating, prosecuting, adjudicating, and punishing offenders. There was considerable variation, however, in the response depending on the type of law or custom that was violated, who the offender and victim were, the specific geographic location of the incident, and the exact historical time period.

Nearly every society has had some arrangements for the temporary confinement of offenders. Some ancient civilizations, such as the Greeks and Romans, also had facilities designed to hold offenders for longer periods of time. In general, however, punishment in premodern Western societies and colonial America primarily involved the use of monetary compensation or corporal punishments. This is not to suggest that imprisonment did not occur, but it was far from the most common or most important form of punishment. When incarceration did occur, it was for the purpose of holding the offender until the corporal or capital sentence was to take place, usually within a day or two.

Modern societies are structured by the formal organization and routinization of social tasks and social life. One of the social tasks that has been increasingly controlled and managed has been the enforcement of laws and punishment of law violators. With the spread of democratic values and market capitalism came growing criticism of the use of physical punishment. In the late 1700s, severe forms of punishment were being questioned by those adhering to the Classical school. Furthermore, existing punishments and facilities of the day were perceived as ineffective and counterproductive. As society shifted from a top-down power structure to one based on the sovereignty of the people, new forms of punishment were needed to reflect these new social relations. It was during this time that the modern-day penitentiary was born, and with it the beginning of formal organizational structures designed to carry out punishments (see Morris and Rothman 1995; Rothman 1971).

Several major penal institutions were created in the United States between 1790 and 1830. Although there were differences in the design and operation of these early penitentiaries, they were more similar than not. In less than 100 years, punishment changed from the rather arbitrary use of physical punishment to a model emphasizing the confinement and correction of individual offenders through segregation, regimentation, and control. Offenders were increasingly separated based upon personal characteristics. As a result, female offenders, juvenile delinquents, and the mentally ill were placed in facilities independent of male adult criminal offenders.

> **Web Activity**
>
> To learn more about the unique circumstances and history of women and institutional corrections, go to the textbook website (www.oup.com/he/lab6e).

ERAS OF PUNISHMENT

The purpose of punishment and the use of different types of punishment have largely reflected the needs of a particular society. As a result, there have been different eras of punishment in the United States that used varying mechanisms for punishment.

The Era of the Penitentiary

Incapacitation and deterrence were the philosophies that dominated the purposes for confinement in the 1800s to 1860s. This was known as the **penitentiary era**, so called because of the development of a formal penal system and a heavy reliance on incarceration. Two different styles of penitentiaries became symbols of this era: separate and congregate. These styles are more commonly known as the Pennsylvania and Auburn systems, respectively.

The Eastern State Penitentiary in Philadelphia, Pennsylvania, was said to be a separate system because of its heavy reliance on silence and the separation of inmates from one another in individual cells. Eating, working, and sleeping were performed in the confines of the cells. The purpose of silence and solitude was reflected in the belief that the only way to repent and reform for one's wrongdoings was to reflect silently on one's deeds. Inmates were also denied visits from family members and friends and access to newspapers, and correspondences of any kind were forbidden (Rothman 1971).

The Auburn Prison in New York also operated under the rule of silence but differed from the Pennsylvania prison in that inmates could congregate with one another during the day while eating or working. Auburn prisoners returned to separate cells at night, and silence, even while in the presence of other inmates, was strictly enforced. Inmates in New York were also secluded from the outside world; there was no sight, sound, or contact with anyone or anything beyond the prison walls (Rothman 1971).

Penitentiaries sprang forth in other parts of the United States following the procedures and philosophies of their predecessors, despite the criticisms lodged against the imposition of silence, corporal punishments to keep inmates under control, and restriction of access to the external society. This so-called old prison discipline led some inmates to suffer from mental, emotional, and physical illness and, in some cases, even death.

The Era of Reform

The Civil War detracted attention from the plight of prisoners housed in the penitentiaries that were built in the 1800s. By 1870, however, the harsh environment of these institutions again came to be scrutinized. A more humanitarian approach to the practice of incarceration was advocated based more on the philosophy of rehabilitation rather than pure incapacitation or deterrence. The National Prison Association, which is known today as the American Correctional Association, was formed in 1870 to address the problems of the penitentiary system. Prison administrators, members of Congress, and prominent citizens from the United States and abroad gathered in Cincinnati, Ohio, and issued a set of declarations by which prisons would be reformed. These principles emphasized the value of treatment for inmates based on their individual needs, an indeterminate sentencing scheme by which inmates could earn their way out of prison, vocational and educational training, labor that was purposeful rather than punishment oriented, and noncorporal methods of discipline that made use of rewards rather than punishment for conformity (Pisciotta 1994). In addition, the reformers abolished the rule of silence. A system whereby released inmates could continue their treatment in the community was also introduced during the **reform era**. Today, this practice is better known as parole, and it will be discussed in more detail in the following chapter.

The Elmira Reformatory in New York was the prototype institution whose mission was to carry out these principles. Inmates were classified based on their conduct and success in the interventions available at the facility, such as training for trade and academics. Similar to Elmira's predecessors, the reformatory was criticized for the means used to control inmates, inhumane working and living conditions, and rigid order. Thus, the intentions of the reforms appeared to be sound but, in the end, poor implementation and a lack of funding required a new approach to the use of institutions for punishment.

The Era of Industry

The idea of convict labor was not new to the world of incarceration: the Pennsylvania and the Auburn systems required inmates to engage in craft-oriented or factory-oriented labor, respectively (Conley 1980). The goods produced by inmates were often sold in the open market. Inmates at the Auburn Prison actually built Sing Sing Prison, New York's second state institution for the incarceration of convicted offenders. Chain gangs were developed during this era, with inmates working on road or canal projects and prison construction for the states. Inmates were also tied to the private sector by being employed contractually with private-sector businesses in the making of furniture, clothing, brooms, baskets, and hosiery. In addition, some inmates were contracted out to work in the stone quarries and coal mines (Mancini 1978; Sellin 1976).

These latter practices, known as **convict leasing**, were a Southern development, and some authors have suggested that convict leasing was basically another way to enslave Blacks following the Civil War (Johnson 2002; Sheldon 2001). Convict leasing of inmates often led to illness, suffering, and even death. For example, in Georgia, convicts were beaten if they did not produce the designated amount of coal per day (Mancini 1978).

Despite such horrific consequences associated with convict labor during the **industrial era**, states and their officials continued their labor programs for inmates until the 1930s, when state legislatures and Congress passed a number of measures banning the sale of inmate-produced goods to the public (Sexton 1995). The major impetus for such legislation was complaints advanced by workers in the organized labor force that inmate-made goods undercut the price at which free-market products could be sold. Once the Great Depression hit in the 1930s, pressure from workers increased considerably to prohibit inmate labor from interfering with their profits; thus, inmate labor was curtailed.

Legislation was reintroduced in the late 1970s that permitted products produced by prison industries to be sold in the open market once again. Today, inmates continue to work while doing their time in various industries connected to the private and public sectors. Inmates have been involved in such jobs as assembling graduation gowns for Jostens, Inc., making embroidered emblems for Lyon Brothers Manufacturing Company, and even sewing garments that were later purchased by J.C. Penney and Victoria's Secret for retail sale for Third Generation, Inc. (Sexton 1995).

The Era of Rehabilitation

By the early 1930s, there was a strong sense of urgency that something needed to be done about the harsh punishments faced by inmates in US penal institutions. The Depression contributed to discontent among the general public, and dissatisfaction in prisons was also on the rise. Several major prison riots in Illinois, Colorado, New York, and Kansas City prompted the government to take notice. Even prison officials began to understand the hopelessness that prisoners experienced. With a report issued by the Wickersham Commission in 1931, inmate grievances were officially recognized. State prisons did not provide anything more than capricious rules and coercive punishments for inmates, and meaningful programs to assist inmates in their reformation were lacking. In fact, inmates spent most of their time inactively engaged in simply doing their time.

Web Activity

Explore the worst prison riots of all time here: https://www.worldatlas.com/articles/10-worst-prison-riots-of-all-time.html. What characteristics did these riots have in common? Now, do a web search and find which prison had the longest riot in history. Why do you think it did not make the top 10 list of worst riots of all time?

The Wickersham Commission called for a new philosophy to guide the prison system; the philosophy of **rehabilitation** soon replaced the philosophies of deterrence and incapacitation that had dominated since the inception of the penitentiary. The major players in the move toward more rehabilitative efforts were the progressives, who were most active during the first couple of decades of the 20th century. The progressives were known for their indeterminist view that social problems, including crime, were often beyond an individual's control, much like having a disease that needs treatment. The medical model dominated the **rehabilitation era** with a focus on the needs of the individual offender and less reliance on prisons to carry out the criminal sanction. Probation, indeter-minate sentences, classification systems, vocational and educational training, and release from prison based on treatment success were some of the significant practices devised and implemented to carry out the goal of rehabilitation. Many of the recommendations from the 1870 National Prison Association finally came to fruition.

Corrections would follow the rehabilitation philosophy for over 40 years, with reported success in some jurisdictions and failure in others. It appeared that states were just not equipped to carry out the rehabilitative ideals. This latter statement es-pecially held true for prisons where the correctional officers were mandated to keep order within the institution while simultaneously attempting to create an environ-ment that was amenable to treatment (Rothman 1980). It soon became clear that the premise of rehabilitation could not climb over the hurdles blocking its proper implementation.

When we couple these ideological struggles with the social and political con-text of the 1960s and 1970s, it should come as little surprise that the philosophy of rehabilitation would soon be replaced with a more punitive philosophy, better known as the get-tough movement. Student uprisings over Vietnam, civil rights demonstrations, increases in poverty and crime rates, and the Watergate scan-dal led people to question the government, social institutions, law enforcement, courts, and corrections. The catalyst that provided further justification for aban-doning the philosophy of rehabilitation was the publication of a report by Robert Martinson finding that "with few and isolated exceptions, the rehabilitative ef-forts that have been reported so far have had no appreciable effect on recidivism" (Martinson 1974: 25).

The Era of Retribution

The "nothing works" doctrine associated with Martinson's publication provided the impetus to close the book on rehabilitation. During this era, and even in the 2010s, some sanctions and criminal justice practices continue to reflect cor-rectional policies that were based on more punitive ideals such as an increased reliance on secure confinement for more offenders for longer periods of time, determinate sentencing models, and the abolition of parole. Offenders are now sentenced to a finite amount of time and release is not necessarily tied to ref-ormation or rehabilitation. Under the auspices of get-tough practices, offenders who commit crimes will get their just desserts.

Now in the **retributive era**, during the past 35 years, there has been a gen-eral trend in the United States and western European countries to respond to law violators with more severe penalties and a decreasing support for rehabilita-tive efforts. In the United States, this has resulted in most jurisdictions enacting lengthier prison sentences, more punitive sanctions (such as three-strikes policies that stipulate life sentences for offenders convicted of their third felonies), and at-tempts to limit the discretion of judges or correctional administrators to reduce sentence lengths. Although these changes apply to a wide variety of behaviors, violent crimes and drug law violations have been particularly affected by these changes (Blumstein and Beck 1999). Perhaps most important has been the "war on drugs" that has been fought during the past 30 years. As a result, drug law violators make up a significant percentage of offenders in criminal courts and under correctional supervision. This is a considerable change from just 30 years ago (Blumstein and Beck 1999).

The Era of Reentry

While not a traditional purpose of punishment like many of the eras we explored above, the reentry movement was a necessary response to decades of sanctioning practices based on retributive and incapacitative philosophies whereby more and more persons were behind bars for lengthier periods of time, which is a costly enterprise. The release of inmates will happen regardless of sentencing motivations. Consider that at a minimum, 95 percent of state inmates will be released from incarceration at some point (Hughes and Wilson 2002). In 2010, over 700,000 inmates were released from state prisons; in 2011, the number was nearly 689,000 (Carson and Sabol 2012). **Reentry** is the transition period of persons who are soon to be released or have recently been released from prison or jail back into the community. It involves providing services and assistance to these individuals and their families. After 9/11 states were in debt, the economy was souring, and unemployment was fairly high compared to the booming years of the late 1990s. When the recession hit between 2007 and 2009, states had to devise ways to defray costs, and imprisoning offenders is very expensive. Couple the budget cuts with the fact that the get-tough policies in the 1980s led to overcrowded prisons, and states had to come up with alternative models to save money while trying to maintain the relatively low crime rates the nation had been experiencing for several years.

In general, there are two mechanisms to reduce prison crowding and its cost. There are **front-door options** that involve community-based sanctions like probation instead of prison or jail. **Back-door options** involve early-release mechanisms such as parole, transitional placement in a community-based correctional facility, or simply being released from prison without any assistance or supervision. The focus on reentry programs and services, most notably in the areas of employment, housing, and behavioral health, becomes important when back-door options are implemented. Given that four in ten offenders return to prison within three years after release, concentrated reentry efforts are vital (Pew Center 2011). Of specific concern are individuals with substance abuse and/or mental health disorders, who have an even greater risk of recidivism. It is estimated that over 70 percent of state prisoners have struggled with either one or both of these conditions (James and Glaze 2006). Research has shown that without appropriate community-based treatment, employment, housing, and other relevant support systems in place, rearrests and reincarcerations of this population are highly likely, especially in the first few months after discharge (Fontaine, Gilchrist-Scott, Roman, Taxy, and Roman 2012; Hartwell 2010; Lurigio, Rollins, and Fallon 2004).

Web Activity

Two exceptional documentaries on the issue of mental illness in state prison systems are *The New Asylums* (http://www.pbs.org/wgbh/pages/frontline/shows/asylums/view/) and the follow-up production *The Released* (http://www.pbs.org/wgbh/pages/frontline/released/view/).

Offenders face a multitude of barriers, such as finding employment, obtaining stable housing, adjusting to life outside prison or jail, and repairing broken ties with friends and family members. Numerous local, state, and federal agencies and nonprofit organizations across the country provide reentry programming and assistance. Reentry efforts that make connections even before inmates return to the community and that continue over the first year after release are essential.

Depending on the jurisdiction where offenders will be returning post-release, local, state, and federal agencies and nonprofit organizations may provide reentry programming and assistance. Efforts that make connections even before inmates return to the community and continue over the first year after release are essential. Some state departments of corrections and the federal government have reentry planning services or programs for inmates preparing for release from custody. During this planning, which can occur upon admission with updates made during their prison stay and just prior to release, inmates are asked to note:

1. Where they will live immediately upon release, and what will their longer-term housing arrangements be?
2. What their transportation plans are from the prison and thereafter?
3. What agencies in the community can provide resources they need such as employment, education, mental and physical health services, and identification such as driver's license, social security card, and/or birth certificate?
4. What they will do during their leisure time?
5. Who they can rely on for social support such as family, friends, or community members?

With the passage of the **Second Chance Act of 2008**, financial support through federal grant funding has increased the number of formalized reentry programs across the US State, local, and tribal governments and nonprofit agencies and organizations can apply for grant funding to develop and implement programs to assist individuals being released from prison, jails, and juvenile institutions. Recently funded projects have included programs that provide assistance for adults with co-occurring substance use and mental disorders, the creating and supporting reentry courts, and mentoring and transitional services for juveniles. A major key to success in reentry programming is to develop coordinated partnerships with state and local

Critical Thinking

With the rampant transmission of COVID-19 in congregate housing units like jails and prisons, planning reentry into the community has become more important not only for the individual being released, but for the communities to where they return. The Council of State Governments Justice Center and the National Sheriffs' Association developed a checklist (https://csgjusticecenter.org/wp-content/uploads/2020/05/DischargePlannerChecklist_6MAY2020508accessible.pdf) that can be used by jail and prison officials to assist in reentry planning in times of this health pandemic. Do you think all the topics were adequately covered in the checklist? Why or why not? What would you add? What community partners would be important for a successful reentry?

criminal justice and social services agencies, organizations, and health service providers to efficiently and appropriately deliver needed support and services to formerly incarcerated populations.

Web Activity

To explore some promising practices, programs, and the populations served, go to https://csgjusticecenter.org/topics/reentry/. What is happening in your state?

PRISON POPULATIONS, DISPARITIES, AND COSTS

Prison Populations and Disparities

In 2018 (the latest date for which data were available at press time), there were 1,465,200 individuals imprisoned in the United States in state and federal facilities, which is a rate of 431 sentenced inmates per 100,000 US residents (Carson 2020). For the most part, prison populations have been decreasing around 1 percent per year for the past four years. Despite these incremental decreases, what continues to be problematic is the disproportionate imprisonment of persons of color. As you can see in Figure 5.1, Black residents continue to be incarcerated at higher rates compared to Hispanics or Latinos and whites. According to 2019 US Census estimates, Blacks comprise a little over 13 percent of the US population and yet make up almost 33 percent of state and federal prison populations. Similarly, though not as wide of a gap as Black inmates, 23 percent of prisoners are Hispanic or Latino, and represent 18.5 percent of the US population. Thirty percent of inmates housed in state and federal facilities are white, yet whites make up over 75 percent of the US population.

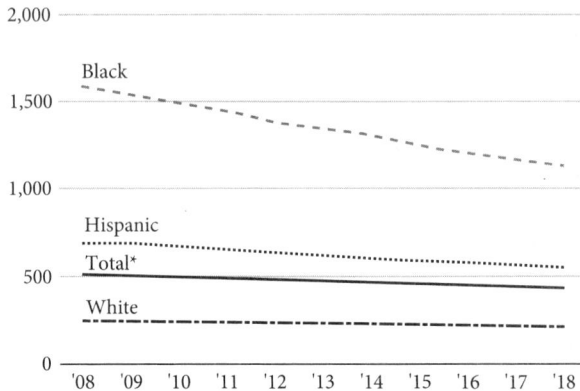

Figure 5.1 Combined State and Federal Imprisonment Rate per 100,000 US Residents of a Given Race or Ethnicity, 2008–2018

NOTE: Rates are based on prisoners sentenced to serve more than one year in state or federal prison. See table 5 for rates from 2008 to 2018.

* Includes all races, including those not shown separately in the figure.

SOURCE: Bureau of Justice Statistics, National Prisoner Statistics , 2008-2018.

Web Activity

Go to https://www.sentencingproject.org/the-facts/#map and explore five states from different regions of the country. Compare and contrast the racial disparities. Detail at least three patterns or observations across the states that you found surprising.

Costs of Imprisonment

In the United States, compared to other nations, imprisonment is a common sanction imposed on offenders. Not only does the United States incarcerate more convicted individuals than anywhere else in the world, the imprisoned also serve longer prison terms as a result of the adoption of determinate and mandatory sentencing models by state and federal governments. These practices have consequentially contributed to the long-lasting phenomenon of **mass incarceration**. To keep up with the constant flow of offenders formally processed in the criminal justice system, jurisdictions have had to increase their funding for various justice agencies. While the funding for all aspects of the criminal justice system has increased, the increase for correctional spending has been the most dramatic. To illustrate, recent cost analyses from the Bureau of Justice Statistics (Hyland 2019) for 2016 (the most recent years available for comparison at time of writing) found that state and local correctional budgets in the United States totaled over $80 billion, which is an increase of over 370 percent since 1980 when costs hovered around $17 billion.

Web Activity

Explore the Vera's Center on Sentencing and Corrections Incarceration Trends Tool. First, view this video: https://www.vera.org/research/incarceration-trends-demonstration-video

and then go to http://trends.vera.org/incarceration-rates?data=pretrial&fips=39067 and explore incarceration rates jails and prisons across states and counties across the United States. Starting in the 1970s, select one year from each decade (i.e., 1970s, 1980s, 1990s, 2000s, 2010s) and examine prison and jail incarceration trends for five states and one county from within each of the five states you selected. What patterns do you see? Describe.

Corrections is a costly business and, as we noted earlier, states are grappling with both a large institutional population and budget constraints. To reduce prison overcrowding, many states and the federal government have greatly increased the bed space within their prison systems through massive prison construction programs. The rationale behind the boom in building more secure places of confinement is the idea that eventually, the more offenders we incarcerate, the less crime we will have (Austin and Irwin 2001). Unfortunately, it also appears that even with such a high incarceration rate, recidivism and crime rates have not been reduced as significantly as many policymakers and the public had expected. Indeed, we continue to incarcerate people at levels disproportionate to actual offense counts (Pew Center on the States 2008).

In 2015, the mean cost of incarcerating one person in prison for one year averaged $33,274 (Mai and Subramanian 2017). Figured into these costs are expenditures for housing, feeding, clothing, and supervising inmates. If we include capital expenses and employee wages and benefits in the calculation, the total annual cost per inmate could run as high as $65,000 in a medium-security prison. To put these numbers in perspective, consider that in the academic year 2017–2018, per-pupil expenditures in state schools averaged $12,602 (National Education Association 2019). As you can see, on average, states spend nearly three times the amount per inmate as per pupil in a given year.

On a global scale the United States, although it is the number one country in incarceration, spends fewer dollars per inmate annually on average (using the $33,274 figure) than other Western nations. For example, to date, Australia's average per-person incarceration cost is around $109,000 a year, followed by Canada at over $91,000, and then England at $70,000 (Bushnell 2018). These other nations greatly outspend the United States per inmate, and yet these three nations' total prison populations combined do not even compare to that of the United States: 167,101 versus 2.1 million (World Prison Brief n.d.), respectively. Indeed, the United States prevails as the "winner" in the total number of persons imprisoned and expenditures on incarceration.

By this point in our discussion, it is obvious that corrections is "big business," with high overhead and human costs. Some states are beginning to realize that something must be done to curb the amount of money allocated to institutional corrections, especially with the serious state budget crises that have occurred over the past few years. For example, Massachusetts, Michigan, Missouri, Arizona, New Mexico, and Mississippi legislators have either repealed minimum mandatory sentencing laws that were the cornerstone of the get-tough era in the 1980s and 1990s or are considering modifications to existing legislation (Shy 2004). Although many of these laws targeted drug offenders, few, if any, states have observed significant decreases in the number of drug crimes occurring with the adoption of minimum mandatory sentences for these offenders. The proposed changes to these types of sentencing systems involve either a reduction in time spent in prison or widening the eligibility standards for parole. Thus, get-tough stances are being replaced by "smart-on-crime" strategies that enable states to conserve both monetary and material resources for already taxed social systems (Shy 2004: 1).

Critical Thinking:

There are more than monetary costs to governments and taxpayers expended due to mass incarceration practices. There are also collateral costs, known as **collateral consequences** to the individuals who have served time in prison that are long-lasting and stigmatizing, often hindering successful transitions post-confinement. One example of a collateral consequence is unable to secure employment due to having a criminal record. What are some others? How do they interrelate to one another? What can we do to offset these challenges?

JAILS

Currently, there are over 3,300 jails in the United States. **Jails** and **detention centers** are facilities designed to hold a variety of offenders for a relatively brief period of time, usually less than one year. The size of a jail varies depending on the geographic and legal jurisdictions it serves. While jails in rural areas and small communities may hold relatively few prisoners, those in cities can be immense. Counties or municipal governments operate most jails, while some jurisdictions such as the federal government have special facilities for their own detainees in certain areas of the country.

Jails perform several important functions. First, jails are where most offenders are housed following arrest. After arrest, a local judge or magistrate reviews the offenders' charges and flight risk and sets a bail amount, orders the offenders held without bail, or releases the offenders on their own recognizance until their next court date. Second, jails house defendants who have been sentenced to less than one year of incarceration. Some jail sentences are served on weekends, or the offenders may be released to the community for work while residing in the jail. Finally, jails may serve as detention centers to temporarily confine a variety of offenders until their cases are resolved or until authorities from the proper jurisdiction assume custody. Therefore, juvenile and adult, misdemeanor and felony, and state and federal offenders may all be housed briefly in the same facility, but sometimes in different units within that facility.

Although there are exceptions, jails tend to be chaotic environments and face a number of problems. Jails have historically been the "dumping grounds" for the poor, deviant, and marginalized individuals in a community (Sheldon 2001). They seem to be continually under pressure from overcrowding, a lack of resources and training, and the issue of local politics. Many individuals processed into the jail are intoxicated or under the influence of behavior-altering substances, highly agitated, suicidal, or mentally unstable when they arrive. Jail personnel often do not have adequate information on an arrestee's needs and risks when he or she is first booked into the facility. This lack of knowledge may lead to otherwise preventable problems. Finally, the continuous movement of prisoners in and out of the jail presents logistical and safety challenges to jail staff and administration. Inmates are frequently moved for court hearings, community service work, and other activities. The high volume of visitors can also provide opportunities for violence or smuggling of contraband.

Jail administrators are constantly facing a number of problems in the management of their facilities. Jails are often impersonal, with little contact between the guards and the inmates. Jails also lack necessary services such as medical, psychological, and substance abuse treatment for inmates. It should come as no surprise that stress levels are often heightened in the jail setting, with violence and safety issues in constant need of resolution. To overcome some of these problems, there has been a movement to replace existing jails with what are known as **new-generation jails (NGJs)**. These are built to house fewer inmates in what are known as pods or modules that contain 16 to 30 separate cells, with one or two inmates per cell. Inmates do not have access to other pods in the jail, and the staff does not have to be concerned with managing more than 60 inmates at any given time. In other types of jails, staff may have to monitor hundreds of inmates at once, thereby decreasing safety for all involved. In the NGJs, inmates eat, sleep, make phone calls, and engage in activities such as playing games or watching television in the pod (Zupan 2002). The staff is in closer contact with the inmates and consistently monitors inmates' behavior, which not only attenuates problems among the inmates and within the facility but can also provide inmates with more positive social exchanges between inmates and staff (Bayens, Williams, and Smykla 1997). One earlier evaluation of an NGJ found that recidivism did not increase and, for some offenders, actually decreased when compared with inmates housed in traditional jails (Applegate, Surette, and McCarthy 1999).

According to a recent report (Austin 2014), compared to state prisons, with over 1.3 million persons incarcerated and serving an average of 2.5 years, jails house 55 percent fewer individuals, with an average length of stay around 23 days. The majority of jail inmates have not been convicted, meaning they have yet to plead or be found guilty of any offense (i.e., they are in the pretrial process). With rare exceptions, offenders go to prison only after they have been convicted. Demographically, nearly 46 percent of jail inmates are white males; in contrast, African American males are the most represented racial/ethnic group in prisons.

A major concern facing our nation's jails are the increasing numbers of individuals with mental illnesses and how jail administrators and staff can effectively deal with this population. Approximately 80 percent of jails conduct mental health exams upon intake (James and Glaze 2006), and it is through this initial screening that persons with mental illnesses are identified. These assessments find that 23 percent of inmates had been treated for a mental illness the year preceding arrest, 17 percent used medication that affects their mental illness, and 7 percent had at least one overnight stay in a psychiatric hospital (James and Glaze 2006). Other than some jails providing psychotropic medications, most facilities lack appropriate treatment for affected inmates, and the political, physical, and administrative realities of jails are often counterproductive to any treatment efforts that might be effective (Treatment Advocacy Center 2014).

Critical Thinking Exercise

Given the problems faced by jail administrators and staff, what approaches and strategies could be tried to better manage the needs of the jail population both while incarcerated and after release? What are some strengths and weaknesses of your recommendations? Why would some strategies work better than others?

MODERN PRISONS

While felony offenders in the United States are more commonly sentenced to community supervision rather than incarceration, prisons are financially and symbolically important forms of punishment. Prisons are also socially and politically important because they are used to house those individuals who are determined to be unresponsive to community supervision, who pose a considerable risk to the community, or who have committed offenses so serious that they deserve to have their freedom taken away for a given period of time. Prisons are also known as penitentiaries, correctional institutions, and penal institutions. To reduce confusion, the term *prison* will be used in this section.

Characteristics of Prisons

In most American criminal justice systems, offenders who have been convicted and sentenced to more than one year of incarceration for a felony offense are generally held in **prisons**. Although many jurisdictions have a juvenile version of a prison system, the majority of prisoners are adults held in state or federal institutions. At any one time, the prison population is composed of offenders sentenced for a variety of offenses as well as those sentenced to prison for probation violations and those returned for parole violations. Individual states and the federal government tend to have a number of prisons within their prison systems. Each prison has certain features that make it more suitable for particular types of offenders. Once an inmate is sentenced to prison, personnel from the corrections department usually conduct an initial **classification** review, in which they evaluate the needs and risk of the offender to determine the best placement for him or her within the prison system. Common topics evaluated in this assessment are the danger posed by the prisoner, the length of sentence, any gang affiliation, physical or mental health needs, and whether treatment programs are available and considered important for the prisoner. Based on this assessment, prisoners are sent to an institution that is classified by its security type.

Critical Thinking Exercise

Prisons house offenders who have committed a variety of different offenses. Research the types of crimes for which offenders have been incarcerated and the demographics of offenders (the textbook website has some suggestions on where to look, at www.oup.com/he/lab6e). Describe the types of offenses and offenders in prison. What does this suggest about crime that is committed and who commits it?

Security Classifications

Most American jurisdictions have three to five different types of prisons, distinguished by their security level. **Supermax prisons** are primarily found in the larger jurisdictions and represent the most restrictive and secure prisons in the country. Because of their extremely high cost of operation and strict limitations on the number of prisoners they can hold, supermax prisons are generally reserved for the most incorrigible and dangerous prisoners in a correctional system. Prisoners in these facilities tend to be continuously confined to their cells except for very brief periods of exercise. Supermax prisons use the most sophisticated security systems and most rigorous safety procedures.

Maximum-security prisons represent the highest level of security in many states. These facilities tend to hold the most violent and disruptive prisoners in those jurisdictions without supermax facilities. Inmate movement within the prison is restricted by numerous checkpoints and gates. External barriers such as walled perimeters, several rings of razor-wired fencing, or armed guard towers are also common.

Some jurisdictions use a third security classification known as **close security**, which lies between maximum- and medium-security prisons. Such facilities may house individuals convicted of violent offenses who do not require a maximum-security setting or disruptive inmates who do not pose as great a physical threat to inmates or staff. **Medium-security prisons** hold a diverse inmate population and can have a variety of architectural styles. Inmates may have some degree of movement within the institution during certain times of the day and participate in a range of activities. However, the specifics of inmate life and the amount of security can vary considerably, even within different prisons in the same jurisdiction.

Finally, **minimum-security prisons** represent the most open and least restrictive type of institution. These can house prisoners convicted of nonviolent offenses, those who pose a minimal security risk, or those nearing final release. Minimum-security prisons tend to allow the greatest freedom of movement and offer a range of programs and services for inmates to participate in.

Some jurisdictions have **specialized prisons** that primarily house inmates with specific characteristics that pose unique challenges to institutions. These facilities offer treatment programs or services that are tailored to meet the needs and risks posed by particular populations. Examples of these institutions include those dedicated to substance-abusing prisoners, sex offenders, and mentally handicapped or psychiatric prisoners. Each jurisdiction typically has a facility dedicated to housing prisoners with severe psychological disorders because of the unique problems such inmates present to the operation of an institution.

Private Prisons

Another characteristic that can distinguish prisons is whether they are privately operated or managed and staffed by a jurisdiction's own personnel. Historically, it has not been uncommon for some degree of private interest to be involved in the operation of jails and prisons. Since the birth of the modern penitentiary around the turn of the 19th century, American correctional systems have had a variety of relationships with private for-profit businesses and nonprofit agencies. However, during the 20th century, the funding and operation of most American prisons has primarily been the responsibility of the public sector. During the push for increasing privatization of government services in the 1980s, American jurisdictions began increasingly to contract out some of their correctional services (Gowdy 2001).

To date, treatment services, community service, and smaller residential programs are more commonly privatized than major prisons. With rising incarceration rates, prison overcrowding, and increasing operating costs during the 1980s, governments were interested in alternatives that could increase the cost-effectiveness of correctional budgets. While the term **private prison** is often used to indicate a correctional facility that is managed and operated by a private corporation, the privatization of correctional services can take a number of forms. The authority to operate these facilities is granted through a contract awarded by a jurisdiction's government. There is considerable debate about the validity of incorporating a profit motive in the punishment of offenders (Gowdy 2001). There are also real questions about whether private prisons are actually more cost-effective and about the quality of services they provide. Despite this, punishment is a major for-profit enterprise, and several states have private prisons that are used in conjunction with the state-run institutions. Only time will tell whether privatization becomes a permanent and growing feature of American corrections or a passing trend that is remembered primarily in history books.

Critical Thinking Exercise

Investigate the use of private prisons in your state. How many people are in private institutions (nationally and in your state)? Should states be turning over control and supervision of prisoners to for-profit companies? What advantages and disadvantages do you see?

Custody and Security within Institutions

The primary goal of a prison is maintaining custody of inmates within the institution. In fact, nearly every decision affecting the operation of a prison must take into account the safety and prison control consequences. Even within the most secure facilities, inmates outnumber the **correctional officers** (or guards) who supervise the prisoners. This is particularly true in large, lower-security facilities.

Secure custody of inmates involves several components. First, prisons must ensure that they are physically secure and can prevent escape and the introduction of contraband into the institution. Second, prison officials want to reduce the occurrence of inmate assaults on staff. Limiting the frequency of inmate-on-inmate violence is another important goal for both the safety of the inmates and the impact such events have on institutional operations. Finally, prison administrators want to secure the efficient functioning of the institution. Procedures such as head counts and activities such as feeding, clothing, and work details create a structure to prison life. The smooth operation of these activities is vital to a manageable environment.

A symbiotic relationship is thought to exist among prisoners, correctional officers, and prison administrators. Though prison personnel have official (and unofficial) mechanisms at their control to ensure discipline, prisoners can create considerable disruption in the operation of a facility. Therefore, all sides tend to engage in activities and relationships that will maintain the status quo and reduce disruptions to daily life and routines. Clearly, the most destructive and disruptive event is a prison riot. In riots, prison officials lose all but the most basic control over some or all inmates and institutional operations. As a result, staff and inmate safety can be in serious jeopardy and considerable damage can be done to the physical structure of the institution.

Web Activity:

Go to the textbook website (www.oup.com/he/lab6e) to explore models used to explain how inmates adapt to life in prison.

Prison Violence and Prison Discipline

Violence, or at least the threat of violence, is a common concern among both inmates and staff. After all, prisons tend to be filled with people who have already demonstrated a willingness to engage in violent or otherwise unlawful acts. Knowledge about violence within prisons is limited by concerns over the validity and reliability of prison records and the limitations of other methodologies used to study **prison violence**. The level and extent of violence will greatly vary from prison to prison and for different prisoners. Different features of the prison, such as its architectural design, inmates' freedom of movement, and group and individual dynamics, can affect the level of prison violence (Adams 1992; Bottoms 1999).

Research suggests that most prisons are not characterized by the systematic and rampant violence often portrayed in the popular media (Bottoms 1999).

Of course, there have been and continue to be prisons and prison systems that are plagued by higher levels of violence. Coercion and the threat of violence appear to be more common than actual physical assaults. Coercion may be used by physically dominating inmates to obtain items such as food, money, personal services, and sexual favors. This threat of violence, including sexual assault, is very real to prisoners. Furthermore, prisoner assaults on staff and other prisoners do occur and can result in serious injury or death. Female prisons tend to have less explicit violence than male prisons, though violence and the threat of violence are clearly a reality in women's prisons as well. Similar to male prisons, there tend to be female convicts who are more willing to use instrumental violence and cause disruptions within the facility (Johnson 2002).

Prison officials have a number of tools to deal with violence and other violations of institutional rules. For violations that are criminal offenses, administrators can refer the matter for criminal prosecution. However, the difficulty in obtaining a conviction in many of these cases and the logistical problems involved often discourage such attempts (Jacobs 1982). A more common response is to use one or more of the sanctions that prison officials have at their disposal. These include the loss of certain privileges such as visitation, solitary confinement (often called segregation) for a period of time, or a change in the inmate's classification status or location (Jacobs 1982). Prison officials may also have the discretion to reduce an inmate's good-time credit. In jurisdictions with indeterminate sentencing, parole officials will examine an inmate's behavior and may reject a parole application if an inmate has a history of disruptive behavior while incarcerated.

Prison Programs

With the exception of the highest security prisons, most prisons offer **programs** that are promoted as helping with offender rehabilitation and increasing the structure and activities involved in an inmate's daily routine. The number and types of programs will vary across different institutions and jurisdictions. In many facilities, inmates can receive good time credits (i.e., days reduced from their sentence) by productively participating in approved activities. In some states, participation in certain programs could improves their chances of an earlier release from custody. The categories of programs offered typically fall under the headings of education, vocational, mental health/substance abuse treatment, religious, and recreation. Specific programs falling under the education and vocational headings that might be available in some facilities include: GED classes, literacy, parenting, post-secondary education classes and carpentry, welding, electronics, computer programming, and landscaping training, respectively. Religious programs include bible studies, access to prison chaplains, weekly spiritual services, and prison fellowships. Exercise courses, intramural athletics, open gym, outdoor yards, music and band, and other leisure activities would fall under the recreational program category.

Web Activity

Explore some prison programs being offered across the country and create one pre-sentation slide based on what you learned about one of the options below, or find one offered by your state's department of corrections.

- **Offender Change Washington State:**
  https://www.youtube.com/watch?v=CRKhlhi7Rj0&app=desktop.
- **Wild Horses Rehab Program:**
  https://fusion.tv/story/4996/rehabilitation-program-pairs-prisoners-with-wild-horses-its-life-changing/.
- **Substance Abuse Program for Female Offenders:**
  https://www.youtube.com/watch?v=y-042l7NeD8&app=desktop.
- **Arizona Corrections Prison Programs:**
  https://www.youtube.com/watch?v=yUh_TAag3qc&app=desktop.
- **Pathways to Rehab Solano Prison**:
  https://www.youtube.com/watch?v=WwgbCeTEipY&app=desktop.
- **Prison Inmates Train Dogs for Disabled:**
  https://www.youtube.com/watch?v=zvyTw37Alzg.

At a minimum, in many institutions, inmates are given a particular work assignment that constitutes a major part of their day. Many basic prison operations such as food service, laundry, and groundskeeping are carried out by prisoners with varying degrees of staff supervision. Involvement in other prison programs, like those noted in the previous paragraph, are voluntary and are available in some prisons for interested and eligible inmates. While the funding for such programs tends to be a relatively low priority, many scholars and practitioners consider these types of activities important in helping prisoners cope with the stresses of prison life and improving their likelihood of successful reintegration after release (e.g., Gaes et al. 1999).

Web Activity

An important influence on corrections has been the emergence of technology. For a discussion of this issue, go to the textbook website (www.oup.com/he/lab6e).

PROBLEMS, RIGHTS, AND IMPLICATIONS IN MODERN PRISONS

In addition to the challenging composition of inmate populations, institutional corrections will continue to deal with the problems of crowding, violence, and decreased availability of effective programs to reduce recidivism. Of course, these issues existed in the past, and given the heavy reliance on institutional facilities for punishment over the past few decades, will most likely persist in the future. Many of these issues have been brought to the attention of the courts by prisoners seeking to lessen the impact that the unique features of prison have on their lives. Even though many decisions set forth by the courts could be considered in favor of such solutions as reducing inmate crowding, the reality is that changes to rectify these problems have been more the exception than the rule. Indeed, some argue that problems surrounding inmate rights, crowding, violence, and inmate social systems have actually worsened over time.

Inmate Rights

Traditionally, appellate courts took a hands-off approach to the problems and grievances of those incarcerated (Haas and Alpert 1989). The reasons for this hands-off approach were that (1) the courts felt that they should not interfere with the operations of the prisons; (2) the judiciary offered a type of checks and balances; and (3) the judiciary could not possibly understand the problems of prison administrators because judges lacked a coherent knowledge of penology (Haas and Alpert 1989). In 1941, the Supreme Court ruled in Ex parte *Hull* that the Fifth and Fourteenth Amendments to the Bill of Rights granted everyone, even inmates, access to the courts (Haas and Alpert 1989). However, not until 1964 did the courts really begin to lift the hands-off policy with the *Cooper v. Pate* decision.

Until the mid-1960s, most prisons were homogenous institutions in which strict control, sometimes rehabilitation, and structure were the rule (Sykes 1958). With the advent of the civil rights movement, many groups began to seek legitimacy for their grievances and remedies to their problems through court decisions. The courthouse door opened for inmates and granted them access to address their grievances similar to that of other groups in society. This hands-on approach to inmate rights has led to lessening a number of deprivations but also paved the way for inequitable sentences, which could undermine other goals or philosophies of the criminal justice system in general and the corrections system in particular.

The prisoners' rights movement led to the establishment of certain new privileges. For instance, inmates now could buy televisions or radios, wear what they wanted in some prisons, or have visitors bring in amenities (Carroll 1974). This led to a situation of the "haves" versus the "have-nots" in which the have-nots could burglarize or victimize the haves to obtain what they wanted. The purpose of using correctional facilities for incapacitation is to prevent offenders from committing any further crimes. If crime continues in the prison, the goal of incapacitation is weakened.

Another result of the prisoners' rights movement is increased freedom of movement and the elimination of the requirement that inmates must participate in treatment programs. Lack of structure means idle time for some inmates, which occasionally leads to violence (Wooldredge 1994). This means that some inmates will experience a rougher time in prison than others because they are being victimized. Therefore, the philosophy of retribution is undermined in that no longer will punishment for similar crimes be the same for all inmates (Hawkins and Alpert

1989). Rehabilitation as a goal may be impossible to meet because inmates must be able to concentrate on their treatment; if they are constantly worrying about being victimized, they cannot actively participate in their own reformation. Deterrence— the idea that imposing severe punishments will create enough fear that the costs will outweigh the benefits of committing crime—may also be undermined because some inmates will be victims and some will continue to be offenders. Correctional officers often look the other way for most infractions because they do not want to attract the attention of administrators who are primarily concerned about the effective control of prisons (Zimmer 1986).

Legislation passed by Congress in 1995, however, may change the current state of affairs for both correctional philosophies and prisoners' rights. The Prison Litigation Reform Act (PLRA) establishes that inmates must exhaust the internal prison grievance procedures before accessing the federal courts. The PLRA also requires inmates to pay their own court filing fees, thereby further limiting access to judicial review of complaints by inmates. In addition, the PLRA reinforces the right of the courts to dismiss any lawsuit deemed by judges to be frivolous or malicious or to state an improper claim. An inmate who receives three such determinations (i.e., three strikes) regarding his or her petitions is restricted from filing further lawsuits without paying court fees in advance. Prisoners also face the possibility of losing good-time credit if judges find that the purpose of their grievances was harassment or a presentation of lies or false information. Further, the PLRA has a provision mandating that inmates must show physical injury in order to file a claim for mental or emotional injury. State inmate petitions filed in US district courts, for both civil rights and prison-conditions grievances, did decline after the passage of the PLRA. Despite these reductions in inmate lawsuits, several key cases did make their way to the US Supreme Court and further affected life in prison and correctional operations.

Crowding

Due to the growing trend of incarcerating and managing large numbers of offenders because of the fall of rehabilitation, more punitive sentencing policies, and increasing the number of offenses eligible for incarceration, prison crowding has become an endemic problem in the United States. For example, it is estimated that 44 percent of the prison population can be accounted for due to the war on drugs (Blumstein 1995). The rise in prison populations is indicative of the trends that can be attributed to judges and prosecutors in convicting more persons and sending them to prison. Prison populations will vary according to (1) how many people are sentenced to prison; (2) how long offenders are sent to prison; and (3) the rate at which they return (Joyce 1992).

Crowding leads to a number of problems within the institution, such as elevated blood pressures, more trips to clinics, difficulty sleeping, suicides, homicides, and other types of assaultive behaviors (Gaes and McGuire 1985; Harer and Steffensmeier 1996). In addition, crowding adds to the uncertainty, apprehension, and cognitive overloads of inmates. These emotional difficulties can interfere with treatment because inmates need to concentrate on their reformation; if they are constantly living in fear, this becomes a near-impossible task. Crowding can also undermine rehabilitation, in that classification of inmates into appropriate housing, programs, and the like is made more difficult and can deplete resources, leaving some inmates to be placed on treatment waiting lists or leading to the elimination of rehabilitation programs altogether.

In addition, crowding can undermine incapacitation due to the early release mechanisms that are relied upon to reduce the population. In effect, inmates are on the streets sooner and may return to crime due to shorter sentence lengths. Inmate crowding can also weaken the goal of general deterrence because would-be offenders see that crowding has led to limited space in facilities, which means that they may not receive prison sentences at all. Crowding can also weaken the objectives of specific deterrence due to the harsh living conditions of the prison environment. Finally, crowding can negatively affect retribution because no two sentences will be served equitably due to crowding.

Violence

As noted, violence in prison has become more and more pervasive due to the ever-changing composition of the prison population, such as the entrance of gangs and the mentally disordered, and the pervasive impact of the prisoners' rights movement (Irwin 1980). Inmates are free to move around the facilities, which leads to more opportunities for victimization. In addition, due to increased crowding, classification efforts may be ineffective at separating violent inmates from the nonviolent (Van Voorhis 1994). Further, because inmates are not required to participate in treatment programs, they have plenty of free time. It has been found that inmates who spend less time in educational activities are more likely to commit personal crimes (Wooldredge 1994). The impact of determinate sentencing, the entrance of younger inmates into the prison, decreases in furloughs, lack of visitation, and longer time until parole dates can also lead to increases in violence (Burke 1995).

Violence undermines retribution because some inmates are offenders and some are victims; this is not equal time for equal crimes. Violence weakens the goals of deterrence and incapacitation because the mere existence of violence in prison means that threats of punishments and preventing further crimes are ineffective at suppressing violence. Rehabilitation efforts may also be unsuccessful because some inmates live in fear of being victimized, and inmates must feel in total control of their being and safety in order to gain anything from treatment efforts.

Critical Thinking Exercise

You are the Director of Criminal Justice for your state. The governor has just informed you that you need to devise a plan to reduce prison crowding by 30 percent in year one, by 40 percent in year two, and by 10 percent each year thereafter until prison crowding in your state's facilities is near 0 percent. How will you accomplish this task? What policies would you propose to reduce incarceration rates? Why do you think these would work? What are some of the problems you might face when implementing your policies? Remember to take into account special offender populations when designing your plan.

Solutions

Possible solutions to these problems have been studied and found to be promising. For example, smaller, more efficiently designed prisons are better able to alleviate the problems posed by violence, inmate subcultures, and crowding. New designs are being used in jails such as the new-generation or direct-supervision jails. Such facilities make better use of design to promote a safer and more controlled environment for correctional officers. Smaller facilities may also encourage inmates to engage in activities such as treatment, vocational training, or education in a manner that can be replicated on the outside when they are released. Housing inmates in huge, dark, noisy prisons is not beneficial for any goal, let alone the well-being of inmates.

If classification systems, which have been found to be valid in dividing prison populations into manageable subgroups, are used more effectively, there may be reductions in violence, crowding, and favorable offender treatment outcomes (Van Voorhis 1994; Makarios and Latessa, 2013). Arguably, some inmates do not belong in prison in the first place, and classification systems can dictate which offenders would be better served in the community. More emphasis might be placed on separating the violent from the nonviolent, the aging from the young, and the mentally disabled from the general prison population. These types of separation could reduce levels of violence and other misconducts, dilute the inherent inequities that resulted from the prisoners' rights movement, and counterbalance the challenges of housing such varied groups in correctional institutions. More adequately classifying inmates can also increase successful treatment outcomes thereby increasing the probability of decreases in future reoffending after release from custody (Latessa, Listwan, Koetzle, 2013). To achieve such positive outcomes, however, we need to ensure we are targeting the (1) right offenders and (2) their criminogenic needs who are (3) amenable to the elements of matched treatment programs. This triad is best known as risk, need, responsivity, respectively, and together are known as the "principles of effective classification."

Principles of Effective Classification

As originally developed by Andrews and Bonta (2006), there are three principles of effective classification: (1) risk; (2) need; and (3) responsivity.

The **risk principle** states that we only target offenders who are medium-high to high risk in terms of their propensity to reoffend. Too often, individuals of low risk are placed in institutions and programs with more serious offenders. Low-risk, often situational (i.e., first crime committed is likely the last), offenders in these settings will be influenced by the higher-risk individuals in terms of the justifications and rationalizations, "tools and tricks of the trade," so to speak, for behaving in antisocial, criminal manners. In turn, this exposure can increase the chances that the low-risk offenders will engage in future crimes since low-risk individuals will learn from their more "experienced" counterparts. In order to reduce the chances of these negative influences on those who are and will likely be law-abiding, a one-size-fits-all approach is not advised. Rather, we should concentrate our efforts on those most likely to recidivate.

The **needs principle** focuses on two types of needs. One is **general needs**. Think of these as more like deficiencies in conduct or life, such as lack of employment or educational skills, substance abuse problems, and relationship issues. The second category is the **criminogenic needs**, which are anti-social attitudes, anti-social friends, substance abuse, lack of empathy, and impulsive behavior. We will surely see greater failure rates if we do not address the factors that have been shown time and time again to lead to offending. Successful programs will target the individual needs of each offender relative to those variables that influenced their law-violating behaviors.

Finally, the **responsivity principle**. Many offenders are assessed for risk and needs, but few are assessed relative to how responsive, or amenable, they will be to any given treatment or programmatic approach, as well as to correctional placement. In other words, the responsivity principle tells us that we should determine how amenable a person will be to a specific program or practice before we subject him or her to it. Aspects to consider when addressing responsivity are a person's personality, maturity level, intelligence, psychological state, learning style, cognitive abilities, and other interpersonal qualities.

To illustrate, let us assume there is a program for offenders that requires a journaling component, but several of the individuals the Department of Corrections would like to place in this program are unable to read or write past a third-grade level. These individuals will likely not be as successful in this type of program and therefore, we will not see promising outcomes for these offenders. Too often, we hear that programs do not work, when in reality they do work for some offenders but not for others, but because we are comparing all of the participants to one another, the successes are often masked, or canceled out, by the failures when the program is evaluated.

There are instruments available to assess the three principles of effective classification available. Most jurisdictions consider offenders' risk and needs, albeit frequently neglect criminogenic needs, but few assess for responsivity. This situation is unfortunate; especially given that studies have shown for over 25 years what programs can work, for what types of offenders, and in what types of settings.

In addition to classification systems, alternatives to incarceration such as community-based correctional facilities, intensive supervision probation, and home confinement coupled with treatment interventions could also be used. Better use of administrative "good time" and sentencing guidelines to reduce sentence lengths may also help alleviate crowding as well as violence and other problems (Joyce 1992). Perhaps limiting parole supervision to one year could be implemented if prison is used as the sanction of choice or if community corrections are used. The conditions required of offenders could be limited to those that are necessary to ensure public safety.

SPECIAL OFFENDER POPULATIONS

Similar to the general public, the prison population includes individuals with substance abuse problems, mental illness, physical disabilities, and diseases. There has also been an increase in the number of aging offenders in correctional institutions due to the get-tough sentencing policies adopted and implemented during the 1980s. Inmates are a unique population in that they are one of two groups in society that are entitled to medical treatment based on decisions handed down by the US Supreme Court (the other group is the military).

Inmates and Infectious Diseases

Offenders are considered a high-risk group for infectious diseases, most notably HIV/AIDS, Tuberculosis, and Hepatitis-C. Today, we can add SARS-Cov2, a type of coronavirus that causes COVID-19, to the list of severe health conditions that are can spread rapidly in congregate living conditions. The rapid spread of COVID-19 in state and federal prisons has resulted in 386,765 inmates testing positive with 2,459 inmate deaths as of March 5, 2021. Prison staff have also been afflicted resulting in over 105,000 cases and 191 deaths (The Marshall Project 2020). Jails were also affected heavily by COVID-19 and because individuals are often entering and exiting jails daily, the spread of the virus both inside the jail and in the community has also been problematic, though exact numbers of cases are difficult to identify.

Web Activity

COVID-19 in prisons in 2020 was widespread. To learn more and see the numbers in your state, go to https://www.themarshallproject.org/2020/05/01/a-state-by-state-look-at-coronavirus-in-prisons.

Since the 1980s, the prison population, like the general population, has witness a sizeable number of individuals diagnosed as HIV positive or with full-blown AIDS. Today, there are approximately 17,150 inmates in state and federal prisons who are HIV positive or have confirmed cases of active AIDS (Maruschak and Bronson 2017). Prior to 1999, it was estimated that prisoners were seven to nine times more likely to have confirmed cases of AIDS than the general population. The good news is that since 1999, the number of inmates who have HIV/AIDS is decreasing.

The number one method of transmission of HIV in the United States is through the sharing of needles or other equipment used to ingest illegal substances. The increase in mandatory minimum sentencing practices arguably led to an increase of substance users in prison, many of whom had already been exposed to HIV. In secure facilities HIV is most often spread through sexual contact between inmates, who were most likely exposed prior to their incarceration via unclean drug-taking methods.

Correctional administrators and staff across the country have implemented several approaches to decreasing the number of new cases within the prison. Some institutions focus on education in terms of how the disease is contracted and treatment options available. A few institutions have provided condoms for those inmates engaged in sexual activities; however, this option is controversial, as sex between inmates is usually prohibited. Voluntary or mandatory testing to determine who is infected with HIV has also been used. Special housing for inmates at different stages of the disease has also been attempted. It has been proposed that at a minimum, infirmaries should be established where inmates already confirmed to have AIDS can be held to protect them from airborne infections such as tuberculosis and pneumonia.

Web Activity

You can explore more about HIV in prisons and women and HIV in prisons on the textbook website (www.oup.com/he/lab6e).

Many state corrections systems have been proactive in collaborating with public health agencies to increase the knowledge about how to take care of not only HIV/AIDS in the prison but also other sexually transmitted diseases, tuberculosis, and Hepatitis-C, which are widespread among correctional populations disproportionate to the general population. Tuberculosis is a bacterial infection that primarily affects the lungs and is highly contagious, especially in crowded and densely populated conditions like prisons and jails. The key to limiting the spread of tuberculosis is identifying, reporting, isolating, and starting therapy for active cases. On average, we see about 4 percent of inmates testing positive for tuberculosis according to the Centers for Disease Control.

Another illness that is prevalent in correctional facilities is Hepatitis-C (HCV). HCV is one of the most common blood-borne illnesses in the United States affecting around 1 percent of the population. In prisons, however, it is estimated that between 17 to 23 percent of inmates are infected (Varan et al. 2014, Edlin et al. 2015). HCV is typically spread by drug users who share needles. The cost to treat HCV ranges from $70,000 to $25,000 per patient for an 8- to 12-week course of treatment with medication. Left untreated, HCV can lead to liver diseases.

Given that many inmates will eventually be released into society and the gravity of these communicable diseases, there is a definite need to provide appropriate treatment, prevention, and post-release programs to curb further transmission of these conditions. Thus, it would be remiss to ignore what goes on in the prison merely because the population affected is made up of offenders.

Critical Thinking Exercise

What should be the response of prisons to HIV/AIDS and other highly communicable diseases? What alternatives make the most sense? What do institutions in your state do to deal with these problems?

Inmates and Substance Use

Nearly half of offenders housed in jails and prisons across the United States admit to having been under the influence of alcohol or drugs when they committed the offense that led to their incarceration. Drug and property offenders are more likely than other types of offenders to engage in crime to acquire money to feed their substance addiction. The mentally ill are more likely to be under the influence at the time of their offenses than those who are not mentally ill. Overall, approximately 70 to 80 percent of incarcerated offenders report that they have used drugs in their past. Younger offenders, particularly those who are first-time or minor drug offenders, make up a significant proportion of jail populations. Since the war on drugs in the 1980s, the United States has seen unprecedented increases in incarceration rates for drug crimes that carry longer sentences than was typically the case prior to "getting tough."

Given that "kicking the habit" is difficult for those seeking treatment in the general population and their success rates are low, the environment of the prison often complicates effective service delivery for inmates who want to rid themselves of their substance addictions. Treatment in correctional facilities can involve counseling, therapeutic communities, detoxification, and 12-step programs such as Alcoholics Anonymous or Narcotics Anonymous. Of these treatment options, recent research shows that in-prison therapeutic community interventions (TCI), especially if coupled with continued treatment after participants are released from prison are especially effective (Galassi, Mpofu, and Athanasou 2015). The introduction of drug courts as alternatives to incapacitation since the late 1980s has provided yet another avenue for handling offenders with substance abuse problems.

Overall, some treatment programs have been found to be ineffective in reducing recidivism. However, only about 20 percent of inmates in secure confinement actually participate in the alcohol- or drug-treatment programs that are offered; in contrast, over 70 percent of inmates in state prison have substance abuse problems with and without co-occurring mental health disorders (James and Glaze 2006). Recidivism rates are two to four times higher for individuals who abuse substances compared to those who do not, so providing and encouraging completion of effective treatment programs while incarcerated increases the probability of higher success rates after release (Bennett et al. 2008).

If inmates do participate, they usually do so during the last six months of their sentences. The length of time in treatment could be one of the hurdles standing in the way of reducing recidivism. In fact, a review of the literature demonstrates that programs that do work are intensive, last 9 to 12 months, focus on offenders who are younger and more at risk, and maintain services after release. They actually work quite well and save money, too. Several recent studies have observed that offenders who participate in treatment programs both in prison and in the outside community have a lower incidence of drug use relapse and criminality (see McCollister et al. 2004).

Inmates and Mental Illness

Historically, asylums held society's misfits, whether they were insane, poor, or criminal. In 19th-century America, asylums were institutions where the mentally troubled were held until a cure for their sickness could be found. Once tranquilizers became available, asylum patients were basically sedated into a stupor. Essentially, this practice continued into the 20th century. Long-term institutionalization in a secure hospital setting became the primary method of care in the United States until the early 1970s.

With the passage and implementation of community mental health acts by states across the country, patients housed in the asylums who were no longer considered to be a threat to themselves or others were released into general society, a process called **deinstitutionalization**. Soon, many city streets in America were occupied by thousands of mentally ill former hospital patients, many of whom were unable to function in ways that were deemed appropriate law-abiding behaviors. Most jurisdictions responded to the problem by confining these "offenders" in correctional institutions. This process is known as **transinstitutionalization**; the mentally ill were first placed in secure confinement in a hospital setting, then they were released, and then they were reconfined, this time under the auspices of the criminal justice system.

Web Activity

Mental health among the offending population and those in correctional facilities is a growing concern. More information can be found on the textbook website (www.oup .com/he/lab6e).

Today, it is estimated that 15 to 20 percent of inmates housed in jails or prisons can be classified as having a mental disability (Pollock 2004; Treatment Advocacy Center 2014). Symptoms of mental health disorders most commonly observed in jails and prisons are mania, followed by major depressive disorder, and psychotic disorder. Nearly all of the state public and private correctional facilities in the United States have reported that they provided some sort of treatment to meet inmates' mental health needs (Beck and Maruschak 2001). Treatment forms range from therapy or counseling services to psychotropic medications and separate care units within the facility.

Inmates with mental disabilities are often at most risk for victimization, both physically and psychologically. These inmates are also found to be difficult for staff to control because many correctional officers do not have the training or educational background to deal with the compounded problems inmates with mental illness face in correctional facilities, especially when officers must give inmates orders of compliance to maintain security and control within the institutions. For example, correctional officers may be required to distinguish between those inmates who truly do not understand the orders that they are given, and as a result act out irrationally, from those who understand the expectations but become upset because they do not want to comply (Pollock 2004).

Inmates with **co-occurring disorders** are also becoming a major concern for management issues in the nation's prisons and jails and then for communities after release. These inmates are those who can be classified as having both substance abuse and mental health problems. These inmates are especially problematic for jails, since the majority of these offenders are purportedly arrested more frequently for less serious offenses (Alemagno et al. 2004). In addition, some of these individuals suffering from co-occurring disorders may seek treatment in a traditional psychiatric center for their mental illness, but they are often turned away because some centers or programs prefer not to deal with patients who also have drug addictions. Whatever the reason, a large number of individuals will return to the community still needing treatment to improve their chances for successful reentry. Further complicating matters, mentally ill offenders are more likely to be homeless, jobless, and alcohol or drug dependent during the year preceding their offense (Ditton 1999).

Critical Thinking Exercise

To what extent should correctional institutions be responsible for handling mentally ill individuals? Why does the criminal justice system assume responsibility for these individuals? Should it continue? What alternatives exist (or should exist) for handling these individuals?

Secure institutions in the criminal justice system have been facing an increase in the number of inmates with characteristics that require special assistance and programming. There has been progress in providing services for the mentally ill in terms of screening for problems and treatment availability, but more needs to be done. The same can be said for aging inmates, inmates with diseases, particularly HIV/AIDS, and inmates with substance abuse issues. These special populations, however, will continue to grow as long as legislation increases sentence lengths for various offenses and broadens the types of offenses punishable by incarceration.

Aging and Elderly Inmates

One prominent issue in the United States over the past 10 to 15 years has been a surge in the percentage of the population over the age of 55. News reports and politicians have often highlighted this fact with an emphasis on government programs in need of reform such as Social Security and Medicare, long-term care, and prescription drug costs. Special housing such as assisted-living communities and retirement communities has been a significant money-maker for construction companies, investors, and real estate developers alike. Few cities over 50,000 residents are without such properties.

Recall that what happens in the general society soon occurs inside the prison walls. With the mandate to provide medical treatment for inmates, the costs and unique problems posed by an aging prison population are an ever-pressing dilemma for an institution that traditionally held convicted offenders between the ages of 18 and 49. The number of state and federal prisoners aged 55 and older is growing at twice the rate of their younger counterparts. Between 1980 and 2010, inmates age 55-plus increased by nearly 1.400 percent. According to the American Civil Liberties Union (2012), if this rate of growth continues, inmates age 55 and older will make up 33 percent of prison populations across the country by 2020. Figure 5.2 displays the increasing trend in the percentage of inmates in state prisons who are 55 years of age or older. There is no epidemic of older persons committing crimes; rather, the increase in this age group is a result of longer sentences, life-without-parole sanctions, and mandatory minimum provisions. As a result, state and federal corrections systems need to allocate three times the expenditures to care for aging inmates compared to their younger counterparts (Faiver 1998). Some state prisons have created special wings that are essentially nursing homes to provide for older prisoners.

When people age, in or out of prison, they change physically, socially, and mentally. For offenders who are aging behind bars, however, many of the issues associated with aging are aggravated. Although aging inmates are entitled to healthcare, the quality of that care may not be sufficient to take care of many of the problems

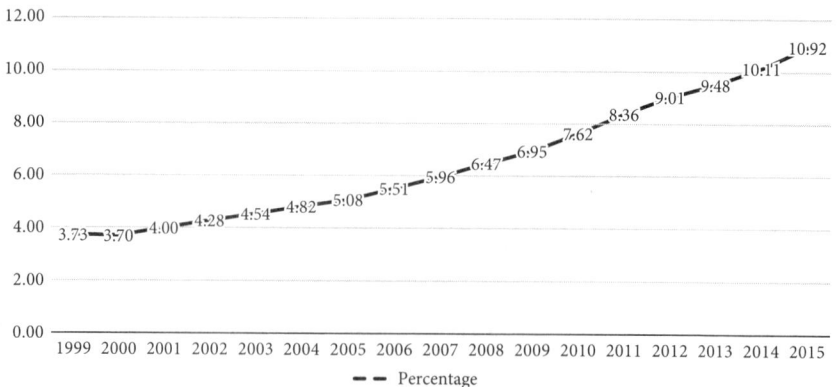

Figure 5.2 Percentage of Inmates 55 and Older, 1999–2015
SOURCE: National Corrections Reporting Program, 2015, https://www.prisonpolicy.org/data/older_prisonpopulations.xlsx (accessed August 28, 2020).

associated with old age, such as dementia. In addition, older inmates may not be able to take care of themselves if they are harassed or assaulted by younger inmates.

Possible solutions to these problems involve early release on medical parole, also known as compassionate release, sentences served in the community for older offenders who do not pose a significant risk to the community, increases in funding to serve aging inmates, and the creation of geriatric units within existing and proposed facilities. Certainly, the former two alternatives would be the most cost-effective for the administration of corrections, considering that offenders serving their time in the community are responsible for their own housing, medical treatment, and daily care. Government allocation of more funds to correctional budgets would be helpful but is not practical or economical based on the fiscal crises over the past several years. In general, most states already spend more on corrections than on education and other social programs.

Web Activity

To learn more about compassionate release for elderly inmates, go to https://www.youtube.com/watch?v=GGGI11LAnK4.

Creating geriatric units and even geriatric prisons is becoming the major approach for dealing with the aging inmate population. These facilities look like mini-hospitals that are staffed with registered nurses and are equipped with appropriate medical devices, which are more readily available than they would be in the typical prison infirmary. Some states have developed prison hospice facilities. Similar to hospice facilities in the community, prison hospices care for terminally ill inmates who are not eligible for or who were denied medical parole. Certainly, as the prison population continues to gray, different approaches, programs, and facilities will be needed to house this population, especially if other back-door options are not available.

FUTURE DIRECTIONS FOR INSTITUTIONAL CORRECTIONS

Like all components of the criminal justice system, correctional systems reflect the characteristics and environment of the society they serve. It is only natural that as society changes, so will the institutions designed to reinforce and protect it. While there is inadequate space to cover the considerable number of important issues facing corrections in the next few decades, the following discussion will briefly touch on some of these issues.

Perhaps the most compelling issue is what will happen with the prison population and incarceration rate, which has seen a fourfold increase over the past 30 years. The wars on crime and drugs have taken an enormous toll on government budgets, often to the detriment of other human services such as education and social services. It is unclear whether jurisdictions can maintain the level of spending on corrections indefinitely or whether public and political support will continue for such expenditures. The wars on crime and drugs have also had a considerable impact on the social fabric of communities and society in general that we are only beginning to understand (Hagan and Dinovitzer 1999). Removing such a large number of persons from society will have an observable impact on the children, families, and communities of offenders. This impact will likely include a number of negative consequences. Expanding the prison population also increases the number of prisoners who will eventually return to the community with additional burdens, especially when mental illness and substance dependency issues are present. The steps that are taken to reintegrate this population into the community and the success of those efforts will be important issues for the country as a whole.

A second major issue is how institutional supervision will deal with the special-needs offenders who are increasingly becoming part of the correctional population. One population demanding special attention is the growing number of persons afflicted with co-occurring substance and mental health disorders in jails and prisons. Although prisons have always had a disproportionate number of substance abusers among their populations, quality drug-treatment programs have never been a high priority within correctional budgets. Most programs tend to be understaffed, underfunded, poorly designed and implemented, and simply too short in duration to adequately address the multifaceted problem of substance abuse. The relatively high percentage of HIV-positive and HCV inmates presents another set of unique legal, medical, and operational challenges to correctional institutions. How prisons respond to these inmates and the measures they take to limit the spread of infections within institutions will require balancing the needs and rights of the individual with the needs of the other inmates and the institution. Medication and treatment for illnesses also increase medical costs for correctional budgets further compounding an already overwhelmed system.

A third population that will increasingly become a fixture in institutions is the elderly. As jurisdictions have increased sentence lengths and decreased the discretion to reduce those sentences, the percentage of older inmates has increased. Incarcerated elderly inmates will require additional medical resources and have special physical and psychological needs.

Critical Thinking Exercise

Corrections has witnessed several eras in terms of the punishments used and the purposes for which they were instituted. What do you think the next era of corrections will be like? For example, will there be an even greater reliance on institutions for punishment? Will more rehabilitation programs be developed? Will special offender populations be effectively served? Will we see more technological advances and less human interaction between corrections officers and inmates? What will our future prisons look like? Who will be housed in them? How can you be confident that your predictions are accurate?

CONCLUSION

Clearly, there are problems and challenges that correctional systems face. The nature of the problems is a function of the society that a correctional system serves. Exploring alternatives to secure confinement and methods to improve existing conditions within institutions should be seriously considered. Currently, it could be argued that none of the goals of the criminal justice system has been achieved due to the problems and characteristics of current correctional environments. Crowding, violence, gangs, and even the unforeseen consequences of the prisoners' rights movement have helped to diminish further the prospects for effective rehabilitation, retribution, incapacitation, and deterrence. These realizations should be at the heart of policies and reforms; there are no short-term solutions to problems that have lasted for decades, especially when they were exacerbated during periods when crime rates were decreasing.

KEY WORDS

back-door options
classification
close security
collateral consequences
convict leasing
co-occurring disorders
correctional officers
deinstitutionalization
detention centers
front-door options
industrial era
jails
mass incarceration

maximum-security
  prisons
medium-security prisons
minimum-security
  prisons
needs principle
new-generation jails
  (NGJs)
penitentiary era
prison programs
prisons
prison violence
private prison

punishment
reentry
reform era
rehabilitation
rehabilitation era
responsivity principle
retributive era
risk principle
secure custody
specialized prisons
supermax prisons
transinstitutionalization

SUGGESTED READINGS

Bernstein, N. (2007). *All alone in the world: Children of the incarcerated*. New York: New Press.

Hurley, M. (2018). *Aging in prison: The integration of research and practice*, 2nd ed. Durham, NC: Carolina Academic Press.

Jacobson, M. (2005). *Downsizing prisons: How to reduce crime and end mass incarceration*. New York: New York University Press.

Latessa, E. J., S. J. Listwan, and D. Koetzle. (2013). *What works (and doesn't) in reducing recidivism*. New York: Routledge.

Mears, D. P., and J. C. Cochran. (2014). *Prisoner reentry in the era of mass incarceration*. Thousand Oaks, CA: Sage Publications.

Montross, C. (2020). *Waiting for an Echo: The madness of American incarceration*. London: Penguin Press.

Petersilia, J. (2003). *When prisoners come home: Parole and prisoner reentry.* New York: Oxford University Press.

Pew Center on the States. (2008). *One in 100: Behind bars in America in 2008.* Public Safety Performance Project. http://www.pewcenteronthestates.org.

Pew Center on the States. (2009). *One in 31: The long reach of American corrections.* Public Safety Performance Project. http://www.pewcenteronthestates.org.

Pratt, J. (2002). *Punishment and civilization: Penal tolerance and intolerance in modern society.* Thousand Oaks, CA: Sage Publications.

Pratt, T. C. (2009). *Addicted to incarceration: Corrections policy and politics of misinformation in the United States.* Los Angeles, CA: Sage Publications.

Prendergast, M. L., E. A. Hall, H. K. Wexler, G. Melnick, and Y. Cao. (2004). Amity prison-based therapeutic community: 5-year outcomes. *The Prison Journal,* 84(1), 36–60.

Roth, A. (2018). *Insane: America's criminal treatment of mental illness.* New York: Basic Books.

Santos, M. (2004). *About prison.* Belmont, CA: Thomson/Wadsworth.

Senghor, S. (2016). *Writing my wrongs: Life, death, and redemption in an American prison.* New York: Convergent Books.

Terry, C. (2003). *The fellas: Overcoming prison and addiction.* Belmont, CA: Thomson/Wadsworth.

CHAPTER 6

꙳

Community Corrections

CHAPTER OUTLINE

After reading this chapter, you should be able to:

- Provide a brief history of community corrections
- Explain different correctional sanctions used in the United States
- Relate how restorative justice fits into a community supervision approach

- Discuss the extent and operation of probation
- Define net widening and discuss why it is problematic
- Define and discuss intensive supervision probation
- Discuss home confinement and issues in using electronic monitoring
- Differentiate day reporting centers and residential centers
- Outline the issues related to the use of boot camps
- Discuss the responsibilities of community supervision officers
- Identify different types of supervision violations
- Discuss the effectiveness of probation and intermediate sanctions
- List and define different forms of prison release
- Discuss issues related to reentry and reintegration
- Identify different special-needs populations
- Relate what is meant by best practices

INTRODUCTION

Community corrections constitute the various punishments and forms of supervision that occur within the community rather than in an institutional setting. Contemporary forms of community corrections include probation, **intermediate sanctions**, and parole supervision. Although some types of intermediate sanctions, such as boot camps and community residential programs, occur in institutional settings, stays in such facilities are generally brief and often include an element of community supervision. Therefore, they are typically included in discussions of community corrections. While jails and prisons may be the most familiar forms of punishments in the United States, far more offenders are supervised in the community than in institutional settings (Pew Charitable Trusts 2018). In fact, almost 70 percent of the American correctional population is in the community (Glaze and Kaeble 2014). Thus, community corrections is an important aspect of the criminal justice system that requires further discussion.

Although correctional agencies and institutions are primarily responsible for administering the penalties imposed on convicted offenders by the courts, correctional agencies actually provide a range of services to the criminal justice system. For example, probation officers in many jurisdictions are responsible for conducting court-ordered presentence investigations and submitting reports to assist in judicial decision-making. In addition, they may collaborate with a variety of criminal justice and human service agencies through such activities as drug treatment courts and programs, afterschool programs for juveniles, and partnering with local law enforcement.

A variety of agencies may provide community correctional services depending on the legal and geographic jurisdiction. There are community correctional programs at the local, state, and federal government levels. Furthermore, local and state governments have community correctional programs for both juveniles and adults. The decentralized nature of criminal justice in the United States makes it difficult to generalize about specific practices and policies. Because the purpose of this text is to introduce readers to the essential features of the criminal justice system, this chapter discusses community corrections generally, with an emphasis on sanctions and supervision of adults in the community (see Chapter 7 for discussions about penalties imposed on juvenile offenders). While specific practices and the types of sanctions that are available will differ across jurisdictions, the underlying principles and issues are often quite similar.

HISTORY OF COMMUNITY CORRECTIONS

For most of human history, punishment has been community-based. With the exception of banishment, most punishments were carried out in a public setting or in a manner that involved community members, especially victims, to a far greater extent than today. Punishing offenders by incarcerating them for a specified period in a facility built exclusively for that purpose is largely a modern practice. Readers will recall that Chapter 5 described the numerous changes in the late 18th century and early 19th century that were associated with the birth and development of the modern prison. However, by the middle of the 19th century, additional changes were occurring that also led to an increased use of **community supervision** for offenders (Vanstone 2008). Many of these community correctional practices had their roots in historical practices, such as judicial reprieve and release on recognizance, that were designed to mitigate the severity of criminal punishment (Clear and Dammer 2003).

By the 19th century, the ideas of the Enlightenment, the growth of capitalism, and democratic principles were influencing attitudes about crime and punishment. These changes led to new approaches to dealing with problems of social order, especially in the new American republic. In particular, the social environment was increasingly identified as an important contributor to crime and disorder (Rothman 1971). Within this context, the notion of individual reform, whether based on moral repentance or changing environmental factors, influenced attitudes on what to do about criminal behavior, especially among less serious offenders. Such ideas would have a direct impact on the development of two of the major forms of community corrections: probation and parole.

Of increasing concern in the new republic were drunkenness and the perceived problems associated with it (Rothman 1971). During the 19th century, those arrested for public drunkenness were frequently sentenced to periods of confinement in local jails, which were often overcrowded and characterized by filth and disease. It was in just such a case that John Augustus, a Boston bootmaker and philanthropist, asked a Boston court to release an offender into his custody in 1841. Motivated by humanitarian interests, Augustus allowed the defendant to reside in his home and assisted him in securing employment while requiring that the offender abide by certain conditions. It was from this humble beginning that

probation started. After Augustus returned to court with the defendant several weeks later, the court was impressed with the apparent change in the offender and agreed to continue to suspend his sentence as long as he remained in good conduct. Augustus soon returned to court to select additional offenders whom he supervised under certain conditions in exchange for the court delaying the imposition of their original sentences (Abadinsky 1997).

For the next 18 years until his death in 1859, Augustus developed a set of procedures that remain essential features of probation today: interviewing defendants to determine their suitability for release, requiring conditions for offenders to obey in exchange for their release, and notifying the court if an offender violated a condition of his or her supervision (Clear and Dammer 2003). In 1878, the Massachusetts legislature created a paid position for a probation officer assigned to the Boston court (Abadinsky 1997). By the early 20th century, formal probation organizations existed in numerous local, state, and federal jurisdictions. By the middle of the 20th century, probation was available for adult felony offenders in all US states and all federal jurisdictions and could be found, in some version, in many countries across the globe (Abadinsky 1997; Vanstone 2008).

Dissatisfaction with the newly created penitentiaries to achieve their intended goals lead to the development of both probation and parole, in the United States as well as internationally (Rothman 1971; Vanstone 2008). Innovations by prison administrators in Australia and Ireland had a considerable impact on the development of parole. In 1840, Alexander Maconochie became administrator of the Norfolk Island penal colony off the coast of Australia (Abadinsky 1997). Maconochie arrived at a penal colony that had experienced a number of disruptions and set about instituting changes to encourage individual reform. He developed a system based on "marks" that prisoners earned toward early release. Prisoners would pass through stages of increasing liberty on the island after periods of good conduct. Eventually, prisoners could earn an early conditional release from the colony (Abadinsky 1997).

Maconochie's mark system was politically controversial and lasted for only a few years (Abadinsky 1997). News of his experiment and its apparent success, however, eventually reached Britain. Soon after, laws were passed that allowed for awarding "tickets of leave" to prisoners, during which time they were to be supervised by the local police. In 1854, Walter Crofton became head of the Irish prison system and instituted policies based on Maconochie's earlier experiment. Under the Irish system, prisoners progressed through four stages of incarceration, each providing a greater level of freedom within the institution, resulting ultimately in early release through a ticket of leave. Importantly, released prisoners were given conditions of release and were supervised by either local police or a civilian who was assigned this responsibility (Abadinsky 1997).

The policies implemented by Maconochie and Crofton were rooted in a penal philosophy emphasizing individual reform that held prominence among many leading American prison experts during this period. The notion of individualized punishment by use of an indeterminate sentence was promoted at an important conference of the National Prison Association in 1870 (Clear and Dammer 2003). Dissatisfied with the current state of prison operations, scholars and practitioners called for a system of incarceration that encouraged reform through offering incentives for early release dependent upon evidence of good conduct and individual reform (Clear and Dammer 2003). Based on these ideas, New York passed an indeterminate sentence law in 1876 for inmates sentenced to the Elmira Reformatory (Abandinsky 1997). The superintendent, Zebulon Brockway, assisted in drafting legislation that imposed sentences with a maximum term of incarceration but allowed inmates to earn early release after demonstrating good conduct and accumulating a specified number of marks by participating in various activities. This became the first official version of parole in American corrections. Appointed guardians, rather than the police officers of the Irish system, supervised released prisoners, and failure to abide by certain conditions of release could result in their return to prison (Abadinsky 1997).

The notion of the indeterminate sentence spread slowly to other states, most of whom used it initially only for youthful offenders and those sentenced for less serious offenses. By the early part of the 20th century, the majority of states used indeterminate sentences for at least some types of offenders (Bottomley 1990). As Rothman (1980) notes, the growth of the use of parole was likely as much a matter of convenience as principle. Urbanization, increasing immigrant populations, and the Great Depression contributed to prison overcrowding and strains on correctional resources (Abadinsky 1997). The increasing use of parole, while consistent with penal theories of the day, was also a useful mechanism for controlling both inmate behavior and prison overcrowding (Bottomley 1990). By the middle of the 20th century, the indeterminate sentence and parole had become standard features of American criminal law and corrections.

CONTEMPORARY COMMUNITY CORRECTIONS

While there are a number of community correctional programs, offenders on regular probation and those under parole supervision constitute the largest portion of the community correctional population. Approximately 6.4 million people were under some form of correctional supervision in 2017–2018 (Maruschak and Minton 2020). Of this total, almost4.4 million people were under community supervision—approximately 3.5 million on probation and nearly 900,000 under parole supervision (Maruschak and Minton 2020). After several decades of increasing correctional populations, the United States has recently experienced a period of declining correctional populations. In fact, the number of persons under probation, jail, or prison supervision has decreased each year since 2008. These numbers, however, must be interpreted cautiously. Itis far too early to tell whether this trend will continue. Furthermore, recent decreases have been relatively small, especially when considered in the context of more than 25 years of annual growth.

Web Activity

Detailed information on correctional populations in the United States can be found in the Bureau of Justice Statistics reports *Correctional Populations in the United States, 2017–2018* and *Probation and Parole in the United States, 2017–2018*, which are available on the textbook website (www.oup.com/he/lab6e).

Though there may be similarities, each jurisdiction has its own model for organizing its criminal justice system. The federal government has a specific criminal justice system for defendants arrested and prosecuted for violating federal criminal statutes and a correctional system to carry out the punishments ordered by the federal courts. When it comes to violations of state law, the picture becomes more complex, as each state has its own criminal justice system and various subsystems within that larger framework. Defendants convicted of state felony statutes and sentenced to prison are sent to facilities run by state correctional agencies. Defendants convicted of misdemeanors and sentenced to time in jail are held primarily in facilities funded and run by city or county governments. The responsibility for supervising defendants convicted of misdemeanor or felony offenses and sentenced to nonprison sanctions, however, varies greatly. In some jurisdictions, supervision of defendants sentenced to community supervision is the responsibility of court employees, while other jurisdictions use state agencies, such as the state departments of corrections, to handle supervision duties. There are also combination or hybrid models of organizing correctional services in which the sanction imposed or the jurisdiction determines who supervises an offender. In addition, the supervision of parolees or those on supervised release may be the responsibility of a department that also supervises probationers or an agency that exclusively handles parolees. Due to the diversity of organization and practice of community corrections in the United States, the following discussion emphasizes the most common features and general principles of community corrections.

Jurisdictions vary greatly in the number and types of sanctions that they can use for law violators. The term *sanction* is often used interchangeably with *punishment* and refers to a specific punishment (e.g., fine, probation, prison) imposed by a court. Although prison is the first punishment that comes to mind for many Americans, it is not the most common punishment used for violations of the law. Incarceration in a state correctional institution is reserved typically for the most serious or habitual offenders and those who cannot abide by the rules of other previously imposed penalties. On a daily basis, courts that deal primarily with misdemeanor crimes handle a far greater volume of offenders than courts that deal exclusively with felony offenders. However, even among offenders convicted of felonies, a probation sentence is imposed in more than one-fourth (28%) of all such cases (Reaves 2013).

Available sanctions for felony offenders include a range of penalties that vary in severity. Table 6.1 provides a brief description of the most common sanctions

Table 6.1 Types of Correctional Sanctions

Fines	Fines are often a part of a larger probation sentence. Some jurisdictions have developed more rigorous monetary penalties called "day fines" that require payment of a percentage of an offender's income over time rather than a flat fee.
Community service work (CSW)	CSW requires that a set number of volunteer hours be completed within a specified period of time. Some jurisdictions use CSW as a stand-alone punishment, especially for misdemeanor offenders. CSW for felony offenders is most commonly a special condition of a probation sentence.
Probation	A term of court-ordered supervision during which offenders remain in the community provided that they follow certain conditions.
Day reporting center (DRC)	A form of community supervision requiring offenders to report to a DRC on a daily or near-daily basis. DRCs may house a variety of services and programs for which offenders are required to participate such as drug testing, GED courses, and counseling.
Intensive supervision probation (ISP)	A form of supervision involving frequent contact, perhaps several times a week, between offenders and probation officers. Some jurisdictions may require offenders' confinement to their residence (i.e., "house arrest") when not engaged in approved activities. ISP may involve electronic monitoring or global positioning system (GPS) devices in some jurisdictions.
Community correctional facilities	Refers to a wide variety of facilities designed to hold offenders for relatively brief periods of time. May serve as a work-release facility in which offenders go into the community for work or other approved activities but are otherwise required to remain in the facility. Such facilities can be used for residential treatment programs for special-needs offenders. May also serve as halfway house facilities for recently released prisoners.
Jail	Offenders who are sentenced by the court to less than a year of incarceration (the maximum may be less in some jurisdictions) usually serve their sentences in jails or detention centers run by the county or municipality. Jail sentences may involve work-release provisions or be followed by a period of community supervision.
Shock incarceration	Some states give judges or correctional authorities the authority to grant early conditional releases to eligible offenders sentenced to a period of regular incarceration. This release typically follows a brief period of confinement (30–180 days) and is conditional upon the offender remaining on community supervision for a specified time upon release. Also known as "shock probation" in some jurisdictions.
Boot camps	Also referred to as shock incarceration programs in some jurisdictions, boot camps involve a brief (less than six months) confinement in a secure facility in which inmates go through a period of drill and instruction modelled on basic military training. Common features include the use of physical exercise and instruction to instil discipline and self-control, and encourage pro-social behavior. Most boot-camp programs now include varying degrees of rehabilitative interventions such as educational and drug treatment programs. Typically followed by a period of community supervision.
Prisons	Also referred to as penitentiaries or correctional institutions. Typically hold felony offenders sentenced to incarceration for more than one year and those returned to prison for parole violations. Security levels and the types of services and offenders hold vary among prisons. Prisoners under sentences of death may be held on "death row," a wing in a high-security institution in or near where executions are carried out.

found in the United States. While not all of these sanctions are available in every jurisdiction, the variety of sanctions in most jurisdictions has increased in the past several decades. Courts may also use a combination of punishments rather than simply relying on one sanction. Parole supervision is not a sanction imposed by a court; instead, prisoners are released from incarceration to parole supervision by a correctional agency (e.g., a parole board). Perhaps the most important distinction is that parolees typically remain under the jurisdiction of the correctional system, whereas probationers and others on community supervision remain under the legal jurisdiction of the original sentencing court. In practice, parolees and probationers may have many of the same conditions and may even have the same officer in a given jurisdiction. Violations of the conditions of supervision for either group may result in the offender having a hearing before the authority that retains jurisdiction in his or her case. Because parole involves the supervision of the offender in the community or a community-based facility, it is generally considered a form of community corrections. Therefore, parole supervision is included in this chapter.

Beginning in the 1980s, many jurisdictions began to create new sentencing options that are less expensive than incarceration but more punitive than regular probation. Often referred to as intermediate sanctions, these provide an alternative to either traditional probation or prison. As shown in Table 6.1, sanctions such as intensive supervision probation and community residential centers are forms of intermediate sanctions increasingly used for a variety of offenders. Such programs are touted as more cost-effective than prison, more restrictive and punitive than regular probation, and offering a better opportunity for a rehabilitative or deterrent impact on offenders (Tonry and Lynch 1996). In addition, courts and correctional departments have begun increasingly to use sanctions and programs consistent with restorative justice. Box 6.1 describes the role of restorative justice in community corrections.

Critical Thinking Exercise

Examine the different types of criminal sanctions found in Table 6.1. Identify which philosophy of punishment—retribution, deterrence, rehabilitation, incapacitation, or restorative justice—is the best justification for each of these sanctions. Is there more than one possible justification for some of the sanctions? If yes, how might having multiple justifications be a potential benefit or problem?

BOX 6.1

Restorative Justice and Community Corrections

Restorative justice represents an alternative vision of the purposes and goals of criminal punishment. Although not incompatible with retribution, deterrence, or rehabilitation, restorative justice focuses on repairing the harms associated with criminal offending. The key attributes of restorative justice are its emphasis on holding offenders accountable by requiring them to take meaningful steps in the healing process for victims and the community to which they may eventually return. Restorative justice has its roots in the treatment of deviant community members by indigenous populations. Restorative justice has become increasingly important as a method of conflict resolution and responding to criminal offenders and their victims. Restorative criminal justice policies have become institutionalized in many Western countries such as Canada, New Zealand, and Australia, especially for cases dealing with youthful offenders (Prison Fellowship International 2012). Restorative justice practices in the United States appear to be expanding beyond the juvenile justice system and are increasingly used in cases with adult offenders. Today, many adult correctional departments highlight the role of restorative justice in their supervision of convicted offenders.

There is both a theoretical and a practical basis for a continuing relationship between community corrections and restorative justice. The nature of community corrections has made its mission susceptible to changing trends and pressures. As such, the focus of community corrections frequently shifts to different responsibilities and practices depending on the sociopolitical environment (Duff 2003; Pease 1999; Tonry 1999). Restorative justice can be used in a manner that holds offenders morally accountable, improves public safety, and promotes meaningful opportunities for rehabilitation (Duff 2003). While there are a number of challenges to restorative justice becoming a central theme of community supervision (Smith 2001), advocates see promise in the role that community corrections can have in creating a more just response to law violations—for offenders, victims, and the community (Duff 2003; White and Graham 2010).

Restorative justice programs can be found in institutional settings, but they remain most common for offenders whose punishment takes place in the community. Common restorative justice programs such as family group conferencing, victim–offender mediation, sentencing circles, and forms of community or victim service often take place in a community setting (National Institute of Justice n.d.; Prison Fellowship International 2012; White and Graham 2010). As a result, community correctional officers may have the responsibility for ensuring that offenders under supervision comply with the conditions of a restorative justice program. At a minimum, agencies and supervising officers can have a significant impact on the organizational and public support for restorative justice programs.

Web Activity

There are some excellent resources on the internet about restorative justice programs with criminal offenders. Students are encouraged to visit the Prison Fellowship International Centre for Justice and Reconciliation at http://restorativejustice. org/#sthash.Po9FpHdx.6n1V6tMP.dpbs, especially the page dedicated to probation at http://restorativejustice.org/restorative-justice/rj-in-the-criminal-justice-system/ courts/probation-and-parole/#sthash.HN1Qybul.dpbs. In addition, the newly established National Center on Restorative Justice (NCRJ) will serve as a clearinghouse of information and promote education, research, and service activities related to restorative justice practice and policy. See more about the NCRJ at https://www. vermontlaw.edu/ncrj.

PROBATION AND INTERMEDIATE SANCTIONS

Probation

All forms of probation represent a term of conditional supervision imposed by a sentencing court. The frequency of contact required between the offender and the probation officer varies depending on the jurisdiction, the offender, and the specific type of probation supervision that the court imposes. Although traditional probation is often the subject of political and media criticism, it remains the most frequently imposed penalty for criminal offenders (Petersilia 1997). In 2017–2018, there were approximately 3.4 million adult offenders under some form of probation supervision in the United States (Kaeble and Alper 2020). Almost 60 percent of those on probation have been placed on supervision for a felony (Kaeble and Bonzcar 2016). Only a small fraction of all offenders sentenced to community supervision are placed on intermediate sanctions, though the exact number is not known. For example, Florida has approximately 90,000 offenders on regular probation compared with only 9,000 on intensive supervision probation—a ratio of 10 regular probationers for every offender on intensive probation (Florida Department of Corrections 2017).

In recent decades, a recurring theme has been the lack of proper funding for regular probation that has resulted in increasing caseload sizes and a reduction in the amount of contact between offenders and officers (Jacobson, Schiraldi, Daly, and Hotez 2017; Kleiman 2015; Petersilia 2002). While there is no universal level of supervision for offenders placed on regular probation, a common practice is that offenders must report once a month to their probation officers. In addition, officers may be expected to have direct contact with offenders at least once a month, whether in the office or in the field. However, due to budgetary constraints and concerns about officer safety, officers may go several months between direct contacts with offenders in some jurisdictions. Furthermore, some departments use a form of unsupervised probation that does not require personal contact between offenders and officers except for special problems or concerns. Scholars and practitioners criticize the deterrent or the rehabilitative function of probation when so little supervision actually takes place or when there are few consequences for technical violations (Alm 2015; Jacobson et al. 2017; Kleiman 2015; Petersilia 1997, 1998). However, others have highlighted the efficiency of unsupervised probation, especially when used with kiosk reporting machines (Jacobson et al. 2017). The argument is that by placing the lowest risk offenders on unsupervised probation, officers can spend more time on active supervision strategies with higher-risk offenders (Jacobson et al. 2017).

Intermediate Sanctions

Intermediate sanctions claim to achieve a number of often competing goals (Tonry 1990). These include decreasing costs, increasing offender accountability and public safety, and increasing rehabilitative effectiveness (Tonry 1999; Tonry and Lynch 1996). Intermediate sanctions can also be justified by both retributive and utilitarian penal philosophies; however, the targeted population and function of the sanctions may differ depending on the perceived value of these goals (Harris 1996; von Hirsch 1998). Although scholars and critics are correct to point out the challenges intermediate sanctions face, support for alternatives to traditional probation and reducing our overreliance on prison remains strong (e.g., Klingele 2015; Larkin 2015; Petersilia 1997, 2002; Tonry and Lynch 1996). The following sections discuss some of the more important intermediate sanctions currently used (see Clear and Dammer 2003, Chapter 7). Community service work and fines, although potentially important forms of intermediate sanctions, are more commonly a special condition of community supervision rather than as a stand-alone penalty and are not discussed here (but see Morris and Tonry 1990).

Intensive Supervision Probation

After early experiments with intensive supervision in the 1960s, the notion of **intensive supervision probation (ISP)** gained increasing support in the 1980s (Clear and Dammer 2003). Today, ISP is perhaps the most common intermediate sanction and is available, in some form, in most US jurisdictions. Some jurisdictions use intensive supervision primarily for parolees, while other jurisdictions have ISP available as both a sentencing option for the courts and as a form of early release (Clear and Dammer 2003). Most ISP programs have several common features. A central premise of ISP is that it provides closer supervision by frequent contact between offenders and officers and greater restrictions on the freedom of offenders. Those on ISP may have contact with their officer several times per week, including interactions at the probation office as well as the offender's home and place of employment. Due to the increased supervision, ISP officers have smaller caseloads than officers with a regular probation caseload. Although the exact number may vary, ISP officers typically have fewer than 40 offenders under their supervision, whereas regular probation officers may supervise more than 100 offenders. Those on ISP often have more, and more restrictive, conditions of supervision and violations tend to be dealt with in a more immediate and punitive manner.

ISP is promoted by supporters as a "real" form of supervision and contrasted with the comparatively lenient requirements of regular probation. A primary goal of many ISP programs is the reduction of institutional overcrowding by diverting appropriate offenders from prison and jail. Proponents claim that ISP can improve community safety by increasing surveillance and contact with offenders and providing a more meaningful opportunity for rehabilitation. Recent research indicates that it is the ability of ISP to ensure participation in more intensive treatment, and not merely enhanced surveillance, which is critical to reducing recidivism and increasing offender success (Lowenkamp et al. 2010; Paparozzi and Gendreau 2005).

Critical Thinking Exercise

Intensive supervision programs are more restrictive and provide much greater contact and oversight of offenders. One result from this closer supervision is that more technical violations are discovered. As a result, a higher percentage of ISP offenders fail to complete their supervision. If a goal of ISP is to keep offenders out of prison, what should officers and courts do in response to technical violations?

House Arrest and Home Confinement

In some jurisdictions, ISP may also involve a period of home confinement and/ or electronic monitoring. Other jurisdictions may use these as penalties independent from ISP. Also referred to as **house arrest**, **home confinement** is a specified period of time during which offenders may not leave their places of residence except for previously approved activities such as work, treatment programs, food shopping, and visits to the doctor or the probation office. Offenders are typically required to submit a weekly schedule in advance, and any activities outside the home approved by supervising officers. Officers can use this schedule to make random field contacts to verify that offenders are at home or at an approved activity. The rationale behind the use of home confinement is fairly simple—the likelihood of offenders violating their supervision can be reduced by confining them to their residences. Thus, offenders are essentially incarcerated, except for approved activities, without accruing the costs associated with incarceration. Of course, like any form of community supervision, offenders can easily choose to ignore the requirements of the program. In particular, home confinement (and electronic monitoring) cannot prevent crimes and violations that occur within residences. Confined to their residences, however, offenders are less likely to have access to targets and opportunities for many types of crimes.

Electronic monitoring seeks to improve compliance with home confinement, whether as a form of pretrial release, court ordered supervision, or as a condition of parole release (DeMichele and Payne 2009) (see Box 6.2). The primary types of electronic monitoring systems currently used are programmed contact or continuous signaling devices (Clear and Dammer 2003). Programmed contact devices use random automated telephone or beeper calls that require offenders to contact a centralized call center within a limited period of time. Offenders then must verify their identities by video or voice identification or use special bracelets that attach to their legs or wrists that transmit a signal or insert similar bracelets into special receivers placed in the offenders' homes that transmit a signal to verify their presence. Continuous contact devices use bracelets that emit a continuous signal to receivers placed within offenders' residences. Such bracelets typically have a limited range (e.g., 200 feet) and, once a bracelet leaves that area, the receiver automatically contacts a centralized computerized system to note the offender left the premises. The computer system is thus able to keep records of when offenders leave their residences and when they return, which officers can compare against approved schedules (DeMichele and Payne 2009). Bracelets are typically tamperproof and send an automatic notification to the computer system if removed.

BOX 6.2

Technology and Community Supervision

Early technologies used in the community supervision of offenders, such as defensive weapons and communication technology, were typically adapted from their initial use in law enforcement. The use of alcohol- and drug-testing equipment became more common as policymakers supported efforts that to enhance surveillance and enforce compliance with supervision conditions. For example, some jurisdictions use remote alcohol detection devices. These require the offender to submit to random alcohol tests, and the results are transmitted electronically over cellular, wireless internet, or phone lines to a computer monitoring system (see DeMichele and Payne 2009). Most significantly, however, community corrections' increasing emphasis on public safety has led to dramatic increases in the use of technology to verify the location of an offender under community supervision (DeMichele and Payne 2009).

The most significant increase in technology-enhanced supervision has been with the use of a global positioning system (GPS; DeMichele and Payne 2009). Such systems use satellite technology to monitor the specific location of offenders and communicate that information to a computer monitoring system (Brown, McCabe, and Wellford 2007). These systems are increasingly sophisticated. Programmed with information about the community, they can indicate whether offenders are entering prohibited areas, such as when sex offenders approach schools. One of the more common uses of GPS supervision (and electronic monitoring in general) is for sex offenders under community supervision (see Button, DeMichele, and Payne 2009). The use of GPS technology for supervising offenders grew from less than 500 in 2000 to 90,000 in 2009 (DeMichele and Payne 2009). It is likely that nearly 200,000 offenders are currently supervised with the use of GPS technology.

GPS technology is still being refined, and various options can be added to the programs by third-party vendors (Brown, McCabe, and Wellford 2007). GPS shares some problems and challenges with electronic monitoring but has its own unique technological, liability, and privacy concerns as well (Brown, McCabe, and Wellford 2007; DeMichele and Payne 2009). There are legitimate concerns about the unforeseen social consequences of such invasive surveillance in a democratic society. For example, even before the development of GPS and the widespread use of electronic monitoring, von Hirsch (1998) argued that there are ethical limits to the intrusiveness of community supervision of offenders. Simply because community supervision is less intrusive than prison does not justify any intrusion into offenders' lives. It is important to consider whether the level of intrusiveness is proportional to the seriousness of the original crime as well as the impact on the privacy of third parties (von Hirsch 1998). However, there appears to be considerable political support for the use of the GPS and other technologies to enhance the surveillance of offenders in the community. As a result, it is likely that they will continue to grow in importance as an option for courts and correctional agencies.

Critical Thinking Exercise

Considerable research has supported the practice of reserving intensive supervision, especially electronic monitoring and GPS, for high-risk offenders. The intensive supervision or treatment of low-risk offenders is associated with *worse* outcomes for those offenders. Therefore, the targeting of appropriate offenders for intensive supervision programs is critical. What criteria do you think are important to consider whether a specific offender is appropriate for such supervision? Are there any factors that should exclude an offender from intensive supervision? Why are these important and what should be the alternative form of supervision for these offenders? Remember that an important goal for these programs is to reduce the use of incarceration.

Web Activity

For a detailed discussion of the different technologies, options, and challenges associated with electronic monitoring, see DeMichele and Payne (2009) on the textbook website (www.oup.com/he/lab6e).

For a detailed discussion of the different technologies, options, and challenges associated with electronic monitoring, see DeMichele and Payne (2009) on the textbook website.

For an in-depth discussion of the issues associated with GPS, including different technologies and important implementation issues, see Brown, McCabe, and Wellford's (2007) report on the textbook website. Pay particular attention to the figures on pages 1-2, 1-3, and 1-6.

Day Reporting Centers

Day reporting centers were first established in Great Britain and followed by programs in Massachusetts and Connecticut beginning in 1985 (Clear and Dammer 2003). Today, day reporting centers can be found in a number of jurisdictions. Similar to other community correctional programs, they can be used for a variety of populations. For example, Cook County (Chicago) created a day reporting program for as a condition of pretrial release (Martin, Olson, and Lurigio 2000;

McBride and VanderWaal 1997). In addition, there are day reporting centers used as intermediate sanctions intended to divert appropriate offenders from incarceration as well as those that serve offenders recently released from prison (see Osterman 2009; Marciniak 1999; Vaas and Weston 1990).

Despite the variety of populations they serve, most day reporting centers have several common features. First, they are nonresidential programs that require offenders to report on a daily or very frequent basis to a reporting center. The specific frequency of reporting may vary across programs and individual offenders, but offenders report to their centers far more frequently than probationers or parolees report to their supervising officers. Second, these centers house a number of the required programs and services for offenders, such as drug testing, substance abuse treatment, job training, and education courses. Probation or parole officers are frequently stationed at the center as well. Thus, day reporting centers can serve as a centralized location for offenders to fulfil a variety of their court-ordered conditions, such as drug testing, restitution payments, community service orders, and treatment programs (see Clear and Dammer 2003). The amount of contact between participating offenders and program staff tends to be quite high, and the emphasis of many day reporting centers is to provide a range of services to offenders with identified treatment needs.

Residential Programs

Residential programs that serve as temporary housing for released inmates as they adjust to living in the community are referred to as **halfway houses** because they serve offenders who are halfway between prison and complete freedom in the community. While the public is familiar with such programs, similar programs can be used as an intermediate sanction. The term **residential community correctional program** (Latessa and Travis 1992) is increasingly used to designate residential programs serving a variety of offender populations for a relatively short period of time, typically less than one year. These programs are designed to assist in offender reintegration into the community by targeting particular offender needs with intensive services. For example, some programs focus on substance abuse treatment, mental health counselling, or serve as a work-release center that assists offenders in securing employment and making payments toward court-ordered financial obligations.

The freedom of movement for offenders and the level of security in residential correctional programs vary. Some programs require offenders to remain at the facility except for approved activities, while others allow more freedom of movement. The types and intensity of the services provided at these facilities depend to some extent on the population they serve. It is common for education and employment training, cognitive thinking and life-skills courses, and substance abuse treatment services to be available. Residential programs, especially those emphasizing employment, are frequently located in urban or suburban areas with accessible employment opportunities and public transportation. Most residential programs serve a population that is at greater risk for substance abuse and recidivism than comparison populations (Latessa and Travis 1992). Further-more, there is increasing evidence that residential community correctional pro-grams may have the most benefit for those at highest risk for substance abuse and recidivism (Lowenkamp, Latessa, and Holsinger 2006). Therefore, the targeting of appropriate offenders for these programs appears to be critical to their overall usefulness (Lowenkamp and Latessa 2005).

Boot Camps

One of the more publicized and better known of the community correctional programs, **boot camps**, have been subject to critical scholarly attention since they began as a correctional sanction in the late 1980s. The use of boot camps for of-fenders has intuitive appeal for American society. Most adults are familiar with the basic premise of a military boot camp, and many Americans associate their own military experience with numerous benefits. Some jurisdictions and schol-ars associate boot camps with **shock incarceration**. Not all shock incarceration programs, however, incorporate a boot-camp experience (Clear and Dammer 2003). Some jurisdictions retain the option of early release to community super-vision for eligible inmates. The idea is that offenders' brief experience in prison will "shock" (i.e., deter) them sufficiently to ensure compliance with community supervision requirements. Programs that use a boot-camp experience have been subject to far more public and scholarly attention. Therefore, the following dis-cussion focuses on boot camp programs.

The central premise of correctional boot camps is that their emphasis on dis-cipline, strict adherence to program rules, and physical conditioning is thought to provide an opportunity for constructive change in offenders' attitudes and behavior (National Institute of Justice 2003). The most characteristic feature of boot camps is the quasi-military atmosphere created by physical conditioning, drills, and manual labor enforced with strict rules and program staff who act in a manner consistent with military boot-camp training. Recent modifications to early programs have included incorporating more rehabilitation and treatment services for inmates and increasing educational and life-skills training compo-nents (Kempinen and Kurlychek 2003; National Institute of Justice 2003).

The physical nature of the boot-camp experience naturally limits such pro-grams to eligible youthful offenders. Some boot camps are exclusively for juvenile offenders, while other programs accept young adult offenders. Many programs target offenders with a history of substance abuse and most exclude offenders with a significant history of personal violence. The vast majority of boot camp programs are designed for male offenders (Clear and Dammer 2003). The high prevalence of past physical, sexual, and emotional abuse among female offenders makes boot camps for this population very questionable (MacKenzie and Don-aldson 1996; National Institute of Justice 2003). A common research finding has been that boot camps with longer and more intensive aftercare services yield more positive outcomes in their graduates, though these differences tend to be rather modest (Kempinen and Kurylchek 2003; National Institute of Justice 2003).

Widely popular when initially created, support for boot camps has some-what diminished. Considerable evidence suggests that they do little to reduce recidivism rates and may actually result in higher technical violations and other problems (National Institute of Justice 2003; Wilson, Mackenzie, and Mitchell 2005). Furthermore, incidents of abuse and poor treatment by staff leading to injuries and even and deaths of residents led to public criticism. Some jurisdic-tions, most notably the federal government, have closed their boot-camp pro-grams. Boot camps for offenders, however, remain popular in some jurisdictions, especially for juvenile offenders.

Web Activity

Review the assessment of juvenile boot camps at NIJ Crime Solutions at http://www. crimesolutions.gov/PracticeDetails.aspx?ID=6.

Critical Thinking Exercise

Despite the considerable evidence that boot-camps are no more effective at reducing recidivism than traditional sanctions such as community supervision, such programs remain popular with some politicians and the public. Why do you think this is the case? What explains the apparent disconnect between research on the value of such programs and continuing support for them? What is the impact of such factors on criminal justice policy in general?

Net Widening

A frequent goal of intermediate sanctions is to divert offenders from an unneces-sarily severe sanction given their crime or risk level. In fact, a number of interme-diate sanctions are justified on the premise such programs can divert less serious offenders from prison into less expensive sentencing options. However, scholars have questioned how new sanctions are used by the courts in practice. Research indicates that intermediate sanctions are often applied to offenders who would have received a less severe penalty prior to the availability of the intermediate sanction. As a result, some offenders receive a more severe sanction than they originally would have received prior to the creation of this new sanction. Mean-while, many offenders who were the targets for diversion by the new intermediate sanction continue to be sentenced to the more punitive sanctions that existed prior to the new program. In other words, the new program is used for less seri-ous offenders, rather than the originally targeted population. This is referred to as **net widening**—when a punishment is used on a larger or different population than the one originally intended.

Although some may see net widening as simply an appropriate increase in the severity of punishment for offenders, this ignores a primary rationale for intermediate sanctions and poses a problem for several reasons. First, net widening increases costs rather than decreasing them by placing offenders who would have received a less expensive sanction (generally, the closer the supervision, the higher the costs) on a more expensive form of supervision without similarly diverting prison-bound offenders. Second, because closer supervision programs generally have higher revocation rates for technical violations (Petersilia and Turner 1993), a percentage of the offenders who might have succeeded under a less restrictive program will likely end up in prison because of violations of the stricter rules of the intermediate sanctions. This could add to operating costs rather than reduce them. A third major concern is the larger issue of social control. By using new sanctions to impose more severe penalties on offenders rather than diverting those who do not require a prison sentence, the criminal justice system is further expanding its intrusiveness into and control over the lives of members of the community (Cohen 1985; von Hirsch 1998). While some jurisdictions have implemented structured sentencing schemes to better target sanctions for particular populations, the potential for net-widening exists for many intermediate sanction programs.

POST-RELEASE SUPERVISION AND REINTEGRATION

Types of Release

More than 90 percent of all prisoners will eventually be released from prison (Petersilia 2003). Over 600,000 prisoners are released each year to the community (Carson 2020). This means that a significant number of individuals will need to make the transition from the highly structured prison environment to the relative freedom of open society. Upon release, most prisoners must identify new ways to meet basic needs such as food, shelter, employment, and clothing that were previously provided by the institution. Failure to secure these decreases the likelihood a released prisoner will be able to successfully reintegrate into the community (Petersilia 2003).

Depending on the jurisdiction and circumstances, prisoners may be released from prison in four ways. Perhaps the most important distinction is whether the prisoner will be under any form of supervision after release. First, a small portion of offenders serve their maximum sentences and are released when the sentence expires. Such inmates, who may be in either indeterminate or determinate sentencing systems, have "maxed out" their sentences, and all supervision is terminated upon release from the institution. Although only approximately 20 percent of inmates are released without any supervision, this is a dramatic increase from 40 years ago, when only 5 percent of prisoners were released in this manner (Petersilia 2003; Pew Charitable Trust 2014). Second, some prisoners may be sentenced to **split sentences**, in which they serve a period of probation following their release. Third, several jurisdictions with determinate sentencing models have created a period of supervision for released prisoners called **supervised release**, or post-release supervision. Such prisoners are required to report to community supervision offices located near where they will reside and assigned to a supervising officer. These former prisoners are required to abide by certain conditions following their release to the community. The length of supervision may vary depending on the conviction offense or the length of incarceration. A violation of the conditions of supervision may result in an individual's return to prison. Finally, prisoners given an indeterminate prison term may be eligible for release to **parole supervision** by the parole authority once they have served their minimum sentence. Prisoners must agree to abide by parole conditions in order to obtain their release. Community supervision may continue until the expiration of the released prisoner's original maximum sentence or until the parole authority terminates their supervision. Failure to comply with the conditions of release may result in the parolee's return to prison until the parole authority grants a new parole release or until the expiration of the original sentence. In some jurisdictions, officers who supervise probationers are also responsible for supervising parolees in their geographic area. In other jurisdictions, distinct agencies provide parole officers who supervise only parolees and those released from prison to mandatory supervised release.

Prisoner Reentry and Reintegration

The sheer number of prisoners returning to American communities each year has forced correctional administrators and policymakers to re-evaluate efforts to improve the successful reintegration of prisoners. Prison has not proven to be very effective at preventing future criminal behavior by released offenders. It is an unfortunate reality that a significant percentage of released prisoners will eventually return to prison. Approximately 60 percent of released prisoners are rearrested for serious misdemeanors or felonies within three years of release, and one-half of released prisoners return to prison within three years (Langan and Levin 2002). The consequences of America's imprisonment binge are becoming apparent in the reallocation of public resources (Austin and Irwin 2001; Travis 2004). In addition, scholars are increasingly discovering negative consequences of mass incarceration and failed prisoner reentry for communities (e.g., Rose and Clear 2003), families (e.g., Travis and Waul 2003), and offenders themselves (Maruna and Immarigeon 2004; Petersilia 2003).

Web Activity

The Urban Institute has been a leading public voice in addressing the challenges of prisoner reentry and developing sound policies in response to this problem. For an example of a collaborative community effort to improve prisoner success upon release see http://www.urban.org/research/publication/framework-safer-return-research-based-community-initiative/view/full_report.

Prisoners face a multitude of problems and challenges that they must overcome if they are to avoid returning to prison (Visher and Travis 2011). Research indicates that lack of adequate and meaningful employment is one of the major characteristics associated with a return to prison (Petersilia 2003; Travis 2005). In addition, offenders may face difficulties because of the "ex-con" label that can have a negative impact on their occupational and housing opportunities. A lack of sufficient education, job skills, or life skills may present difficulties in obtaining basic amenities, services, and material goods. Another major concern is reestablishing family and social networks (Garland, Wodahl, and Mayfield 2011). Offenders may be estranged from family and friends who could assist with reintegration into the community (Hagan and Dinovitzer 1999). Though not all former associates will have a positive influence on offenders' lives, social isolation can lead to stress and negative behaviors such as substance abuse and crime. Research indicates that an increasing percentage of inmates have histories of substance abuse and/or mental-health problems. At the same time, the availability of prison programs and the level of participation in such programs have been diminishing (Petersilia 2003). Therefore, prisoners increasingly need access to meaningful treatment services inside prison and upon release.

Prisoner reentry (also referred to as **prisoner reintegration**) is the process of adjusting to a law-abiding lifestyle after returning to the community from prison (Petersilia 2003). A variety of programs to improve prisoner reentry are currently in operation throughout the country. Some of these are informal programs run by nonprofit and faith-based agencies, while other jurisdictions have very structured government programs that may involve a variety of organizations, including correctional staff and resources (see Petersilia 2003; Travis and Waul 2003). To reduce the stress and problems of release, many offenders are released into halfway houses, which may be privately operated or run by correctional departments. Similar to the community residential programs discussed earlier, there is considerable diversity in the types of halfway houses. Most provide inexpensive housing and typically offer only basic amenities. Prisoners may be placed in these facilities as a condition of their release or may elect to reside there because of a lack of housing options and a shortage of money. More structured facilities may provide a range of services and resources such as substance abuse counseling, life-skills training, or other relevant services and may place a number of restrictions on residents.

Web Activity

Visit the National Reentry Resource Center website at http://csgjusticecenter.org/nrrc/. This clearinghouse of information sponsored by the Department of Justice and the Council of State Governments Justice Center is an excellent resource for information, statistics, and tools for criminal justice and community agencies, as well as the general public.

COMMUNITY SUPERVISION

Offender Responsibilities

Those placed under some form of community supervision or in an intermediate-sanction residential program are given a list of conditions that they must comply with in order to remain in good standing with the court or parole board. These **conditions of supervision** state the behavioral expectations while under supervision. Failure to conform to these rules constitutes a violation of supervision and may result in a supervising officer or staff member submitting a violation report to either the court of jurisdiction or the parole board. As a consequence, an individual's supervision may be revoked, and they can receive more severe sanctions or be returned to prison.

Conditions of supervision can be divided into standard or special conditions. **Standard conditions** are rules that everyone placed on this type of supervision must follow. Standard conditions represent the minimum expectations while under supervision. The most prevalent standard condition requires obeying all laws. Other common standard conditions include informing a supervising officer of a change in address or work, not leaving the state or jurisdiction without the approval of a supervising officer, and, in some jurisdictions, submitting to drug testing.

Courts and parole boards can impose **special conditions** depending on the nature of the crime or characteristics of the defendant. Such conditions are based on the needs and risks of a particular offender. Examples of special conditions include sex offender treatment, substance abuse counseling, work toward the completion of a GED, and the payment of restitution to a crime victim.

Web Activity

Examples of standard conditions of probation for federal probation can be found at http://www.dcp.uscourts.gov/Supervision/Conditions_English.pdf, and for the state of New Mexico at http://cd.nm.gov/ppd/ppd.html.

Officer Responsibilities

In many jurisdictions, officers who supervise offenders in the community perform a range of duties. The two major responsibilities are conducting investigations and supervising offenders. The most important investigation conducted by probation officers is the court-ordered **presentence investigation**, which is typically completed after a defendant has pleaded or been found guilty. It summarizes facts about the defendant, the offense, and other relevant information used by the court to determine an appropriate sentence. It is common to include information about the defendant's prior criminal and substance abuse history, employment, and education as well as the financial or emotional harm caused to any victims. Through their investigation, probation officers may identify special conditions that the court should consider imposing if the offender is sentenced to a form of community supervision. Although the courts are not required to follow either the sentencing or the special condition recommendations found in the presentence investigation report, there tends to be a close association between the probation officer's recommendations and the final sentence (Abadinsky 1997). Supervising agencies frequently use presentence reports to assist in the needs and risk assessment for the offender. Other investigations conducted by community supervision officers include helping the court to determine if it is appropriate to reduce a defendant's bail and verifying an offender's plans for transferring supervision to or from another location.

The most important role of a community supervision officer is to ensure that those placed on community supervision abide by the conditions of their supervision. Depending on the type of supervision and jurisdiction, officers may have little personal contact with offenders, or they may have regular office, work, or home contacts. Officers are responsible for verifying that offenders are attending all required programs; making regular payments toward their court costs, fees, and restitution; and abiding by the law while under supervision. Officers may also conduct drug tests on those offenders who are required to submit to drug testing as a condition of their supervision.

Probation officers may also be given the responsibility to supervise offenders who have been placed in diversion programs prior to adjudication of guilt. **Diversion programs** offer offenders the opportunity to temporarily halt the prosecution effort against them. Some jurisdictions have a special form of probation imposed prior to adjudication of guilt. If the offender completes the requirements of the program, the prosecutor's office dismisses the charges against the offender, avoiding an official conviction on his or her record. Violation of the conditions of the program can result in the prosecutor deciding to proceed with a criminal prosecution against the defendant. Diversion programs are typically reserved for juveniles, youthful offenders, or first-time offenders. Offenders with previous felony convictions or those arrested for violent or serious offenses are typically not eligible for participation in diversion programs.

Supervision Violations

Supervision violations are violations of probation, parole, or an intermediate sanction's program conditions. Supervision violations may be either new offense or technical violations. **New-offense violations** occur when offenders under supervision commit a new crime. For new offense violations, the offender may have to appear before the appropriate court for the new crime as well as the court or parole board with jurisdiction for their community supervision to address the violation of supervision conditions (i.e., violation of the condition to obey all laws). **Technical violations** involve conditions of supervision that are not violations of criminal statutes. Positive drug tests, failure to attend treatment meetings, absconding from supervision (i.e. fleeing supervision), and failure to make a good-faith effort toward paying restitution are common technical violations.

How officers respond to a violation of supervision conditions depends on the nature of the violation, the offender's progress under supervision, and the officer's perception of the appropriate response (Clear, Harris, and Baird 1992; Jones and Kerbs 2007). Minor technical violations are often handled informally, perhaps with verbal or written warnings to the offender. More serious violations require officers to consider the nature and context of the violations, the probationer's progress and likelihood of successfully completing supervision, and organizational and office dynamics (McCleary 1992). New-offense violations, especially felonies, are almost always reported to the court or parole board. Serious technical violations, such as those that potentially represent a threat to public safety, are also typically reported to the appropriate authority. Prosecutors, judges, and parole boards have considerable discretion in their response to condition violations, but supervising officers' recommendations can play an important role in the final disposition of the case. For new-offense violations or serious technical violations, offenders' supervision can be revoked and they may be sentenced to a new term of supervision, a more restrictive form of community supervision such as an intermediate sanction, or a term of incarceration in jail or prison (see Box 6.3 for information on probation violations).

BOX 6.3

Swift-Certain-Fair Responses to Probation Violations

One of the most widely discussed innovations in community supervision in the past several decades has been efforts to create a process in which officers and the courts respond quickly to probation violations. These are often referred to as "swift-certain-fair" policies or HOPE-style probation because HOPE is the name of Hawaii's program which has been the most prominently discussed (Kleiman 2016; Larkin 2016). While there are numerous variations across jurisdictions, a common goal is to respond to technical violations, especially failed drug tests, with a judicial hearing within 72 hours of the violation and imposing a modest, but meaningful, sanction at that time (Klingele 2015). HOPE probation began in Hawaii in 2004 after Judge Steven Alm decided that "probation-as-usual" was not working (Alm 2015). A major problem with "probation-as-usual" is that it often takes several violations before an officer may decide it is necessary or worth the effort to seek a revocation hearing with the court (Alm 2015). Furthermore, violation hearings under traditional probation may take several weeks or months to resolve (Kleiman 2015; Larkin 2016). This greatly diminishes the purported deterrent value of punishment for violations. In response to this problem, some jurisdictions have created mechanisms for mandatory reporting of violations to the court for immediate action. The most common sanction is a brief jail sentence (typically 1–5 days), but judges may have the option to impose other sanctions such as community service, curfew restrictions, or residential drug treatment. The response to violations under these programs is argued to be swift, certain, and fair.

Swift-Certain-Fair programs have been widely touted as way to make probation supervision meaningful once again (Alm 2015). Furthermore, early evaluations of HOPE and similar programs reported significant reductions in recidivism and revocation rates (Hawken and Kleiman 2009; Larkin 2015). More recent evaluations of these programs, however, have found little to only modest long-term reductions in recidivism and revocation rates (Lattimore, MacKenzie, Zajac, Dawes, Arsenault, and Tueller 2016; O'Connell, Brent, and Visher 2016). Such results are not surprising to those critical of exclusively deterrent-based strategies with offenders. Some have questioned the effectiveness of merely relying on the threat of additional penalties as a means to change offender behavior, even when those penalties are imposed swiftly and with a degree of certainty (e.g. Cullen, Manchak, and Duriez 2014; Klingele 2015). While swift-certain-fair programs have intuitive and political appeal, they largely ignore the numerous cognitive and social challenges that affect the lives and decision-making of many offenders (Klingele 2015). Furthermore, the attention paid to such programs seemingly minimizes the existing evidence about what actually works to reduce recidivism and revocation rates (Duriez, Cullen, and Manchak 2014; but see Kleiman, Kilmer, and Fisher 2014). Numerous studies have found that incorporating core correctional practices, such as targeting offender risk, reserving intensive programs for high-risk offenders, and utilizing cognitive behavioral strategies, can result in significant reductions in offender recidivism and revocation rates (e.g. Gleicher, Manchak, and Cullen 2012; Lowenkamp et al. 2010; Paparozzi and Gendreau 2006; Taxman, 2008a; Trotter 2006). The challenge seems to be how to respond in a timely and effective manner to significant violations while minimizing the use of incarceration for all but the most necessary cases (Corbett 2015; Kleiman 2016; Klingele 2015). Significant justice reforms frequently require revision and modification in light of practical concerns and evidence of their effectiveness. Whether and how swift-certain-fair policies will be revised in light of recent evidence remains to be seen.

SPECIAL-NEEDS POPULATIONS AND COMMUNITY SUPERVISION

Many offenders have characteristics that place them at considerable risk for recidivism or create additional barriers to successful reintegration. Scholars have identified several "special-needs populations" and the characteristics that pose unique or additional challenges for those in this group (National Institute of Corrections 2011). Examples of such groups include substance abusers (Center for Substance Abuse Treatment 2005), elderly persons under supervision (Aday 2003), female offenders (Belknap 2001; Sheenan, McIvor, and Trotter 2011), and offenders with mental-health problems (Prins and Draper 2009). While not all individuals with these traits experience difficulty in completing their sentence, research has found these populations have a variety of problems that can contribute to higher rates of recidivism and other negative outcomes. Those responsible for the supervision of these populations should be aware of the problems and challenges they experience.

One special-needs population that the criminal justice system has been increasingly responsible for supervising includes offenders with mental-health problems. The percentage of the correctional population with identifiable mental-health disorders has been growing over the past 30 years (Ditton 1999; James and Glaze 2006; Prins and Draper 2009). To date, correctional agencies have been unable to meet the increasing demand for mental-health services for institutional or community-based offenders (Ditton 1999). Offenders with mental-health problems have considerable challenges in abiding by the conditions of their supervision. In addition to the challenges of obtaining and maintaining a stable residence and employment, mental-health problems can make it difficult to comply with even seemingly simple conditions of supervision such as reporting to the probation office. Furthermore, these offenders often have co-occurring disorders of mental-health and substance abuse problems. Such conditions exacerbate already difficult circumstances and place real constraints on offenders' personal and social resources and their ability to use those limited resources.

The criminal justice system has taken steps to improve the success of offenders with mental-health problems. Many probation departments have officers with special training who are responsible for supervising such cases. Also, some communities have mental-health courts, which are designed to provide a holistic response to the challenges facing these offenders (e.g., Justice Center 2008). While considerable variation exists, mental-health courts seek to coordinate the variety of social services thought necessary to improve the lives of individuals with mental-health problems who come to the attention of authorities. They often use a problem-solving and team approach to providing services and supervision. For those cases under community supervision, the probation officer may have an active role in case management (Justice Center 2008). While many mental-health courts are in the experimental stage, results are encouraging. Furthermore, the use of evidence-based treatment strategies and protocols has been found to reduce a variety of negative outcomes for this population (Justice Center 2008; Prins and Draper 2009).

THE EFFECTIVENESS OF COMMUNITY CORRECTIONS

Research has found that community supervision programs have varying degrees of success in reducing recidivism (see Paparozzi and DeMichele 2008; Petersilia 1997; Tonry and Lynch 1996). Given the wide variety of sanctions discussed and the meaningful differences in the same type of sanction across jurisdictions, any conclusions about the impact of various sanctions should be tempered with caution. Furthermore, some programs have been found to be more successful with particular types of offenders. Despite these caveats, there appear to be some common themes in the research on a variety of community correctional sanctions. Interested readers are encouraged to see more comprehensive reviews of the research literature (e.g. Shapland, Bottoms, Farrall, McNeil, Priede, and Robinson 2012).

Depending on the jurisdiction and the exact outcome measure, research has found considerable variation in the effectiveness of community supervision. In general, research has found that probation and intermediate sanctions are moderately effective at achieving several goals. A major issue in evaluation research is determining how program effectiveness will be measured. Measurements of offender success could include the number of offenders who successfully complete supervision, the number of new-offense or technical violations during supervision, or the number of new arrests following the completion of their supervision. How success is measured will greatly affect how successful a program appears.

Morgan (1996) reported that studies have found that 15 to 50 percent of probationers failed under community supervision. A report on probationers in the state of New York found that of the 40,000 probationers discharged across the state in 2006, 22 percent had their probation revoked for a technical violation and 9 percent revoked for new offenses for a total failure rate of approximately one-third of probationers (New York State Division of Criminal Justice Services 2008). Other studies have found evidence of comparable success in other jurisdictions (e.g., Gray, Fields, and Maxwell 2001). The majority of probation failures are the result of technical violations and new misdemeanor offenses. Most studies have found that violations for new felony offenses are far less common than other violations (e.g., Gray, Fields, and Maxwell 2001). Those on misdemeanor probation appear to have a much higher success rate than offenders placed on probation for felonies, but this could be due to the lower risk posed by misdemeanor defendants or the less intense nature of the supervision for those convicted of misdemeanors (Petersilia 1997).

An important question in evaluating the effectiveness of intermediate sanctions is "In comparison to whom?" Determining the appropriate comparison group for offenders sentenced to intermediate sanctions is often a challenge and may affect conclusions about the utility of such sanctions. To some extent, the identification of a comparison group depends upon the goals of a specific program (Lurigio and Petersilia 1992). One goal that most intermediate sanctions achieve is closer supervision and control over offenders compared with regular probation (Petersilia 1998). In many jurisdictions, intermediate sanctions have been incorporated into structured sentencing and, provide more proportional sentencing options between probation and prison (Harland 1998). Another common finding is that offenders sentenced to intermediate sanctions generally have higher levels of participation in treatment programs than those on regular probation or imprisoned (Tonry and Lynch 1996). This is significant because programs that emphasize treatment services are more effective at reducing recidivism than similar programs that focus primarily on surveillance and control (Lowenkamp et al. 2010).

Intermediate sanctions, however, suffer from a number of problems that challenge their ability to reduce recidivism or correctional costs. Perhaps the most significant problem is that net widening plagues intermediate sanctions (Tonry and Lynch 1996). Despite efforts to structure sentencing decisions to reduce net widening, many offenders sentenced to intermediate sanctions were not the originally intended population, resulting in higher costs, limited impact on prison overcrowding, and expanded social control over offenders.

Generally, most evaluations have found only modest differences in the recidivism rates of similar offenders who receive intermediate sanctions versus those who receive either probation or imprisonment. Probationers tend to have the lowest recidivism rates, followed by offenders placed on intermediate sanctions. Released inmates have the highest recidivism rates. However, when offense seriousness and other relevant characteristics are taken into account, the difference in recidivism rates between intermediate sanctions and other populations becomes marginal (National Institute of Justice 2003; Petersilia and Turner 1993; Tonry and Lynch 1996). While the bulk of research on boot camps finds little impact on recidivism (National Institute of Justice 2003; Wilson, Mackenzie, and Mitchell 2005), studies on the impact of electronic monitoring on recidivism are mixed (Bonta, Wallace-Capretta, and Rooney 2000; Padgett, Bales, and Blomberg 2006). Research indicates that community correctional programs with an institutional and staff commitment to treatment and that adhere to demonstrated effective practices have much better success rates (Lowenkamp et al. 2006; Paparozzi and Gendreau 2005; Taxman 2008a; Trotter 2013). Unfortunately, these qualities are not found in every program or jurisdiction, and making such changes is not easy.

While probationers and those on intermediate sanctions may have comparable new-offense violations, offenders on intermediate sanctions typically have higher revocation rates. The increased restrictions and closer supervision involved in intermediate sanctions have resulted in considerably higher technical violation rates for regular probation. The stronger control and surveillance orientation of most intermediate sanction programs also means that such violations may be dealt with more severely and result in revocation and possible imprisonment (Tonry and Lynch 1996). As a result, research has questioned the ability of merely surveillance-focused intermediate sanctions to reduce offender recidivism or correctional costs (see Lowenkamp et al. 2010; Tonry and Lynch 1996).

The COVID-19 pandemic has introduced new problems and issues for community corrections. Its impact on supervision can be seen in Box 6.4.

BOX 6.4

COVID-19 and Community Corrections

It should be no surprise that the COVID-19 pandemic that has affected nearly all aspects of social and economic life, has also impacted the community supervision of offenders. Restrictions imposed by social distancing and other public health protocols have resulted in a number of changes affecting probation and parole. While there have been many significant consequences for community supervision, several are worth noting. First, jails and prisons are taking steps to reduce their populations to minimize the spread of infection within their institutions (Prison Policy Initiative 2020). As a result, it appears that more individuals are being released to pre-trial supervision or post-release supervision. This increases the caseload for officers who were already responsible for large caseloads. Second, to allow for social distancing, many departments have reduced or suspended the required reporting of those under supervision to the office, especially for low-risk offenders. Relatedly, some departments have reduced the number of field contacts that officers are expected to have with those under their supervision (Swan, Campbell, and Lowe 2020; Schwartzapfel 2020). However, it appears that some agencies, such as federal probation and pretrial officers, are conducting social distancing field work to offset the lack of office reporting (US Courts 2020). Many agencies are also using phone, email, and online social media software programs to remain in regular contact with those under their supervision (US Courts 2020; Schwartzapfel 2020). While this cannot replace the value of face-to-face contacts, it is an effort to maintain some level of contact with those under supervision. Finally, with the closure of courts and the expected delay in court hearings, it appears that officers are submitting fewer violation of supervision reports, especially for technical violations that do not involve threats to public safety (Schwartzapfel 2020; White 2020). The changing use of officer discretion does not appear to be in response to official policy, but rather a balancing of public safety concerns with the practical challenges and public health risks associated with certain officer actions.

Although the long-term implications for supervision policy and practice remain to be seen, many see the COVID pandemic as a unique opportunity for community supervision to assess long-standing practices (Schwartzapfel 2020; US Courts 2020). For example, reformers have repeatedly called for minimal supervision for low-risk offenders and less punitive responses to technical violations (Klingele 2015; Jacobson et al. 2017; Pew Charitable Trusts 2018). The current climate offers an opportunity to assess the potential impact of such changes. In addition, many departments have turned to technology to maintain regular contact with those under supervision. This is not necessarily the active monitoring technology discussed in Box 6.2, but rather online meeting platforms such as Google Hangouts and Zoom. For those without internet or sufficient computer resources to connect through video, phone and email communication have been used in place of traditional face-to-face meeting. Few would claim these can gather the quality and quantity of information to be obtained via face-to-face meetings. However, the such technology might be able to be used for occasional meetings or to discuss less significant matters. The extent to which such technology might be able to supplement, in an efficient and effective manner, traditional offender supervision is yet to be determined, but it has been critical to address the significant challenges posed by the COVID-19 pandemic.

Critical Thinking Exercise

Intermediate sanctions do not appear to have met many of their utilitarian goals (cost-effectiveness, reduction of prison overcrowding, reduction of recidivism). However, some argue that such penalties may serve a retributive function of simply being a more appropriate (i.e., deserved) punishment and sentencing option. As a result of this appears to be increased costs to the criminal justice system. Many states have or will be experiencing considerable budget shortages due to COVID-19. How do we balance the budgetary needs of the criminal justice system and other public goods (such as education, healthcare, and transportation) that governments provide? What should be the major questions to determine which government services receive priority in funding decisions and why?

Perhaps the clearest measure of the effectiveness of parole and post-release supervision is whether an offender returns to prison following release. While there is evidence that prisoners who participate in targeted, problem-specific prison programs have significantly lower recidivism rates upon release, the percentage of offenders participating in such programs is rather minimal (Petersilia 2003). Many of the recent reentry programs have not yet been subject to thorough evaluation. However, released prisoners who participate in long-term, well-designed, and well-implemented post-release programs tend to have lower recidivism rates than inmates released without such services (e.g., Andrews 2006; Paparozzi and Gendreau 2005). The extent to which reentry continues to be a politically viable investment remains to be seen (Wodahl, Ogle, and Heck 2011). The history of criminal justice policy suggests caution in assuming long-term commitments to particular policy initiatives, especially those emphasizing rehabilitation. Research indicates that continuing allocation of sufficient resources and proper implementation greatly affect the overall effectiveness of such programs (e.g., Wilson and Davis 2006). It is too early to determine how such issues will affect the future of reentry efforts. Given the tremendous number of inmates released each year and the direct and collateral consequences of imprisonment, however, the benefits of improving prisoner reintegration could be tremendous. On the other hand, the failure of the criminal justice system, social service agencies, and communities to assist this population could have serious long-term negative implications that we are only beginning to appreciate.

Critical Thinking Exercise

Many studies find that most violations of supervision are for technical violations and not for new offenses. How should technical violations affect the perceived success or failure of a program? What are the justifications for sanctioning an individual for a technical violation, especially when the violation does not pose a threat to public safety? What should the courts or parole boards do in such cases?

INCORPORATING BEST PRACTICES INTO COMMUNITY CORRECTIONS

Responding to criticisms about the effectiveness of correctional interventions, a growing body of research has focused on those practices that have demonstrated success in reducing recidivism (e.g., Andrews and Bonta 2006; Bernfeld, Farrington, and Leschied 2001; McGuire 2001). Based upon evaluations of a wide range of correctional practices, scholars have identified important principles for correctional treatment programs (Andrews and Bonta 2006), examples of programs and programmatic elements associated with offender change (e.g., Lowenkamp, Latessa, and Smith 2006), and insights into implementing these in real-world settings (Bernfeld, Farrington, and Leschied 2001; McGuire 2001). For example, studies have demonstrated that intensive programs should be reserved for higher-risk offenders (Lowenkamp, Latessa, and Holsinger 2006). The use of intensive programs for low-risk offenders can actually increase offender recidivism rates, thereby decreasing public safety and increasing costs.

Correctional agencies are increasingly developing and implementing programs consistent with these correctional "best practices" and effective correctional interventions. Websites for many community correctional agencies highlight initiatives organized around the principles of "what works" (e.g., Crime and Justice Institute 2004; Ohio Department of Rehabilitation and Correction 2007; White 2005).

While some offenders will fail to respond positively to even the best-designed programs, the knowledge base about how to improve program success rates has grown considerably in the past two decades. The challenge is how to translate this knowledge into politically, fiscally, and operationally meaningful action (Taxman 2008b). Politically, public officials remain very cautious about supporting policies that may be interpreted as "soft on crime." The use of correctional resources has historically been focused on control and surveillance activities. Even within community corrections, where officer caseloads are often high and resources limited, there is often real skepticism about the development of and resource allocation to new programs and strategies. Finally, research has demonstrated that new programs are rarely implemented in a manner consistent with important underlying principles. Whether the result of budget shortfalls, a lack of staff training or commitment, or changes in administrative philosophy, it is difficult, though not impossible, to maintain long-term program integrity in human service organizations.

Web Activity

Visit the National Institute of Corrections' website on incorporating evidence-based practices into the correctional system at https://nicic.gov/assign-library-item-package-accordion/evidence-based-practices-ebp-ebp-implementation.

CONCLUSION

Ongoing efforts in the international war on terrorism, concerns about homeland security, and continuing economic problems caused by COVID-19 have put a strain on public resources. Recent state budget crises have resulted in many government agencies, including corrections, making budget cuts. In corrections, resources dedicated to rehabilitation efforts typically suffer most during periods of budget problems. It is unclear what long-term impact these forces will have on criminal justice policy. History suggests, however, that the economic implications and political feasibility of any changes will be more important than philosophical considerations of criminal justice policy. As a result, criminal justice reformers are using this context to call for less ideological and more evidence-driven policies. For example, there has been increasing attention to how mass probation contributes to mass incarceration and problems of prisoner reintegration (e.g., Jacobson et al. 2017; Pew Charitable Trusts 2018). Evidence of the financial costs associated with mass incarceration and the failure to provide resources to assist in reentry may lead to meaningful policy changes, but that is far from certain.

While community corrections is increasingly recognized as a vital component of American criminal justice systems, it continues to be viewed by the public and political decision-makers as of secondary importance compared with institutional corrections (Paparozzi and DeMichele 2008). A result has been that community correctional programs have been required to do more with less: supervise more offenders without a similar growth in the funding to provide adequate supervision and services to those populations. Every day, thousands of community correctional professionals try to achieve the difficult balance of helping offenders maintain a crime-free lifestyle and reintegrate into the community while identifying and responding to supervision violations and threats to public safety.

The trend appears to be to increase both the surveillance and the treatment requirements for offenders placed under community supervision. It is unclear if the funding necessary to sustain such changes will continue to be available. Recent attention to the challenges and long-term consequences of prisoner reentry may provide an opportunity for meaningful dialogue about offenders in the community and efforts to reduce their likelihood of recidivism. There have also been calls to reduce the use of supervised probation by focusing on moderate to high-risk offenders who actually require supervision (Jacobson, Schiraldi, Daly, and Hotez 2017). Furthermore, scholars have questioned the necessity of extensive restrictions and impositions on offenders that are unrelated to their criminal behavior and seemingly do more harm than good (Corbett 2015; Horwitz 2010; Klingele 2013, 2015). It is unclear whether such arguments will make much progress in reversing long-standing practices and trends in community corrections. It is certain, however, that community corrections will continue to be an important component of American criminal justice and the community it serves.

Critical Thinking Exercise

The recent COVID-19 crisis has required many state and local governments to make significant cutbacks in services. Although the criminal justice system is often protected from substantial cutbacks, this has not been the case in all jurisdictions. As noted earlier, community corrections is often far more susceptible to cutbacks, due to fewer fixed costs, than institutional corrections. Imagine you are the administrator of a large community corrections agency and are required to make substantial cutbacks to next year's budget. Where would you try to save money and why? How might you save money in those areas? What services would you consider essential? What arguments would you make to protect resources for those activities?

KEY WORDS

boot camps

community corrections

community supervision

conditions of supervision

day reporting centers

diversion programs

electronic monitoring

halfway houses

home confinement/house
    arrest

intensive supervision
    probation

intermediate sanctions

net widening

new-offense violations

parole supervision

presentence investigation

prisoner reentry/
    reintegration

probation

residential community
    correctional program

shock incarceration

special conditions

split sentences

standard conditions

supervised release

supervision
    violations

technical violations

SUGGESTED READINGS

Crime and Justice Institute at Community Resources for Justice. (2009). *Implementing evidence-based policy and practice in community corrections*, 2nd ed. Washington, DC: National Institute of Corrections.

Jacobson, M.P., V. Schiraldi, R. Daly, and E. Hotez, E. (2017). *Less is more: How reducing probation populations can improve outcomes.* Papers from the Executive Session on Community Corrections. Cambridge, MA: Harvard Kennedy School. https://www.hks.harvard.edu/sites/default/files/centers/wiener/programs/pcj/files/less_is_more_final.pdf.

McNeil, F., P. Raynor, and C. Trotter. (Eds.). (2010). *Offender supervision: New directions in theory, research and practice.* New York: Willan.

Shapland, J., A. Bottoms, S. Farrall, F. McNeil, C. Priede, and G. Robinson. (2012). *The quality of probation supervision: A literature review.* Centre for Criminological Research: University of Sheffield.

Travis, J. (2005). *But they all come back: Facing the challenges of prisoner reentry.* Washington, DC: Urban Institute Press.

Trotter, C. (2006). *Working with offenders: A guide to practice.* Thousand Oaks, CA: Sage Publications.

White, R., and H. Graham. (2010). *Working with offenders: A guide to concepts and practice.* New York: Willan.

CHAPTER 7

✦

The Juvenile Justice System

CHAPTER OUTLINE

After reading this chapter, you should be able to:

- Provide a brief history of the development of juvenile justice
- Compare the terminology of the juvenile and adult justice systems
- Identify and define the philosophy of the juvenile justice system
- List key contributions to the growth of *parens patriae*
- List and discuss the different types of general purpose clauses
- Compare and contrast different definitions of delinquency
- Define and discuss the issue of sexting
- Define transfer or waiver provisions
- List different forms of transfer
- Tell the differences found using different ways of measuring delinquency
- Outline issues involved in detention
- Talk about the intake decision and alternatives
- Identify different roles assumed by attorneys in juvenile court
- List and discuss key court cases in juvenile procedural rights
- Define state training school and discuss programming in such institutions
- Discuss the move toward deinstitutionalization
- Identify different issues in community supervision of youths
- Demonstrate knowledge of reentry concerns
- Discuss the gang problem and talk about different efforts to deal with gangs
- Identify restorative justice and family group conferencing and discuss their impact on youths and recidivism
- List different forms of restorative justice
- Address the issues related to capital punishment for juveniles

---

INTRODUCTION

Dealing with juvenile offenders poses unique problems for society and an entire system has been established to address juvenile concerns and issues. Where it is possible to talk about a criminal justice system that attempts to coordinate the efforts of the police, courts, and corrections into a functional whole, the juvenile justice system is often viewed as only an appendage to that system. This is largely due to the fact that juvenile justice was founded on a different set of assumptions about the nature of juvenile misbehavior and the proper responses to deal with juvenile transgressors.

THE DEVELOPMENT OF JUVENILE JUSTICE

The history of juvenile justice is a relatively short one. Until the mid-1800s, there was no separate legal status of "juvenile," nor was there a separate system for dealing with youthful offenders. Throughout most of history, there was no such status as "child." Youthful members of society were considered either property or people. When very young, from birth to age five or six, they held the same status as property. They could be bought, sold, and disposed of according to the needs of the owners (the father), just as a cow or other belonging. Once youths turned five or six, they became full-fledged members of society and were expected to act the same as any adult.

Web Activity

A list of common practices for dealing with the very young can be found on the textbook website (www.oup.com/he/lab6e).

The general view that children were the same as adults extended to the realm of legal sanctioning. Children were subject to the same rules and regulations as adults. There was not a separate system for dealing with youthful offenders. The law made no distinction based on the age of the offender. In fact, youths could be sentenced to death for various criminal actions. While harsh punishments, including the death penalty, were imposed on youthful offenders, few received the sanction and there was a de facto process of **nullification**, or a refusal to enforce the law and sanctions against children.

The concept of childhood began to emerge in the 16th and 17th centuries as medical advances expanded youthful life expectancies. Youths began to be viewed as in need of protection, assistance and guidance in order to grow up uncorrupted. This was largely led by clergy and scholars. Protecting children was a means of assuring a more moral and productive society in the future.

The beginnings of the juvenile justice system are found in the policy changes directed at dealing with poverty and the potential threat the poor posed to society. A primary response undertaken by many communities and religious groups was to take the poor off the streets and provide religious and vocational training, with the expectation that they would eventually be released so they could assume jobs and care for themselves and their families. Many groups focused their attention on dealing with poor children, because they were viewed as better candidates for education and training.

The Growth of Juvenile Institutions

Various institutions were established to assist in this policy of helping the poor while protecting society. The earliest such institutions were the **houses of refuge**, the first of which was established in New York in 1825. This was quickly copied in Boston (1826) and Philadelphia (1828). These institutions handled both adults and juveniles in need of assistance. Central aspects in the handling of youths were education, skills training, hard work, religious training, and parental discipline. Unfortunately, the houses of refuge quickly became overcrowded and failed to provide the training and assistance they promised.

By the mid-1800s, the houses of refuge gave way to a new set of institutions—the **reformatories**. While the basic goal of the reformatories was the same as the houses of refuge—education, training, and parental discipline—the reformatories followed a cottage design that closely resembled homes, each with a set of surrogate parents and a small number of youths. Unlike houses of refuge, the reformatories focused exclusively on youths. The parental figures would provide the love and care needed by the youths. Unfortunately, the reformatories suffered from many of the same problems as the houses of refuge. What makes them important is the fact that they started to recognize the unique needs and issues of young people in society.

Throughout the development of these new institutions, there remained a single system for dealing with criminal behavior by individuals of all ages in society. Youths who broke the law were still taken before the same courts as adults and subjected to the same penal code as anyone else in society. While the houses of refuge and the reformatories handled youths sent to them by the courts, most youths still found themselves jailed with adults and punished in the same ways as adults.

The Juvenile Court

The development of the juvenile court followed the same logic as the establishment of the new institutions, namely that some individuals needed assistance rather than punishment to make them law-abiding, productive contributors to society. The first recognized individual juvenile court was established in Cook County (Chicago), Illinois, in 1899. The legislation that established the Illinois court reflected the general belief that juveniles needed assistance to overcome the disadvantages they faced in society and that they could be reformed through a system of benevolence rather than one that punished problematic behavior. Besides responding to the concern over the poor and destitute, the new juvenile court also emerged as a result of the growth of scientific explanations for behavior, particularly psychology and sociology. These disciplines argued that the problems of youths could be addressed in ways other than by simple imposition of punishment by the criminal justice system. The new court also adopted a new vocabulary for its operations.

Web Activity

Julian W. Mack was one of the leaders of the movement to establish a juvenile court and served as a judge in the Chicago juvenile court for many years. He described the role and methods of the court as one that assists parents in the proper ways to raise their children. You can read his seminal paper on the role of the juvenile court at the textbook's website (www.oup.com/he/lab6e).

The new juvenile court had jurisdiction over all youths aged 15 and younger, no matter what the issue. The court operated in a very informal manner and avoided any resemblance to the adult court. Due process, attorneys, juries, and other elements of the adult system were excluded from the new juvenile system. The juvenile court was supposed to handle youths in a paternalistic manner and offer them help and assistance just like that found in a family. The court also relied on probation, rather than incarceration, for problem youths. The actual procedures and workings of the juvenile court generally reflected the character of the different judges and individuals working in the court.

The Philosophy of the System

Perhaps the greatest challenge to the growth of the juvenile justice system entailed the debate over the philosophy of the new court and the question of a juvenile's constitutional rights. The new juvenile court conformed to a philosophy that was diametrically opposed to the existing tenets of the adult criminal system. The juvenile system took the stand that youths were incapable of forming the *mens rea* (criminal intent) required for criminal acts. Instead, youthful deviant behavior was the result of forces that were beyond a juvenile's control. Alternatively, youths were simply too immature to understand the consequences of their behavior. Rather than take a strict legal response to juvenile misbehavior, which included concerns over the constitutional rights of youths, the juvenile court adopted the ***parens patriae*** philosophy that focused on protecting, nurturing, and training the youths so that they could make better decisions and avoid problems.

Parens patriae, or the state as parent, is based on the English Chancery Court, which was tasked with looking after the property rights of orphaned children, among other things. The court was to act as a parent to those juveniles who were in need of assistance. *Parens patriae* opened the door to increased involvement in the lives of juveniles and their families. This is probably best exemplified in the passage of statutes specifically outlining status offenses. For example, the original Illinois statute establishing the juvenile court addressed criminal activity, dependency, and neglect. By 1903, however, the state added incorrigibility, curfews, and other status offenses to the court's mandate.

The *parens patriae* philosophy was not new to the juvenile court. Indeed, it had been used in an early court case in which a young girl was incarcerated against the wishes of her father. In Ex parte *Crouse* (1838), a woman asked the court to incarcerate her daughter because she was incapable of taking care of her. The father objected and argued it was illegal to incarcerate a child without the benefit of a trial. The Pennsylvania Supreme Court, however, rejected the father's argument, stating that when a parent is incapable of doing his or her job, the state has a duty, under *parens patriae*, to step in and take action for the betterment of both the juvenile and the community. More importantly, the court noted that the rights of the parents are superseded by the rights and interests of society. This stance was reaffirmed after the initiation of the juvenile court in *Commonwealth v. Fisher* (1905). In this case, the Pennsylvania Supreme Court noted that when the objective of the state is not to punish or simply restrain a youth, but rather to provide care and protection, the state has a right and duty to step in and take custody of a youth. In essence, if the intent is to help the youth, *parens patriae* allows the juvenile court wide latitude to intervene in the life of the youth and the family.

The *parens patriae* philosophy has remained the dominant view in the juvenile justice system. It was not until 1966 that the philosophy was seriously questioned in *Kent v. United States*. While the US Supreme Court did not rule specifically on the philosophy of the juvenile justice system, Justice Abe Fortas argued that

> there may be grounds for concern that the child receives the worst of both worlds: that he gets neither the protections accorded to adults nor the solicitous care and regenerative treatment postulated for children. (*Kent v. U.S.* [1966])

Justice Fortas was suggesting that the philosophy allowed the juvenile court unfettered involvement in the lives of juveniles without granting them due-process rights, despite the fact that the court was also failing to provide the help and care that the philosophy mandated. Changes in the juvenile justice system over the past 30 years show a gradual diminution of *parens patriae* in juvenile proceedings.

Despite *parens patriae's continuing influence*, other philosophical rationales also help drive juvenile justice. The general purpose clauses for juvenile courts that appear in state statutes outline the primary intent or focus of the juvenile court. These clauses fall into five categories: (1) the balanced and restorative justice orientation that focuses on the needs of all parties involved, including the youth and the victims; (2) the Standard Juvenile Court Act clauses that emphasize care, guardianship, and control of the youth; (3) the legislative guide clauses that focus on care, protection, supervision, and rehabilitation of children; (4) a criminal court orientation clauses that focus on deterrence, punishment, and accountability; and (5) traditional child welfare clauses where the emphasis is on the best interests of the child. *Parens patriae* is a key in all of these but the criminal court orientation.

Web Activity

You can look at the general purpose clauses for your state and others at http://www.ncjj.org/pdf/1State_Juvenile_Justice_Profiles_2005.pdf.

Critical Thinking Exercise

Research the general purpose clause for the juvenile court in your state.

DEFINING DELINQUENCY

The development of a separate system for handling problem youths also meant that a new set of laws and terminology was not far behind. Primary among these changes was the fact that "delinquency" replaced "crime" as the focus of the juvenile court. "Delinquency" did not exist prior to the establishment of the juvenile court. Youthful offenders had always been processed in the same criminal system as adult offenders. The juvenile court now handled youths under a different set of laws and policies.

One way to define **delinquency** is to simply use the **criminal law definition** of illegal behavior. In other words, a delinquent is any juvenile who violates the criminal code. Thus, a juvenile who commits a robbery, burglary, assault, or any other criminal offense is considered a delinquent. This definition is used throughout the United States.

These are also actions that are illegal only for persons of a certain status, such as juveniles. These are usually referred to as **status offenses**. Typical status offenses for juveniles include the use of alcohol or tobacco, curfew violations, truancy, disobeying one's parents, running away, or swearing. Adults who participate in any of these actions are not subject to sanctions by the criminal or juvenile justice systems. Different jurisdictions have different terms for status offenders. Common terms are "incorrigible," "unruly," "dependent," "PINS" (person in need of service), or "CHINS" (child in need of service). Some of these terms refer both to juveniles who have done something wrong and to youths who have been subjected to poor parenting or are victims of a crime and are in need of protection.

Critical Thinking Exercise

Look up the delinquency and status offense statutes for your state and at least two other states. How are they similar and different?

Web Activity

The legal definition of delinquent and unruly child for the state of Ohio can be found on the textbook website (www.oup.com/he/lab6e).

In defining delinquency, it is important also to note that the definition of a juvenile varies from jurisdiction to jurisdiction. In 41 states and the District of Columbia, a juvenile is anyone under the age of 18. Eight states define juveniles as those under age 17 and one state defines juveniles as individuals under age 16. While these ages set an upper limit for juvenile court jurisdiction, many states also set a minimum age for handling cases in the juvenile system. Thirty-three states have no minimum age, while 11 set age 10, three set it at age 7, one sets it at age 8, one sets it at age 11, one sets it at age 12, and one uses age 6 as the minimum. Besides the minimum age, there are often provisions whereby the juvenile system can retain jurisdiction over an individual who was adjudicated in the system but has since passed the age of majority. States accomplish this under what are generally known as **youthful offender statutes**. The majority of states (35) extend jurisdiction to age 20 and four extend it to age 24.

Web Activity

A breakdown of the age jurisdiction in the states as of 2018 can be found on the textbook website (www.oup.com/he/lab6e).

Despite the existence of a separate system to handle youths, states also have provisions for handling juveniles in the criminal justice system. These provisions are known as **transfer** or **waiver**. Transfer, or waiver, is a process whereby someone who is legally a juvenile is determined to be beyond the help of the juvenile justice system. Thus, there is a need to invoke the adult criminal process to handle the youth and protect society. Most jurisdictions set a minimum age at which transfer can be invoked.

It should be evident that defining delinquency is not a straightforward endeavor. The definition varies greatly based on the age of the youth and the jurisdiction. This situation also leads to variation in the measurement of youthful misbehavior, since the level of delinquency varies according to how the problem is defined.

Critical Thinking Exercise

Explore your state's statutes and find the definitions and guidelines for juveniles and transfer or waiver used by your state. How do they compare with what is presented here? Randomly pick one or two other states and compare those results to your state.

MEASURING DELINQUENCY

There are a number of different ways to measure delinquency, each of which produces a different picture of the delinquency problem. The two primary approaches to measuring delinquency are the use of official records and the administration of self-report surveys.

Official Measures

Official measures of delinquency are based on the records of various justice system agencies. The level of delinquency, therefore, reflects both the behavior of the juveniles and the activity of the agencies. Official statistics can be obtained from law enforcement, the courts, and corrections. Perhaps the most recognized official measure is the **Uniform Crime Reports (UCR)** which provides information on offenses coming to the attention of the police. The traditional UCR reports (now referred to as the **Summary Reporting System or SRS**) focuses on the Index, or Part I, offenses and the 21 Part II offenses. The greatest detail appears in the arrest figures for the Index offenses. Since many crimes are not reported to the police, and only a fraction of all crimes are cleared by arrest each year, little information is known about the offenders in most crimes. Arrest data by age for 2019 reveal that over 428,000 juveniles were arrested, reflecting 10.8 percent of all those arrested for Index crimes. The arrest data reveal that youths represented 9.8 percent of the arrests for the violent crimes of murder, rape, robbery, and aggravated assault and 11.1 percent of all property crime arrests in 2019.

The use of arrest data for measuring youthful offending is problematic mainly due to the focus on the Part I crimes listed in the UCR SRS. Beginning in 2021, the **National Incident-Based Reporting System (NIBRS)** will replace the SRS and provide much more detailed information on 23 categories of crimes with 52 total offenses. It is unclear to what extent this shift to a new system will have on police counts of youthful behavior.

Web Activity

Extensive UCR data can be found at https://ucr.fbi.gov/crime-in-the-u.s/2019/crime-in-the-u.s.-2019/topic-pages/persons-arrested for information on age, sex, race/ethnicity, and other factors related to offending.

Information on the NIBRS system can be found at https://ucr.fbi.gov/nibrs/2018.

Other source of official delinquency data come from the courts and correctional system. Most youths reaching the courts enter after contact with law enforcement, although many also come from other agencies as well as direct from family referrals. In 2017, 744,451 youths reached the juvenile court for delinquency offenses and over 101,000 status offenders appeared in courts. Compared to both police and court data, the number of youths who appear in correctional statistics is relatively small. Correctional data are typically presented as an average one-day count, with actual daily totals varying around figures. In 2017, public and private facilities combined held roughly 35,000 juveniles on a typical day (Sickmund, Sladky, Kang, and Puzzanchera, 2019), with public facilities holding roughly 70 percent of the youths.

Web Activity

Extensive court and correctional statistics can be found at http://www.ojjdp.gov/ojstatbb/.

These data present a slightly different picture of juvenile offending. The key point to remember is that these figures reflect not only the behavior of the youths but also the behavior and decision-making processes of the agencies. In all official measures, the data fail to consider juvenile behavior that does not come to the attention of the juvenile justice system.

Self-Report Measures

Self-report measures attempt to gauge the level of delinquency by asking individuals to admit to their participation in deviant activity. Where official measures reflect information on those offenses that have been reported to the authorities or where an individual has been arrested, self-reports do not need any involvement of the criminal justice system.

Self-report surveys have a long history in juvenile justice. One of the earliest self-report surveys was developed by Short and Nye (1958) to tap the level of misbehavior by youths. Their survey asked youths to note the frequency with which they committed each of 23 items. The items in the scale were dominated by status and minor property offenses, and it is common to see only a subset of the items used in analyses. Dentler and Monroe (1961) offered a similar self-report survey that focused on minor delinquent offenses.

Most self-report surveys uncover a great deal of delinquent activity. Indeed, various studies using scales such as that of Short and Nye show that virtually every juvenile is a delinquent. This is due to the many minor transgressions that appear in them. Defying parental authority and trying alcohol at some time are pretty universal activities for juveniles. Asking if the individual has "ever" committed an act contributes to the high levels of positive responses. Compared to official counts of delinquency, such self-reports show a great deal more deviance.

More recent self-report surveys, such as the **Monitoring the Future Survey** (MTF) and the **National Youth Survey (NYS)**, include many more serious offenses that elicit significantly fewer positive responses. Both the MTF and NYS include questions on hitting teachers, group fighting, use of weapons, robbery, and aggravated assault. Whereas most self-report surveys are done at a single time on a sample of youths, the MTF gathers data on a national sample of eighth, tenth and twelfth graders, as well as young adults, every year. The NYS used a panel design with a group of 11- to 17-year-olds from across the United States and re-interviewed those individual repeatedly over a period of years. Data from these projects provide an historical picture of offending and reveal that few youths commit the more serious offenses.

Web Activity

Survey items from both the MTF and NYS can be found on the textbook website (www.oup.com/he/lab6e).

Self-report studies can provide information not available from official data. One example of this is that self-report surveys can ask a wide array of questions about the individual's behavior and factors that may contribute to the behavior. Such information is not available in official measures of delinquency. Another advantage of self-reports is that it is possible to examine new or unique behaviors not specifically addresses in official data. On example of this would be the growing interest in crime on social media, such as sexting.

Web Activity

An illustration of the kinds of information available from self-report surveys in relation to sexting can be found on the textbook website (www.oup.com/he/lab6e).

Like official data, self-report measures are not without fault. As already noted, many survey instruments tend to err on the side of recording numerous minor criminal acts and status offenses but often fail to tap into more serious actions. Exceptions to this problem, such as the NYS and MTF, which include serious criminal acts, find results much more in line with those revealed in official arrest statistics. A second major problem with self-report data is the fact that most surveys are one-time efforts, which makes it difficult to know what changes (if any) are taking place over time.

Critical Thinking Exercise

What measure of delinquency is the best, and why?

THE JUVENILE COURT PROCESS

Most youths come to the juvenile court by way of the police. Other youths are referred to the court by parents, schools, or other agencies and individuals. Cases can be petitioned to court and handled in a formal capacity or not petitioned and subjected to informal interventions. Estimates of the number of delinquency cases and the movement of cases through the various alternative processes for 2018 appear in Figure 7.1. In 2018, approximately 57 percent of all delinquent youths were petitioned to the juvenile courts. Of these, 1 percent were waived to adult criminal court. Once a juvenile is referred to court, the case can follow a range of different paths through the system. In addition to these cases, another 100,000 status offense cases were petitioned to juvenile court.

No matter how youths reach the court, the process and decision points are the same. In general, there are five key stages in juvenile court processing: the detention decision, intake, transfer (or waiver), adjudication, and disposition. Within each stage, various issues and processes arise.

744,500 estimated delinquency cases

Waived
3,600   1%

Placed
62,100   28%

Adjudicated
220,000   52%

Probation
139,000   63%

Other sanction
19,000   9%

Petitioned
422,100   57%

Probation
71,900   36%

Not Adjudicated
198,400   47%

Other sanction
17,900   9%

Dismissed
108,600   55%

Probation
49,400   15%

Not petitioned
322,400   43%

Other sanction
142,600   44%

Dismissed
130,400   40%

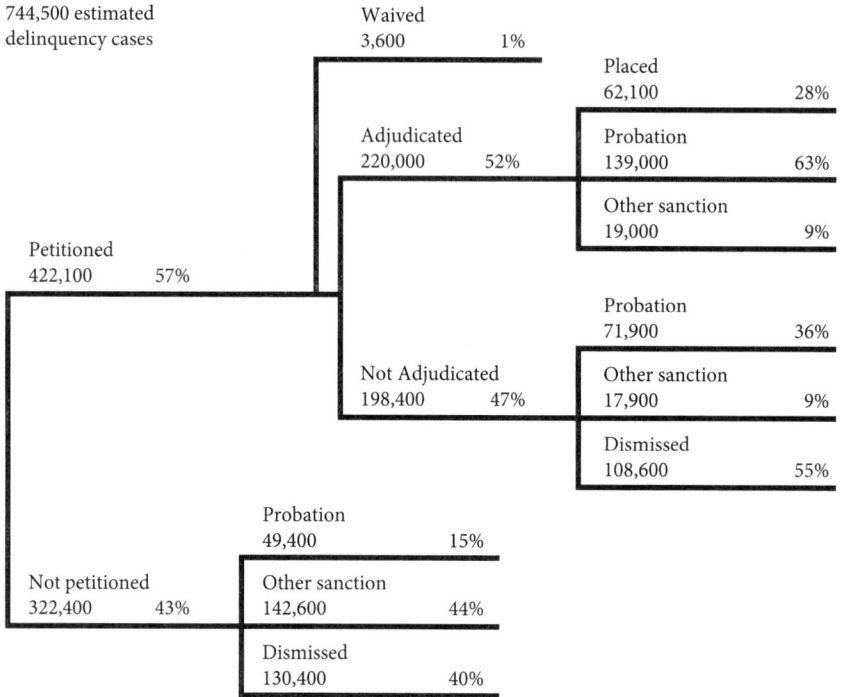

Figure 7.1 Juvenile Court Processing of Delinquency Cases, 2018
SOURCE: Hockenberry and Puzzanchera (2020).

Detention

The initial decision to be made by juvenile court personnel is whether to hold a youth in custody or allow the youth to go home until further action is taken. A **detention** decision is the counterpart to the bail decision in adult court. The detention decision considers whether the individual will appear at a later date, whether the person is a threat to others, and whether the juvenile is in danger himself or herself. That is, detention is considered for the good of society *and* the good of the juvenile.

Detention decisions are initially made by probation officers or special detention workers, although the final decision on whether to continue detention is up to the juvenile court judge. The Model Juvenile Delinquency Act, a guideline for state codes, stipulates that a detention hearing be held within 36 hours. Critics of detaining youths who are at high risk for future offending generally claim that many youths who are held do not really constitute a threat, and therefore, the detention is a violation of their rights. Such preventive detention, however, has been declared constitutional by the US Supreme Court (*Schall v. Martin* [1984]).

In 2018, approximately 203,000 (27%) of the delinquency cases involved detention. For status offense cases, roughly 5 percent involved detention. Most youths are released to their families. The choice of which youths to detain raises concerns for some observers. As a result, many courts now use risk-assessment instruments to base the detention decision on proven risk factors.

Web Activity

An example of a risk-assessment instrument can be found on the textbook website (www.oup.com/he/lab6e), as well as a reference to other risk-assessment instruments.

The youths who are not released to their parents or guardians are placed into either secure or nonsecure detention facilities. **Secure detention** is the equivalent of the local jail for adults. While youths are in a locked facility, they must be isolated from adults, both physically and audibly. That is, youths are not supposed to be able to see or hear confined adults. In **nonsecure detention**, the youths may be placed in group homes, halfway houses, foster care, or other community-based alternatives. Youths in these facilities may still attend their normal schools and other functions as allowed by the court. Both secure and nonsecure detention facilities must provide food, a place to sleep, healthcare, educational programming, and appropriate treatment programs. Both the educational and treatment components respond to the *parens patriae* doctrine of helping youths rather than punishing them.

Because of the relatively short periods that most youths spend in detention, treatment interventions within the detention facilities are often very simplistic and do not address the underlying needs of the youths. Instead, the interventions tend to address the need to keep order in the facility. Perhaps the most common form of detention programming is a **token economy**. Under this approach, youths receive points or tokens for acting appropriately and lose them for inappropriate behaviors. The tokens are good toward extra privileges or purchases from a store or vending machine. Other interventions, such as counseling and vocational training, may appear in some facilities but are not very common due to the relatively short stay for many youths.

The cost involved in housing youths and providing for their constant care while in detention has led many jurisdictions to seek out alternative modes of supervision. **Day–evening centers**, one option, provide educational programming, treatment programs, or other activities during the day but send the youths home at night. This alleviates the need to provide beds, clothing, and three meals a day. The parents or guardians provide oversight at night. A second option is to use **home detention**, which involves ordering youths to remain at home at all times, unless given permission by the court to leave the premises. Youths are monitored by probation or court personnel through frequent visits, phone contacts, or even electronic monitoring devices. This is a cost-effective alternative to the use of a detention facility. A final alternative to detention is to allow youths to post **bail**, as in adult court. While a seldom-used alternative, due mainly to the inability of most youths and their families to raise the required funds, bail is receiving greater attention as a method for handling serious youthful offenders.

The Intake Decision

The second major decision point in the juvenile court is intake. The **intake decision** is the juvenile system's counterpart to filing charges or a grand jury indictment in the adult system. It is at intake that the decision is made to file a petition with the court to hear the case or to handle the youth in another way. The petition alleges that a child is either delinquent, neglected, abused, incorrigible, dependent, or otherwise in need of court intervention. The decision to file a petition is typically made by a probation officer or intake officer after he or she has reviewed the facts of the case, met with and talked to the youth and his or her family, gathered background information about the youth (including prior offending, school records, and so forth), and considered alternatives to formal court processing. Many jurisdictions mandate that all decisions to file or deny a petition be reviewed by a prosecutor in order to ensure that there is legal standing for the court to take action and guarantee that serious juvenile offenders are not moved out of the system. Despite the move to include prosecutorial oversight, fewer than half of all juvenile cases reaching the intake stage are *not* petitioned to the court.

Youths who are not petitioned to court are not simply let go by intake. Most of the time some form of **informal adjustment** is mandated by the intake or probation office. An informal adjustment means that the youths will be required to participate in something short of a court procedure. Interestingly, 59 percent of the youths not petitioned to court were still placed on some form of probation or received some form of sanction (Hockenberry and Puzzanchera 2020). Alternatives may include making restitution or attending counseling or treatment programs. It is not unusual for such informal adjustments to require the participation of the parents and other family members, especially if counseling or treatment is mandated. Various restorative justice practices fit into this realm of informal adjustment.

Restorative (reparative) justice seeks to use interventions that return victims, offenders, and communities to their pre-offense states (Bazemore and Maloney 1994). Restorative justice programs seek to bring offenders, victims, and various members of the community together to identify the types and levels of harm suffered, allow victims to express their concerns about the crimes and their losses, and allow offenders to explain why they committed the acts. The ultimate goals are to identify ways to repair the harm done to victims, help victims heal, restore communities to their precrime states, and reintegrate offenders into society.

Family group conferencing (FGC) is one form of restorative justice targeted at youthful offenders and often occurring at the beginning stages of system processing. FGC has become a part of police and pretrial diversion programs in many jurisdictions. FGC came to prominence in 1989 when New Zealand removed all youths aged 14 to 17 from formal court processing and mandated that they be diverted to conferencing (Kurki 2000). Facilitators lead family members, close friends, and other support groups of the victims and offenders through a discussion of the facts of the cases, the impact of the events on all parties, the feelings of all participants toward the actions and the offenders, and the development of mutually agreed-upon resolutions.

Research uncovers high levels of satisfaction by those participating in FGC. However, the results are based only on those who volunteer to participate, so there is a built-in bias favoring FGC. In terms of recidivism, McGarrell et al. (2000) report a 40 percent reduction in recidivism for program youths compared to youths in regular juvenile justice programs. Similar recidivism findings appear in a range of other FGC evaluations.

Another alternative to formal juvenile court processing at the intake stage is referral to a specialty court. Two forms of specialty courts, teen courts and drug courts, have developed in recent years to address special populations. **Teen courts (or youth courts)** rest on the restorative justice philosophy, which seeks to help the offender, the victim, their families and friends, and society at large. There are roughly 1,050 teen court programs handling more than 100,000 cases (National Association of Youth Courts 2017). These courts focus on first time offenders and rely on peers to assess the behavior and impose sanctions on offenders. Youths act as judges, attorneys, and jury members. The most common penalty from teen courts is community service, although writing apologies, composing essays on offending, and restitution are also common types of outcomes. Teen courts tend to be used effectively with status offenses and other minor transgressions.

Drug courts involve a strong collaboration among the judge, prosecutor, defense attorney, and drug treatment specialists. The goal is to address the youthful offending and the concurrent drug use. The courts use treatment, coordination of interventions, and intensive monitoring. Youths appear frequently so the judges can monitor their progress, offer encouragement, and admonish the youths if needed. There is frequent drug testing, with penalties for positive tests. Recent evaluations of drug courts show modest positive results. Mitchell et al. (2012) report that juvenile drug courts reduced recidivism from 50 percent to 43.5 percent.

The Transfer (or Waiver) Decision

One option available to the juvenile court when faced with a serious juvenile offender is to **transfer or waive** the youth to the adult system for processing. This is an important decision, since the transfer means that the youth will be dealt with as an adult and will incur an adult criminal record if convicted. A criminal record may have serious ramifications for future employment opportunities, whereas a juvenile record is typically confidential and not subject to disclosure. In 2018, approximately 3,600 juveniles were waived to the adult criminal court (Hockenberry and Puzzanchera 2020). This is significantly below the peak of 13,300 cases waived in 1994.

The traditional and most common method for transferring a juvenile was through **judicial waiver** (allowed in 46 states as of 2018). Judicial waiver is typically made at a hearing analogous to a preliminary hearing in adult court. At this hearing, the prosecutor asks the juvenile court judge to transfer the youth to the adult court for processing. The prosecutor must show probable cause that the juvenile committed the alleged offense. He or she must also convince the judge that the youth is not amenable to treatment in the juvenile system—that the juvenile justice system is not capable of helping the youth. This is typically demonstrated through past failures of the juvenile system to correct a problem or the particularly heinous nature of the offense.

Web Activity

A list of different forms of transfer and state-by-state information on waiver can be found on textbook website (www.oup.com/he/lab6e).

Concern over the increasing number and seriousness of juvenile crimes, particularly since 1990, has led to a greater reliance on two other types of transfer—prosecutorial waiver and legislative waiver. **Prosecutorial waiver** (or **direct file**) refers to the ability of prosecutors to directly file the case in adult court (possible in 14 states). The decision is at the sole discretion of the prosecutor within the boundaries set by state statutes. The third form of transfer is **legislative waiver** or **statutory exclusion**. Legislative waiver means that state legislatures determine that certain offenses or cases automatically go to adult court. Twenty-eight states have legislated immediate transfer to adult courts. The case is excluded from juvenile court processing by statute. The typical cases addressed by legislative waiver are serious personal offenses, such as murder, or those involving serious repeat offenders. **Once/always provisions**, which exist in 35 states, stipulate that once a youth is adjudicated as an adult, he or she will remain under the jurisdiction of the adult court for any future transgressions. Finally, 28 states allow for **reverse waiver**, where the adult court can return a waived youth to the juvenile system for processing.

The impact of transferring youths to adult court on subsequent offending and crime rates is not clear. There is evidence that transfer has little or no deterrent effect (Jordan and Myers 2011; Mulvey and Schubert 2012). Those who are transferred tend to receive probation rather than being incarcerated or are released earlier than they would have been if kept under juvenile court jurisdiction (Fagan 1995). This may be due to the lack of appropriate places of confinement for youths who are convicted under adult statutes. They cannot simply be placed into adult correctional facilities with adults, but they are not under the jurisdiction of the juvenile correctional system. These results suggest that transferring youths to the adult system is not a panacea for the problem of youth crime.

Adjudication

Actual hearings in the juvenile court are referred to as the **adjudication** stage. During adjudication, the judge must determine whether there is enough evidence to support the petition and what remedy to use with the juvenile. This is comparable to finding guilt or innocence and sentencing in the adult court.

The adjudication stage in the juvenile court is supposed to look a great deal different from what is seen in an adult court. Under *parens patriae*, there is not supposed to be a determination of guilt or innocence. The actual fact that a crime may have been committed is secondary to the needs of the youth and his or her family. Due-process considerations of the admissibility of evidence, the use of hearsay evidence, the presence of attorneys, and similar issues are secondary to determining what is in the best interests of the child. The entire setting of a juvenile courtroom is often configured to suggest a nonadversarial proceeding. Indeed, during the early days of the juvenile court, attorneys were rarely included in the proceedings, with only the judge, the youth, his or her parents, and perhaps a probation or intake officer in attendance. Many hearings are held around a large conference table and the judge does not even wear judicial robes. It is common for the judge to ask all the questions, and the probation or intake officer offers most of the evidence.

This ideal process of juvenile procedure has undergone several changes over the past 30 years. Today, there is a greater emphasis on procedural rights in many cases, particularly those dealing with serious offenses. As a result, both prosecuting and defense attorneys are becoming more commonplace in juvenile court proceedings. The determination of guilt or innocence has also become more common. Many courts have adopted the trappings of adult court, with a judge's bench, judicial robes, defense and prosecution tables, and concern for the due-process rights of the youth. This movement may be due to the increasing levels of serious offending by youths.

The emergence of due-process concerns and the participation of attorneys in the juvenile court process leads to competing roles in the courtroom. The first is the **zealous advocate role** as found in the adult criminal court. The training of most attorneys and the move to more due-process concerns have resulted in attorneys fighting for their youthful clients, even when they know the child is guilty and in need of the help that could be provided by the court. The second role is the **concerned parent role**. This approach often leads attorneys to push youths to admit to petitions in order to secure the help and assistance of the court.

There is conflicting evidence on the effectiveness of defense attorneys in the juvenile court. First, many youths are not represented by attorneys because they do not understand their rights and often waive their right to representation out of ignorance of the law (Brooks and Kamine 2003). Second, where attorneys are used, their presence result in fewer dismissals and harsher outcomes, including out of home placement (Burruss and Kempf-Leonard 2002; Feld 1988; Guevara et al. 2004). Finally, in many cases, the quality of representation is poor or ineffective (Brooks and Kamine, 2003; Miller-Wilson and Puritz 2003). The participation of attorneys in the juvenile court setting, therefore, may not be beneficial for many youths.

Disposition

Once the court has determined that the facts of the petition are sufficiently supported, a **disposition** (the equivalent to a sentence in an adult court) is determined. Most often, the disposition reflects the *parens patriae* philosophy and seeks interventions and treatments that address the needs of the youth and the family. The judge pays a great deal of attention to the recommendations of the probation officers, social workers, psychologists, and others who have examined the youth. Counseling, educational programming, and treatment programs dominate most dispositions, and most of the time there is a strong desire to send youths home for treatment within the community. Indeed, the vast majority of youths are placed on some form of probation.

Many jurisdictions have moved to more punitive sanctions in recent years. This trend has been mandated in many places by legislative attempts to get tough on juvenile offenders by setting minimum sanctions that the juvenile courts must impose for some crimes. It is not unusual for jurisdictions to impose these harsher dispositions on older youths who have been involved in repeat offenses. A good deal of the concern is that these youths will continue their offending once they become adults and are no longer under the juvenile court's jurisdiction.

Jurisdictions also have developed systems of **blended sentencing** whereby the juvenile court or the adult criminal court imposes a sentence that can involve either the juvenile or adult correctional system, or both. Fifteen states have juvenile blended sentencing schemes (OJJDP 2020). Blended sentencing addresses the loss of jurisdiction by the juvenile court before youths can be adjudicated or before treatment can be completed or the needs of young adults that cannot be met by the adult correctional system. Under blended sentencing, the court imposes dispositions that rely on both the juvenile and adult systems. For example, a 17-year-old who is adjudicated in juvenile court may begin his or her disposition in a juvenile facility. Instead of simply being released when he or she turns 18 and the juvenile facility is no longer appropriate, the individual is automatically transferred to an adult facility and supervision by the adult court. Another possibility is for the 17-year-old to be sent directly to adult supervision after adjudication. Alternatively, a youthful adult offender (say age 19) who is found guilty in adult court may be better served in a facility or program run by the juvenile court and, thus, sent to the juvenile system for help. Such blended sentencing grapples with offenders who do not quite fit into one or the other system.

Web Activity

You can see the states and conditions where blended sentencing can be used on the textbook website (URL here).

DUE PROCESS FOR JUVENILES

Juveniles share some, but not all, of the same constitutional rights as adults. Prior to the 1960s, the *parens patriae* philosophy ruled in the juvenile justice system and due-process rights were not a concern in the juvenile court. The 1960s and 1970s saw the growth of due-process protections for youthful offenders. The report of the President's Commission on Law Enforcement and the Administration of Justice (1967) raised serious questions about the juvenile court's handling of youths, its ability to deal with the increasing number of cases and the need to protect both youths and society. During this period, the US Supreme Court and state courts began to take a more active look at the operations of the juvenile justice system. Consequently, youths are now afforded some of the same constitutional rights that adults have in the criminal justice system. At the same time, the courts still recognize the *parens patriae* doctrine as the driving force when dealing with juveniles and have been reluctant to award full constitutional protections to youths in the juvenile justice system.

Four landmark Supreme Court cases opened the door to constitutional due-process protections for juveniles. The first case to seriously question the *parens patriae* doctrine and the lack of due-process rights for juveniles was *Kent v. U.S.* (1966). In *Kent*, the US Supreme Court was asked to examine the rights of a juvenile faced with transfer to the adult court. Kent was a 16-year-old boy accused of rape who had been waived to the adult court without benefit of a hearing, the assistance of counsel, or an explanation of why he was waived. The Supreme Court decided that the juvenile court judge had erred. Specifically, the court should have allowed Kent's attorney to review the evidence and be present at a hearing in order to refute the evidence and offer a counterargument to the court. The denial of counsel was a violation of Kent's Sixth Amendment rights. Further, the Supreme Court ruled that the judge needed to set forth in writing the specific reasons why he transferred the case to the adult court. The *Kent* case is important for two reasons. First, it outlined the procedure by which transfer decisions must be made; no such procedure existed prior to this time. Second, and more important, the case established some due-process protections for the first time in juvenile procedures. While the protections only applied to transfer decisions, they opened the way for further challenges to *parens patriae*.

Web Activity

Excerpts from the court rulings for the landmark Supreme Court cases dealing with youths can be found on the textbook website (URL here).

The year after the *Kent* decision, the US Supreme Court ruled in the case *In re Gault* (1967). In this case, a 15-year-old boy was accused of making obscene phone calls and was sentenced to the state training school until he became an adult. In essence, Gault was given a six-year sentence for a crime that for an adult, could only bring a $50 fine and two months in jail. The appeal, however, was not over the sentence; instead, the questions raised dealt with the procedure followed when imposing the sentence. Gault was taken into custody by the police without any notice being given to his mother. He was detained until his hearing one week later, at which he was denied the right to counsel, no specific charges were ever

filed, the person making the accusation was not required to appear, and no transcripts of the proceedings were kept. The Supreme Court ruled that when there
is a possibility of confinement, a juvenile does have certain rights, including the
right to an attorney, the right to know the charges against him or her, the right
to confront his or her accuser, and the right to remain silent (*In re Gault* [1967]).
The Court specifically noted that the inclusion of due-process rights in juvenile
court would not hinder the court's ability to act in the best interests of the child.

The rights of juveniles to due process were further enhanced in 1970 in the
case *In re Winship*. In this case, a 12-year-old boy was confined to the state training facility for allegedly stealing $112 from a woman's purse. During the juvenile
court hearing, the court adjudicated the youth delinquent using a "preponderance of evidence" criterion. The appeal dealt with whether this standard of proof
was sufficient for incarcerating a juvenile. The US Supreme Court noted that the
higher standard of "beyond a reasonable doubt" as used in the adult court must
also be used in juvenile proceedings when there is the possibility of committing
a youth to a locked facility (*In re Winship* [1970]). The Court also questioned the
use of "preponderance of evidence" based on its lack of accuracy and openness
to interpretation.

Despite the growth of due-process considerations in juvenile court, not all
constitutional rights afforded to adults are applicable to juveniles or the juvenile
court. This was made evident only one year after *Winship* in the case *McKeiver v.
Pennsylvania* (1971). In this case, the juvenile was denied the right to a jury trial
and appealed to the US Supreme Court for relief. The Supreme Court, however,
sided with the lower courts and denied the appeal. It did this for several reasons.
First, the Court ruled that there is no need for a jury trial to ensure fairness;
bench trials are just as capable of ensuring fairness as a jury trial. Second, the
Court did not want to turn the juvenile courts into an adversarial setting, and
a jury trial would be much more adversarial. Third, the Court pointed out that
the juvenile court was capable of fulfilling its mandate without giving full due-
process rights to juveniles. Finally, while it did not mandate jury trials in juvenile
cases, the Court did note that a jurisdiction could allow for juries if it desired to
do so (*McKeiver v. Pennsylvania* [1971]).

These four cases are typically considered the most important cases for the
juvenile justice system. They opened the door to review of the actions of the juvenile court and offered some constitutional protections to youths. At the same
time, they limited the extent of those constitutional rights and reaffirmed the
basic philosophical mandate underlying the juvenile system.

Since these cases were decided, many other challenges have been mounted
on behalf of juveniles. Some of the most notable over the past 15 years have
dealt with sentencing of juvenile and the Eighth Amendment prohibitions
against cruel and unusual punishment. The appropriateness of capital punishment for juveniles has been a matter of debate for several years. Prior to 2005,
statutes allowing the imposition of the death penalty for individuals who committed their crimes when aged 16 or 17 were permissible under the US Supreme

Court ruling in *Stanford v. Kentucky* (1989). The legal status of the death penalty for youthful offenders was overturned in the case *Roper, Superintendent,
Potosi Correctional Center v. Simmons* (2005). In the majority opinion, the
Court noted that the "evolving standards of decency that mark the progress of
a mature society" clearly indicate that imposing death on juveniles constitutes
"cruel and unusual punishment" in violation of the Eighth Amendment. The
Court noted that most states did not allow for the death penalty for juvenile
cases, the majority of states with death penalty statutes for youthful offenders do not carry out the executions, and the prevailing international opinion
is against the use of the death penalty for youths (*Roper v. Simmons* [2005]).
After many years of debate, the death penalty is no longer an issue in relation
to juvenile offenders.

Web Activity

Extensive information on the death penalty can be found at the Death Penalty Information Center's website, http://www.deathpenaltyinfo.org.

Beyond the death sentence, the Supreme Court has issued three rulings
that address sentences of life-without-parole for juveniles. The Supreme court
ruled in *Graham v. Florida* (2010) that sentences of life-without-parole for
youths committing nonhomicide cases violated the Eighth Amendment's prohibition against cruel and unusual punishment. The court ruled that youths
must be given the opportunity to demonstrate their maturity and rehabilitation. This ruling was extended in *Miller v. Alabama* (2012) to prohibit mandatory life-without-parole sentences juveniles that are established by statute. The
Court ruled that sentencing courts has to provide "individualized" sentences
that consider the possibility of rehabilitation in light of "children's diminished
capacity and heightened capacity for change." Finally, in *Montgomery v. Louisiana* (2016), the Supreme Court ruled that *Miller v. Alabama* applies retroac-
tively and that life-without-parole cannot be imposed even in homicide cases
unless the court finds that the child "exhibits such irretrievable depravity that
rehabilitation is impossible."

Throughout the court cases, there is an attempt to balance the rights of juveniles as individuals and citizens with the family and societal needs to protect
and raise children to be law-abiding citizens. The growth of litigation over the
rights of youths can be considered a direct result of changes in both the behavior
of youths and societal responses to that behavior. As society and the juvenile
justice system have taken new steps to address youthful misbehavior, particularly
in terms of more adversarial proceedings and harsher forms of punishment, the
courts have stepped in to outline appropriate safeguards for the rights of youths.
In essence, the courts have established policy through the rulings they have
handed down.

Critical Thinking Exercise

Should juveniles be given full constitutional protections? What would be the consequence of doing so? What would be the consequence of not doing so?

INSTITUTIONAL CORRECTIONS

Juvenile corrections takes a variety of forms, ranging from institutional and residential settings to probation and community-based alternatives. The primary goal throughout the juvenile corrections system is to help youths overcome the problems leading to misbehavior. The history of many correctional initiatives today dates back to the founding principles of the juvenile system. The early houses of refuge and reformatories set the stage for today's residential institutions, while probation has been a cornerstone of dealing with juveniles since before the first juvenile court was established.

Institutional and Residential Interventions

On the latest one-day count of juveniles in residential placement in 2014, over 48,000 youths were being held in some form of residential facility, with over 70 percent in public facilities and 29 percent held for offenses against persons (Hockenberry, Wachter, and Sladky 2016). Females constituted only 15 percent of those in facilities and are held for status offenses and technical violations more often than males.

State training schools are the juvenile justice system's equivalent of the adult prison. These schools house youths who are considered to be a risk to themselves and the community and who are beyond the help of community-based interventions. The actual setup of training schools varies greatly from place to place. Some closely resemble adult prisons, with high walls, fences, barbed wire, locked cells, and heavily regimented activities. At the other extreme are training schools built on the cottage design of the early reformatories. These institutions may be totally open, meaning there are no fences or locked doors to keep juveniles from escaping. The guards in these facilities may actually act more like parents than jailers.

The most important part of training schools is the degree of programming that is supposed to take place. Most training schools offer some combination of academic education, vocational training, and behavior modification. Academic education is required by law for all youths of school age who have not graduated from high school. Vocational training may be offered to older youths who have completed school or who are no longer required to go to school. **Behavior modification** is used ostensibly to teach youths about proper behavior through a system that rewards positive behavior and punishes poor behavior. Most institutions use a formal point system, or token economy. Beyond these three interventions, institutions may implement a wide range of additional programming. Individual, group, and family counseling sessions are popular interventions used in institutions, along with drug or alcohol programs, work release, vocational counseling, and job placement.

A key issue facing institutional programming is its effectiveness at reducing recidivism and helping the youths become productive members of society. Unfortunately, the evidence on effectiveness is mixed (see Whitehead and Lab 2018). The reason for this is not entirely clear, although a large part of the problem may entail the degree to which the intervention is appropriately implemented and carried out (Schubert and Mulvey 2014). That is, did the institution deliver the treatment as it was meant to be delivered and at a level sufficient to bring about a positive change? Among effective programs are Multisystemic Therapy (MST) and those that incorporate proven principles and approaches such as cognitive behavioral approaches. Some of the keys to effective programs is implementing interventions that are intensive and behavioral, target criminogenic need, match offenders to programs, and target risk factors (Andrews 2006; Andrews et al. 1990; Gendreau 1996).

Web Activity

References and materials addressing the effectiveness debate can be found on the textbook website (www.oup.com/he/lab6e).

Alternative Interventions

Traditional state training schools are not the only means of housing delinquents. Many youths are held in open facilities such as shelters, halfway houses, and group homes. These residents typically attend regular schools while receiving counseling and other interventions at the facility. One popular alternative has been the use of **boot camps**. Also known as a type of **shock incarceration**, boot camps are short-term programs that are supposed to handle first-time, nonviolent offenders. The camps are operated on a military model, with strict rules and discipline, physical training and conditioning, and counseling and education. The camps are intended to show youths that with hard work and self-discipline, they can succeed in life and do not need to turn to delinquent or criminal behavior. Unfortunately, the evidence shows that boot camps have little or no effect on recidivism (Aos, Miller, and Drake 2006; Lipsey 2009; MacKenzie and Freeland 2012). Boot camps are part of the more general trend to get tough on crime.

Another approach is **wilderness programs**, in which youths are placed in situations where they must learn survival skills and rely on one another to succeed. These programs can be either short-term or long-term and can take a variety of forms, including sailing trips, wagon trains, or back-country camps. The underlying idea is to build self-esteem and show the youths that hard work and perseverance pay off. Implicit in the approach is that the skills and self-esteem developed in the program can be transferred back into the daily lives of the youths. While research on these approaches is relatively limited, Lipsey and Wilson (1998) argue that wilderness experience programs have little or no impact on recidivism rates and that youths who participate in these interventions recidivate at comparable levels to those who are processed through other juvenile correctional programs. In addition, these programs can be very costly, and there have been problems including serious injuries and even death.

Deinstitutionalization

One of the strongest policy recommendations made by the President's Commission in 1967 was to deinstitutionalize many of the youths held in secure juvenile facilities. One underlying rationale for this suggestion was the fact that many incarcerated youths were there for status offenses and not violations of the criminal law. A second argument was that there was little evidence that institutionalization was effective at correcting the problems of youths. Perhaps the strongest argument favoring **deinstitutionalization** was the belief that involvement in the formal justice system was criminogenic, meaning that youths would be more prone to criminal behavior after system intervention than before.

The move toward deinstitutionalization was codified in the 1974 Juvenile Justice and Delinquency Prevention Act. A major part of this legislation was to remove status offenders from any form of secure confinement. The rationale for this was twofold. First, mixing status offenders and serious delinquents has the potential of causing the status offenders more harm than good. Second, status offenders have committed no transgressions against other individuals; rather, they have exhibited behavior that may lead to further problems. Given the possible criminogenic effects of system intervention, it would be in the best interests of the youths to keep them out of any institutional placement. Interestingly, this legislation could not directly force states to deinstitutionalize status offenses, since the states have the legislative authority over this matter. In order to influence the states, the legislation withheld federal monies from jurisdictions that failed to deinstitutionalize status offenders. In 2017, roughly 1,690 youths were held in residential facilities for status offenses representing less than 4 percent of those in facilities (Sickmund, Sladky, Kang, and Puzzanchera 2019).

Several states, including Massachusetts, Maryland, Missouri, California, Illinois, Ohio, New York, and Texas, have taken steps to close state training schools. Massachusetts incarcerates less than 3 percent of the youths sent to the state by the courts. Nationally, the number of youths in residential placement has dropped by almost 60 percent from 1997 to 2017. Youths are now placed in alternative community programs or in settings run by private agencies under contract with the state authorities.

The deinstitutionalization movement has resulted in mixed outcomes. In terms of cost efficiency, the alternatives used in place of residential placement are significantly cheaper. The impact on recidivism, however, is not as positive. Various evaluations show that the recidivism rate has not significantly changed as a result of deinstitutionalizing youthful offenders. While the move toward deinstitutionalization has been effective at reducing the numbers of youths in confinement, particularly status offenders, the move has not resulted in lower recidivism rates.

COMMUNITY INTERVENTIONS

At the outset of the juvenile justice system in 1899, community interventions were the preferred method for dealing with youths in need of assistance. There were no residential institutions under the control of the court, and the court relied on probation as the primary means of dealing with youths in need of help. Keeping juveniles at home and in the community was considered the best way of helping children.

Probation

The most common form of community intervention today is probation. Roughly 60 percent of all delinquent youths processed through the juvenile court end up being placed on probation. In addition, many more youths handled informally are also placed under some form of probation supervision.

Web Activity

Information on the adjudication offenses for youths placed on probation can be found on the textbook website (www.oup.com/he/lab6e).

Probation departments are active throughout the juvenile system and often fulfill the duties of intake, staff and administer local detention facilities, run informal intervention programs, develop social history reports (the juvenile system equivalent of a presentence investigation), and make recommendations to the judge on dispositions, as well as supervising and working with youths placed on probation. Much of the supervision revolves around making certain that the youths remain in school, obey the law, and become involved in pro-social activities, as well as fulfill any orders to complete counseling, make restitution, or participate in other treatment programs. In general, probation in the juvenile justice system mirrors the process in the adult system. The biggest difference, however, should be a greater emphasis on providing treatment and aid to youths and a reduced interest in simply monitoring and enforcing rules.

Aftercare

Juvenile justice also has a form of parole, commonly referred to as **aftercare**. Aftercare differs from probation mainly by the fact that youths in aftercare have spent some amount of time in secure facilities and are being released back into the community. Many of the rules, regulations, and programming available in aftercare are identical to those found in probation, with supervision being the most important component. Due to the similarity between probation and aftercare, in many communities aftercare is provided by the probation department. Both probation and aftercare use many of the same treatment ideas, including reality therapy, behavior modification, an emphasis on educational achievement, and vocational training.

Reentry Concerns
Community supervision, particularly as aftercare, faces many problems with **reentry** for those youths returning to the community. Youths who have been separated from society need to be reintegrated to normal daily activities when they are released and return home. Studies on reentry programs and other interventions have not found a clear-cut or simple answer to what makes for successful reentry. However, the research does indicate some suggestions for success. First, mental-health services can reduce recidivism. Second, mentoring is related to reduced recidivism, reductions in positive drug tests, and more connections to educational and employment services and mental-health treatment (Nellis 2009).

Issues in Supervision
While supervision appears to be a straightforward idea, there are a number of competing factors that make it a very difficult task for both probation and aftercare. The traditional view of supervision in the juvenile justice system has emphasized the *parens patriae* goals of providing benevolent assistance to youths and their families. Supervision is supposed to help youths identify problematic behavior and uncover means to overcome the problems and issues that push or pull them into delinquency. This approach is sometimes referred to as a "social worker" approach that attempts to find solutions to the problems underlying the behavior.

At the same time, there is a growing tendency to get tough with the youths. Rather than work to help youths, supervision becomes a means of watching for violations and sanctioning youths for additional transgressions. Supervision, therefore, is little more than another method used under a punitive model of juvenile justice. Probation officers and aftercare workers act as extensions of the police and seek to justify ways of placing youths into secure residential institutions.

An emerging middle ground for supervision is the balanced approach. Under this approach, probation or aftercare workers are responsible for addressing youths' needs while simultaneously taking the safety and security needs of the larger community into account. Typical responses under the balanced approach include restitution, community service, counseling, rehabilitation, and punishment. Officers are expected to identify the correct mix of the competing philosophies (*parens patriae*, retribution, restorative, and so forth) to use with each youthful offender.

While it may appear reasonable to use elements of a wide range of philosophies and approaches when addressing juvenile misconduct, this situation causes a great deal of anxiety for system workers. What is the correct approach to use with each individual juvenile? What interests are to be emphasized and when (e.g., youth or society)? What training is the most appropriate for the job? What does the community really want (e.g., retribution or rehabilitation)? How should the impact of supervision be evaluated (e.g., arrests, convictions, number of counseling sessions, improved grades in school)? These and many other questions and issues form the basis for role confusion and discontent for many probation officers and aftercare workers.

Questions of the effectiveness of community interventions are similar to those found with institutional interventions. Many programs have exhibited positive results for some youths, especially when the program has been properly implemented and the proper amount of intervention has been applied. What has not been found is any one program that works all the time. In general, programs tend to be time and place specific.

SPECIAL TOPICS

The juvenile justice system must deal on a regular basis with a wide range of issues and topics related to youthful misbehavior. Three important issues that have not been addressed yet in the chapter are gang behavior, disproportionate minority contact, and calls to eliminate the juvenile justice system. While space does not permit a full discussion of these issues, each is briefly addressed in the following paragraphs.

Gangs

Discussion of gangs and gang membership are an important topic for both the juvenile and criminal justice systems. Gangs and gang members contribute disproportionately to delinquent and criminal behavior. The study of gangs has a long history in the juvenile justice system. A major reason for this is the observation that youths tend to commit offenses when in the company of other youths. Some authors have suggested a **group hazard hypothesis**, which claims that society responds to group transgressions more than to individual violations (Erickson 1973).

The study of juvenile gangs dates back to work done in Chicago in the 1930s. Since that time, a wide range of definitions for a gang have emerged, and writers have not settled on a single definition. In general, the term *gang* has referred to groups that exhibit characteristics setting them apart from other affiliations of juveniles. Curry and Decker (1998) offer six elements as common to most definitions of a gang. First, there is typically a minimum number of members for the group. Second, gangs typically have symbols that can be used to identify them, including certain clothing, colors or hand signs. Third, gangs also are demarcated by both verbal and nonverbal forms of communication, such as hand signs and graffiti. Fourth, there is a degree of permanence to the gang, typically lasting a year or more. Fifth, gangs often claim territory. Finally, and perhaps most importantly, gangs are involved in criminal behavior.

Many jurisdictions have passed laws specifically dealing with gangs and gang behavior. Forty-four states and the District of Columbia have statutes defining a gang. Fourteen states define a gang member (National Gang Center 2016). Typical elements of statutory definitions are criminal activity, a pattern of criminal activity, a hierarchy or leadership structure, an alliance or understanding among members, and some common name or symbol (Barrows and Huff 2009).

While not all gangs look alike, there are some common features of most gangs. Most gangs draw youths from the lower socioeconomic classes, are racially homogeneous, offer their members a sense of belonging and status, and are dominated by youths in their late teens. The degree of organization and the behavior of gangs vary considerably, although most gangs are involved in some type of criminal activity. Physical aggression or the willingness to use physical force has long been a cornerstone of gang activity, although in recent years this aggression has increasingly been expressed using firearms, resulting in the death of combatants. Drive-by shootings, or forays, have become a recognized part of gang violence in many cities.

The extent of gang membership is also difficult to assess. From 1996 to 2012, the National Gang Center conducted annual surveys to assess gang membership and activity. According to the 2012 survey, there are almost 30,000 active gangs with roughly 850,000 members operating in US cities (Egley et al. 2014). The number of gangs and gang members vary greatly from area to area, but they appear in virtually all areas of the country.

Web Activity

Information on gangs and characteristics of gang members and interventions with gangs can be found on the National Gang Center's website at http://www.nationalgangcenter.gov/.

Interventions with gangs have taken a variety of forms. In 1993, Spergel and Curry identified five common intervention strategies: suppression, social intervention, organizational change and development, community organization, and opportunities. While law enforcement respondents to a national survey indicated that opportunities provision was the most promising response to gangs, it is the least used. Suppression is the most common response but is considered the least effective (Spergel and Curry 1993). Vigil (2010) argues that effectively responding to gang and gang problems requires a balanced strategy incorporating elements of prevention, intervention, and law enforcement. This means creating solutions that address the economies of the area, sociocultural factors surrounding youths, and the sociopsychological marginality of the youths (Vigil 2010).

Among the methods used to address gangs and gang behavior are detached worker programs, statutory changes, deterrence strategies, and the G.R.E.A.T. program. **Detached worker programs** place gang workers into the community and free them from heavy paperwork and administrative responsibilities. The workers are supposed to spend time with the gangs and try to redirect their activities to noncriminal activities. While these programs are able to organize noncriminal activities and enhance contact with the gangs, there is evidence that they inadvertently increase gang cohesion among the members and actually make the gangs more attractive to youths.

Statutory changes attempt to make gang membership a crime, such as California's Street Terrorism Enforcement and Prevention Act of 1988 (the STEP Act). These statutes typically enhance civil penalties and injunctions against gang members associating with one another and congregating in public. Local jurisdictions may establish or enhance specialized gang units to enforce these new laws. Another innovative use of legal codes to fight gangs is to employ civil, rather than criminal, codes. **Civil abatement** procedures can be used to control or eliminate locations that gang members frequent or own (Cristall and Forman-Echols 2009). When an address is identified as a gang headquarters or hang out, the police and civil authorities, including health departments and building code enforcement, will bring lawsuits in civil court against the owners that can result in eviction or property forfeiture. Injunctions against gang members can also be used to order them to stay away from the property. In a similar fashion, **civil gang injunctions** involve court orders that prohibit certain behaviors linked to criminal activity. These orders may prohibit gang members from associating in public, marking territory, trespassing, loitering, or other similar activities (Los Angeles City Attorney's Office 2009). These injunctions are typically aimed at specific gangs and gang members, locations, and activities (Hennigan and Sloane 2013).

Web Activity

The G.R.E.A.T. program has developed into multiple components for different aged youths, parents, and schools. Explore the program at https://www.great-online.org.

Deterrence strategies have received a great deal of attention in recent years. These typically involve suppression efforts along the lines of the **Boston Gun Project**, which used an approach called **pulling levers**. Pulling levers sought to deter behavior by taking a zero-tolerance response with regards to any transgressions by any member of a gang. The entire gang was held responsible for the acts of all its members. The Boston Gun Project resulted in a 63 percent reduction in homicides, a 25 percent reduction in assaults with firearms, and a 32 percent reduction in the number of shots fired (Braga et al. 2001). Replications of this approach in Indianapolis, Cincinnati, Stockton (California), and Lowell (Massachusetts) have found similar positive effects.

A final well-known intervention is the **G.R.E.A.T. (Gang Resistance Education and Training)** program, in which police officers teach anti-gang, anti-violence lessons in middle schools. The goal is to provide youths with the skills to identify high-risk situations and resist the peer pressure and allure to take part in gangs and gang activity. The program is geared toward increasing self-esteem, changing attitudes, developing life skills, respecting others, having empathy, making positive choices, and eliminating violent behavior. Conflict resolution is the key part of the program. A recent national evaluation of the program reports positive results, including increased refusal skills, better resistance to peer pressure, less gang membership, and more negative attitudes about gangs (Esbensen et al. 2013).

Unfortunately, the evidence on the effectiveness of interventions with gangs and gang members does not suggest strong positive results. Most methods appear to have little impact on criminal and deviant behavior. Some of the failure may be attributable to the fact that many programs fail to target the key causes of gangs and gang behavior and are poorly implemented. Indeed, most interventions tend to try to suppress gang behavior through arrest and prosecution rather than attacking the underlying causes of gangs and gang activity: the lack of social opportunities, the lack of jobs, poor education, and other key factors.

Disproportionate Minority Confinement

The fact that more minority youth, particularly African American youths, are found in the juvenile justice system that their population representation is on that has long been recognized in the literature. This situation was first formally recognized in the 1980s and labeled as disproportionate minority confinement reflecting the number of youths in secure custody. This term as been expanded to **disproportionate minority contact (DMC)**, which recognizes the overrepresentation of minority youths at almost all stages of the juvenile justice system, including arrest, court referral, detention, and probation.

The extent and level of DMC is evident throughout the juvenile justice system and over time, although the level is not stable across jurisdictions or time. Leiber and Fix (2019), looking at data from 2005 to 2015, report that DMC is found across the states and that the African American contact is often more than three times that for whites and twice African American proportion of the population. Comparing the data over time shows increasing levels of disproportionate contact for African Americans. Similar disparities are also found when considering other minority youths (such as Hispanic youths). Leiber and Fox (2019) claim there is no clear patterns of DMC reductions found in the national data over time. The authors note that the extent of the difference in contact varies across segments of juvenile justice system processing (such as detention, petition, and waiver). Some points in the juvenile justice system have shown reductions in disproportionality while others show increases.

Numerous explanations have been set forth to explain DMC. Among these are selective enforcement of the law, institutional racism, socioeconomic factors, different levels of offending, bias in processes and procedures, and administrative policies and practices that vary across groups. Dawson-Edwards et al. (2020) condense these reasons into two primary explanations. The first of these is the argument that different youths commit more offending than others which results in more system processing. The second is that there is different treatment applied to minority youth compared to white youth. While there is no consensus on the cause of DMC, it does not change the fact that the juvenile justice system needs to address the disparity in processing different youths. Exactly how to address the disparity, however, will differ according to the presumed cause.

Responding to DMC has been mandated in the 2002 amendments to the Juvenile Justice and Delinquency Prevention Act (JJDPA). One major requirement outlined in the Act is for jurisdictions to document the extent of DMC at the different points in the juvenile justice system processing. States are required to report the findings along with how they are addressing the problem. It is important to note that the JJDPA is a federal law and applies directly to federal agencies and cases. States are not required to adhere to the requirements of the Act. In order to coerce states to comply with the DMC requirements, the JJDPA tied federal funding to state compliance. Robles-Ramamurthy and Watson (2019) point out that the ACT does not mandate states to establish specific types of programs or efforts to address any identified disparities. Responses are solely at the discretion of the states. The states are only expected to take some action.

Addressing DMC requires efforts at various points in the criminal justice system, juvenile justice system, and society. The efforts can attack the problem in various ways corresponding to different explanations for the disparities. System and societal decisions to focus on certain types of offenses and selectively enforce behaviors the differentially involve certain groups or segments of society should be amended so that they are bias free. One example of this was the decision to punish crack cocaine use more seriously than other forms of cocaine which resulted in greater incarceration for African Americans. DMC that is the result of beliefs that minority youths commit more serious violent crimes can be combatted through diversity and sensitivity training. If the disproportionality is the result of great offending by poorer minority youths, the response may require social changes to combat income, educational, and employment inequality, among other things. These are only a few examples of ways states can attempt to address DMC. It is important that states examine the extent and causes of DMC and implement changes to ameliorate the problems.

THE FUTURE OF JUVENILE JUSTICE

A great deal of debate has occurred of the past 30+ years on the appropriate approach to dealing with problem youths and the form of the juvenile justice system. One manor argument has been to "criminalize" juvenile court and to make it a scaled-down version of adult criminal court. A **criminalized juvenile court** would entail providing juveniles with all the procedural protections of criminal court. Thus, children would have the right to a jury trial and would have fully adversarial defense attorneys, not attorneys who often slip into the role of a concerned parent trading off zealous advocacy for promises of treatment. At the same time, it would be necessary to scale down penalties out of concern for the reduced culpability of children. The major problem with this suggestion is that it may not satisfy calls for a more punitive approach to juvenile offenders that imposes adult penalties for what some people perceive as adult offenses.

Critical Thinking Exercise

What impact would criminalizing the juvenile court have on youths and the juvenile justice system?

An alternative to basically eliminating the juvenile court is the idea of re-balancing the juvenile court (Bishop and Feld 2012). Rather than go toward a get-tough approach, the court needs to balance *parens patriae* and the need to hold youths accountable for their actions. This argument fits with a softening of the get-tough era. First, crime has declined and three are eased calls for harsh treatment of juveniles. Second, advances in both neuroscience and developmental psychology have provided scientific support for the proposition that youth are less mature and less responsible. Third, advocacy groups have worked to soften punitive demands of the get-tough era. The National Research Council of the National Academies of Science recommends that juveniles be held accountable for offending, but that condemnation, control, and lengthy confinement are not necessary to do so. Developmentally appropriate interventions should focus on implementing evidence-based programs and engage the youth's family and draw on neighborhood resources. There should also be an emphasis on procedural fairness and due-process rights.

One indication of the re-balancing has been a return to a lower bound of criminal court jurisdiction to age 18 in several states. Other states have restricted the offense or offender criteria for transfer to the adult court (Daugherty 2013). Another indication is that the Supreme Court has ruled against life without parole sentences for youths convicted of nonhomicide offenses (*Graham v. Florida*, 2010) and against mandatory life without parole sentences for juveniles (*Miller v. Alabama*, 2012).

Despite the calls for changes in juvenile justice, there remains an overriding belief in the need to help youths rather than punish them. Consequently, eliminating the juvenile justice system makes little sense. The adult system would have to make drastic changes if it were to assume responsibility for juvenile offenders. Many of the changes would probably mirror the current activities of the juvenile system. What is needed is a system that has the flexibility to guard the due-process rights needed to protect the accused and the power to use whatever intervention is in the best interests of both offenders and society. Clearly, the juvenile justice system will continue to undergo change, and that change may include moving closer to the adult system.

CONCLUSION

Juvenile offending raises special problems for society and agents of social control. Indeed, a separate system of justice has been in existence for over 100 years to deal with problem youths. This system operates under a different philosophy from the criminal justice system, although many people have challenged the *parens patriae* philosophy in recent years. The juvenile system generally assumes that youths are in need of help rather than punishment and operates from the premise that the proper intervention can remove the causes of misbehavior. While many have called into question the effectiveness of the juvenile justice system and have called for more punitive responses to offending youths, others have argued for a more balanced approach that maintains *parens patriae* while emphasizing the safety of the community. It does not appear that the juvenile system is in danger of being abolished. Instead, it will continue to adapt to the competing demands being placed on it from various societal constituencies.

KEY WORDS

adjudication
aftercare
bail
behavior modification
blended sentencing
boot camps
Boston Gun Project
civil abatement
civil gang injunctions
concerned parent role
criminal law definition
day–evening centers
deinstitutionalization
delinquency
detached worker
    programs
detention
direct file
disposition
disproportionate
    minority contact
    (DMC)
drug courts

family group
    conferencing
G.R.E.A.T.
group hazard hypothesis
home detention
houses of refuge
informal adjustment
intake decision
judicial waiver
legislative waiver
Monitoring the Future
    Survey
National Incident-Based
    Reporting System
    (NIBRS)
National Youth Survey
nonsecure detention
nullification
once/always provisions
parens patriae
President's
    Commission on Law
    Enforcement and the

Administration of
    Justice
prosecutorial waiver
pulling levers
reentry
reformatories
restorative (reparative)
    justice
reverse waiver
secure detention
shock incarceration
state training schools
status offenses
statutory exclusion
teen courts
token economy
transfer or waiver
Uniform Crime Reports
waiver
wilderness program
youthful offender statutes
zealous advocate role

SUGGESTED READINGS

Empey, L. (1982). *American delinquency: Its meaning and construction*, Chapters 2–4. Homewood, IL: Dorsey Press.

Feld, B. (1993). *Justice for children: The right to counsel and the juvenile courts*. Boston: Northeastern University Press.

Sickmund, M. (1994). *How juveniles get to criminal court: Juvenile justice bulletin*. Washington, DC: US Department of Justice.

Torbet, P., R. Gable, H. Hurst, I. Montgomery, L. Szymanski, and D. Thomas. (1996). *State responses to serious and violent juvenile crime*. Washington, DC: Office of Juvenile Justice and Delinquency Prevention.

CHAPTER 8

✦

Conclusion

CHAPTER OUTLINE

Criminal Justice and Discretion
Technology
Fiscal Austerity and Criminal Justice
Criminal Justice Reform
Criminal Justice as a Processing System

After reading this chapter, you should be able to:

- Discuss how discretion is endemic throughout the criminal justice system
- Relate different points at which discretion appears
- Tell how fiscal austerity has affected the operations of the criminal justice system
- Discuss the impact and challenges of opioid addiction on the system
- Outline technological changes impacting criminal justice
- Discuss how criminal justice is a processing system influenced by a different inputs

---

The criminal justice system is constantly facing enduring and new issues in its efforts to address anti-social behavior in society. Similar themes and issues exist and emerge across the different components of the system and impact the operations of the agencies and units that comprise the criminal justice system. In some cases, the issues are more focused on only one part of the system. Among the themes and issues facing criminal justice are discretion, the impact of technology, fiscal austerity, and criminal justice reform.

CRIMINAL JUSTICE AND DISCRETION

The criminal justice system is multidimensional, so we can think about it in different ways. For example, the system can be viewed as a series of interrelated discretionary decision points where citizens and criminal justice system actors make decisions about reported crimes and the future of suspects, defendants, and offenders. For example, crime victims decide if they will report their victimization, police officers decide if they will arrest a suspect, prosecutors decide if (and how) to prosecute, and so on.

These decisions are made at different levels. At an individual level, each actor decides how to act, given a range of possible actions. There are usually multiple choices available to actors. Judges sentencing convicts usually choose from a range of supervision types (probation, intensive supervision probation, boot camps, or prison), the length of supervision, and the conditions (e.g., will the convict be required to attend substance abuse treatment as a condition of supervision?).

Discretionary decisions are also made at an organizational or aggregate level. Jurisdictions rely upon different balances of actions and options, and some may not have options that others do (e.g., boot camps, a secure detention facility for juveniles). For example, one jurisdiction may rely upon community corrections options, such as probation and parole, to a greater extent than another. One court jurisdiction may plea bargain more cases than another.

Discretionary decision-making by actors is not without constraints. Both policy and substantive law limit and guide how these discretionary decisions are made by system actors. Decisions are also constrained and molded by local norms of appropriate behavior for actors. For example, in some jurisdictions police officers resort to physical force more often than in other jurisdictions. Most organizations exhibit informal, unwritten occupational norms of conduct for their employees, such as the police subculture. Because these norms and subcultures are unwritten, they are hard to change via formal methods, such as changing a law, crafting a written organizational policy, or holding formal training programs. Although hard to see and hard to change, these informal norms have a powerful influence over system actors. At the end of the day, there is still significant latitude in discretionary decision-making despite the constraints imposed by policy, law, and local norms.

TECHNOLOGY

As discussed at different points in this text, technology plays an important role in criminal justice and is constantly evolving. This is not a new situation. The introduction of cars to police patrol was a giant step in using emerging technology. The move to radios from police call boxes is another early example of technology making a change in how the criminal justice system operates. The introduction of new technologies has increased in momentum since 2000 and can be seen throughout the operations of the criminal justice system—from the police to the courts to corrections.

The increase in the use of police body cameras is perhaps the most recognized enhancement in police technology in recent years. This move has been partly a response to the increased use of mobile phones by citizens to document police behavior and the use of force in police-citizen encounters. Many of those events have made their way onto the evening news and have prompted citizen disputes with police actions, sometimes involving violence. The police often point out that the citizen films fail to show the entire event and have responded by issuing body cameras and requiring officers to use them to document the entire encounters with citizens.

The police use both public media (i.e. television, radio, etc.) and social media to solve crimes and gain citizen support of their efforts. Crime Stoppers solicits the public for information about criminal events by showing pictures of wanted individuals or reenactments of crimes (typically on television). There are roughly 1,200 Crime Stoppers programs around the world that have cleared more than 1.6 million cases since its inception in 1976 (Crime Stoppers International 2015). The idea of police soliciting help in solving crimes has moved to the use of social media recent years, with law enforcement using Facebook, YouTube, Twitter, blogs, podcasts, and tools. The International Association of Chiefs of Police (2014) noted that 94 percent of law enforcement agencies are using some type of social media to enhance their crime solving abilities and to encourage public participation in prevention activities.

The courts have also embraced new technologies. Video arraignments and the use of distance technologies for other preliminary hearings is becoming commonplace in many jurisdictions. Instead of transporting accused individuals who are being held in jail to the courthouse for every hearing and appearance, the accused sits in a room at the jail that has been outfitted with a video camera while the judge (and often other court actors such as attorneys and court reporters) remain at the courthouse and the entire proceeding takes place online. This saves time and cost associated with transportation and personnel time, and allows for processing more cases. Another use of technology by the courts is to enhance the place of victims in the court process and proceedings. Given the orientation of the system to protect the rights of offenders, victims are often ignored or relegated to an afterthought. The system often fails to keep victims notified of important events in their cases, including case dates, sentencing hearings, and parole hearings. One major effort to address these problems has been the development of the Statewide Automated Victim Information and Notification (SAVIN) program. This system allows victims and witnesses to identify how (and if) they want to be kept notified about every event related to a case's processing. This system uses automated phone and email notifications.

The correctional system has also embraced technology. Perhaps the best example is the use of electronic monitoring systems (EMS). EMS is an enhancement of home confinement that responds to the lack of space to hold in jail everyone awaiting trial and the need for greater supervision for those released on probation or parole after conviction. This technology dates to the late 1980s, but was initially limited due to the use of land line phone technology and the cost of the systems. While costs are still a concern, the technology has advanced in a number of ways making use of EMS more palatable. EMS systems are not tied to wired phone systems any longer. Today, they typically use wireless phone technology. Another recent innovation making EMS more useful is the coupling of the system to global positioning system (GPS) technology. The use of GPS allows the system to track the exact location of the individual on EMS in real time or retrospectively. EMS is used in countries around the world, and more than 110,000 individuals are on EMS in the United States (DeMichele and Payne 2009).

As technology changes, its impact on the criminal justice system will continue to grow. Advances in technology have increased in speed over the past several decades and there is no indication that they will slow down. Indeed, it is likely the opposite will occur and impact individuals, agencies and society in multiple ways. Certainly, the move to a cashless society has opened the way to new forms of theft, including general identity theft. The criminal justice system can also use the new technologies to improve its functioning and protect society.

FISCAL AUSTERITY AND CRIMINAL JUSTICE

The criminal justice system undergoes changes in response to fiscal pressures and constraints placed on it. The changing fiscal landscape may be the result of general societal economic changes (such as the 2008 recession or the shutdowns of the COVID-19 pandemic) which can curtail tax revenues available to the public sector at all levels. Political change can also lead to both reductions and expansions in public services.

Privatization made inroads into the state's monopoly over the criminal justice system. Burgeoning prison populations resulted from the "get tough on crime" ideology of the 1980s and 1990s. One of the first resorts of states with excess inmate populations was to send their prisoners to other states with unused beds and cells. (This is slightly different from the informal policy of "bus therapy," sending troublesome prisoners from place to place to disrupt their criminal activities and social networks.) The rise of private prisons coincided with outsourcing in the private sector and the use of contractors for logistical support services (among others) by the military.

Sending prisoners to privately run facilities was not only consistent with the reigning political ideology of the time but also made it possible to shift costs away from the state. This can be done in many ways. First, shifting work to the private sector avoids the expensive pension systems of unionized state workers. Second, this shift moves other expenses (e.g., food, utilities) to a private bidding system outside public scrutiny. Third, the private sector can build facilities unencumbered by the demands of state bidding rules and regulations, thus speeding up the process and saving funds. Issues over safety and cost effectiveness have led to state and federal decisions to either cease or scale back on the use of private prisons.

Privatization is also evident in policing. The use of private police officers tends to be an augmented service, with their jurisdiction overlapping that of the public police and sheriffs' departments. They are often employed by gated communities or resorts or other recreational areas. To this point, none has played a significant role in municipal policing in any larger jurisdictions. Unlike their private-security predecessors, however, private police are certified law enforcement officers, empowered by their respective state with powers of arrest. While their jurisdiction tends to be linked contractually to the property rights of their employers, they are actual police officers, better trained and more professional than the "rent-a-cop" stereotype of security guards.

To this point, private courts are restricted to the traditional tribal and ecclesiastical venues, not general criminal justice matters. The restorative justice movement often provides an alternative to public court proceedings, but always with the authorization of the courts themselves. Prosecution remains a possibility should restorative efforts fail or one of the parties choose to withdraw from the process.

Fiscal austerity affects the entire criminal justice system, as well as the social agencies that work with system clientele. The federal largesse of previous decades has shriveled: though operational grants are still available through the Bureau of Justice Assistance, and the National Institute of Justice still provides research and seed money for innovation, far fewer funds are available for special projects like DUI checkpoints.

Police often take drastic steps to maintain core services in the face of austerity. Many tasks once done by sworn officers have been "civilianized" or outsourced. Dispatch services are mostly performed by civilians, and in many cases they are regional rather than locality-based. Crime scene security and prisoner transport duties are conducted by private companies. Increasingly, crime scene technicians are specialists rather than uniformed police officers.

State and local agencies are also affected by deferred maintenance programs, reduced training, fewer equipment upgrades, reduction in benefits, hiring freezes, and even layoffs. Prosecutors' offices have fewer equipment costs, but loss of investigator positions and clerical staff can curtail case preparation, curtailing options for plea negotiations.

Fiscal austerity on the part of states and localities is already disrupting the traditional fixed-benefit pension systems of generations past, even though the private sector abandoned them decades ago. While union contracts have held firm to the model because of their political clout, defined benefits often give way to defined-contributions packages in the public sector as well. Another benefit issue is the cost of medical insurance, and that is also still in flux at the state and national levels. The attractiveness of benefits packages affects the pool of potential candidates, possibly mitigating other potential advantages (a better-educated workforce in public service, for instance) of the contemporary jobless recovery.

It is not just the formal criminal justice agencies that are affected by economic austerity: the social services agencies that formally or informally are partners in the justice system are being hurt as well. Victims' services, prisoner reintegration programs, and rehabilitation services are all vital to the overall effectiveness of the system. As the public's willingness to fund "soft" services deteriorates, there is a tendency to revert to the older investment in punishment as a crime deterrent, despite the lack of clear evidence of its effectiveness and the lack of funds to carry out punishment (whether incarceration or effective community supervision) on the scale called for in the get-tough-on-crime era.

CRIMINAL JUSTICE REFORM

Criminal justice is constantly facing and adapting to new issues. In some cases this may emerge from individual events, such as the 9/11 terrorist attacks the prompted the reconfiguration of many agencies, or from a problem receiving a great deal of media attention, such as the problem of opioid addiction which led to police training in the administration of Naloxone. There have also been point in time where large changes have been made that have led to huge changes across the criminal justice system. Two examples of major changes have been the 1967 President's Commission and the 1994 Crime Bill.

The 1967 President's Commission on Law Enforcement and the Administration of Justice is a prime example of large-scale change in criminal justice. The Commission addressed the growing crime problem and social unrest in the country by investigating causes of crime and all components of the criminal justice system. The multivolume Commission report looked at the causes of crime, the measurement of crime, the actions of all components of the system (including the police, courts, corrections, and juvenile justice), organized crime, drug usage, technology and criminal justice, and other topics. This led to many major change including the development of the National Crime Victimization Survey, the Law Enforcement Assistance Administration and the Law Enforcement Education Program, improved training of the police, the precursors to the Office of Justice Programs and the National Institute of Justice, the development of new technologies for criminal justice agencies, and other important initiatives.

The Violent Crime Control and Law Enforcement Act of 1994, also known as the 1994 Crime bill, ushered in a wave of changes to criminal justice. This Act was passed at a time when getting tough on crime was the approach pushed by both the system and society. One major provision was the expansion of the federal death penalty to cover an additional 60 offenses, including terrorist acts and narcotics offenses. The institution of three-strikes policies (mandating sentences of life in prison for those convicted of their third conviction) was also part of the Act. Another large change was the establishment of the Office of Community-Oriented Policing Services (COPS) and the funding of 100,000 new police officers across the country. The Act also included the Violence Against Women Act targeting the prevention and responses to violence against women. Yet another component was the elimination of funding for college education for inmates.

It appears likely that some type of major criminal justice reform is on the horizon at the time of this writing. A number of things presage such reform. The most notable factor is the deaths of African American suspects at the hands of police officers that have been prominently displayed in the media and the subsequent Black Lives Matter movement. These events have led to calls to "defund the police" or disband police departments. While it appears unlikely that massive defunding or disbanding of the police will occur, it is likely that greater funding and emphasis will be placed on police actions and training that focus on cultural diversity and sensitivity, alternatives to arrest and the use of de-escalation, empathy, mental health awareness, and similar response modalities. Change may also advance in the area of disproportionate minority contact. While some efforts have been made in this area, more needs to be done and the Black Lives Matter movement has shed additional light on disproportionate representation in the criminal justice system. Shifts in the law that recognized the disparate impact on three-strikes laws are also a precursor to addressing disproportionate minority contact. Changing technology, particularly in the use of DNA in the identification of offenders and its use in court, has led to more and more convictions being overturned and growing questions about the need to make changes in court process and procedure.

There is little doubt that questions have been raised about the actions and mandates of the criminal justice system. Changes have been made and there are calls for greater reform. Whether any reforms will appear as separate initiatives or as a major package of reforms like the 1967 President's Commission or the 1994 Crime Bill is unknown. The timing of any changes is also up in the air but will probably be determined over the coming year.

CRIMINAL JUSTICE AS A PROCESSING SYSTEM

How society controls crime is suggested by the different philosophies of criminal justice. These philosophies sometimes contradict each other, and most policies are usually a balance of different philosophies. Such contradiction is unavoidable in a democracy, but discretionary decision-making allows criminal justice actors to implement these sometimes-competing policies while at the same time the system still functions. Usually these philosophies are enacted by legislators as substantive laws. Procedural laws prescribe the methods by which governmental bodies may enact laws and are important because they limit many of the government's powers and thus dictate and constrain the creation and implementation of criminal justice policy. Lawmaking is in turn influenced and constrained by local politics, the media, and public sentiments and voting patterns.

Citizens are the true gatekeepers of the criminal justice system. When they choose to report crimes is a reflection of their belief or philosophy on what society should address. Their actions serve as the inputs for the system. Police officers and police agencies make discretionary decisions concerning what laws to need to be enforced and when to make arrests. These decisions by police officers and agencies are influenced by the communities they serve and by laws and policies. Multiple courts and t jurisdictions mean there are differences in the policies that are created and the decisions made. Prosecutors decide when to release an arrestee without charge or to press charges and when to engage in plea bargaining. Judges and defense attorneys, with their different backgrounds and institutional allegiances, influence the court process and the cases and sentences that result from court action. Prisons, jails, and community corrections all face different forces that influence their actions and beliefs about their roles. Their policies and decisions are influenced by the philosophies of criminal justice (such as the value of rehabilitation as opposed to incapacitation). These philosophies compete with each other for resources and sometimes contradict each other. Compromises often result as actors carry out competing mandates in their day-to-day work.

Discretion, technology, fiscal austerity, and criminal justice reform all play a role in the day-to-day processes of the different criminal justice components. At the same time, each agency or component brings issues, beliefs, and philosophies to the decision-making process. In the end, what we view as the criminal justice system is a complex web of social interactions among a myriad of system actors and the thousands of criminal justice organizations, as the system pursues multiple, competing, and sometimes contradictory goals. Philosophies are crafted into laws and policies, system actors strive to implement these laws and policies via their discretionary decisions, and all of this takes place within an ever changing set of societal issues and demands.

GLOSSARY

A

actus reus the act done; the criminal act

adjudication In the juvenile court, the counterpart to finding guilt or innocence and sentencing in the adult court.

administrative law Law that is created and enforced by administrative bodies.

adversarial system of justice A system, like the criminal justice system, in which two opposing parties (prosecution and defense) work with a neutral body (the judge) to determine the outcome of a case.

aftercare The juvenile justice system equivalent to adult parole.

alternative dispute resolution An alternative to the traditional criminal court, in which victims, offenders, and others work together to settle disputes outside of the criminal justice system.

appeal The opportunity for defendants to challenge their convictions, sentences, and other issues in order to ensure that their cases were handled properly.

appellate courts Court that do not have the jurisdiction to conduct trials. They hear cases on appeal from lower courts; they do not hold trials.

appellate jurisdiction Courts with this jurisdiction hear cases on appeal from lower courts; they do not hold trials.

arraignment Stage of a criminal case where defendants are required to enter pleas to the formal charges against them, usually after a **preliminary hearing** or **grand jury hearing.**

assembly-line justice Term used to describe the fast and efficient movement of cases in and out of the court system.

assigned counsel A court-appointed attorney paid on a case-by-case or hourly basis to act as defense counsel.

B

back-door options Early release options such as parole to relieve prison overcrowding

background checks A standard part of the hiring process in any law enforcement agency. Telephone and in-person contacts with references, criminal history checks, and the like are made to assure that candidates have the appropriate ethics, mentality, and skills to perform a job and to verify that all information provided by the candidates' applications is accurate.

bail A system requiring a guarantee by defendants to return for court dates. Judges decide whether defendants must pay a certain amount of money to be released prior to trial or must be detained due to flight risk, public safety, and so forth.

bailiffs Typically, law enforcement officers who maintain order in the courtroom.

beat integrity The philosophy and administrative priority of assigning specific officers to specific beats for long periods of time, to develop a comprehensive knowledge of the area and establish positive working relationships with the residents and merchants there; replaced an older system that moved officers around to many beats, frequently or haphazardly, in order to reduce the opportunities for corruption.

behavior modification A system that rewards positive behavior and punishes poor behavior as a means of changing or controlling behavior; typical approach used in institutions.

bench trial A trial without a jury, in which a judge hears the evidence and renders a verdict in a criminal case.

bills of attainder Policies that allow the imposition of punishment without a trial. This type of policy is unconstitutional according to the US Constitution.

blended sentencing A disposition that relies on both the juvenile and adult systems, such as when a youth begins his or her disposition in a juvenile facility and is automatically transferred to an adult facility after reaching the age of majority.

blue wall of silence The term for the refusal of police officers to report misconduct of other officers, usually out of a misguided sense of solidarity or a fear of social ostracism and denial of assistance ("backup") on duty. The blue wall is usually composed of nonoffending officers who know of elements of the misconduct, but refuse to "rat" on or testify against other officers, regardless of the seriousness of the offense, thus thwarting effective investigation of police misconduct and crimes committed by police officers.

boot camps Sometimes called **shock incarceration**, boot camps are short-term programs that are supposed to handle first-time, nonviolent offenders. They operate on a military model, with strict rules and discipline, physical training and conditioning, and counseling and education.

Boston Gun Project This project used an approach called **pulling levers**. Pulling levers simply sought to deter behavior by taking a zero-tolerance response with regards to any transgressions by any member of a gang. The entire gang was held responsible for the acts of all its members.

broken windows An informal theory of police responsibility for controlling low-level disorders and the relationship of disorder to more serious crime. First advanced by James Q. Wilson and George Kelling in an article in *The Atlantic Monthly* in 1982, the hypothesis asserted that order maintenance should be the primary police focus, not serious felony crime; reductions in serious crime would follow the reestablishment of civil order in the neighborhoods.

burden of proof Level of proof needed to find a defendant guilty of a crime, to issue search warrants, and so forth (for example, to obtain a conviction, a prosecutor must prove his or her case "beyond a reasonable doubt").

C

campus-based academies Police recruit training facilities that function like college campuses and are frequently located on such campuses. The academies may be self-contained, giving instruction only to new police officers, or may be part of an academic degree course of study, typically a two-year associate's degree. The instructional curriculum is similar to that of stress academies, but without the military boot-camp trappings.

case attrition Cases disappearing from the criminal justice system by being dropped, dismissed, and so forth.

case law Law created by judges through their interpretation of other types of laws.

chain of command A term referring to the command and supervision of the police organization. It is the sequence through which orders are given and information is relayed.

challenge for cause A method of removing jurors during jury selection for a legally prescribed cause (for instance, being a relative of the victim).

citizen patrols Patrols of an area by citizens acting as eyes and ears for the police.

civil abatement use of legal codes to fight gangs is to employ civil, rather than criminal, codes

civil gang injunctions court orders that prohibit certain behaviors linked to criminal activity

civil rights movement A long-standing attempt by the African American community to overturn the legal and social restrictions of Jim Crow segregation and the social attitude prevalent among whites that Blacks were inferior (a legacy of slavery). While the movement has been ongoing since the end of Reconstruction, it was most visible and powerful in the 1950s and 1960s, when televised conflicts with white police galvanized both the movement and attempts to reform the police.

civilian review A special process of handling complaints against police officers by having civilian boards, or mixed police and civilian boards, review the facts and adjudicate the complaint; highly unpopular with police officers. Civilian review boards (CRBs) may work in concert with Internal Affairs or independent of it; the scope of authority given to a CRB is determined locally through the political process. CRBs emerged from strong feelings of dissatisfaction with police internal review of complaints against "their own."

Classical school Eighteenth-century philosophy that contends that humans possess free will and are rational and thus make choices about how to behave. Advocates consider behavior a process whereby people weigh the costs of their actions and the benefits they expect to receive.

classification Review in which the needs and risk of the offender are evaluated to determine the best placement of that individual within the prison system.

close security A security classification representing a middle ground between **maximum** and **medium security**. Facilities with this classification may be used for individuals convicted of violent offenses who do not require a maximum-security setting or disruptive inmates who do not pose as great a physical threat to inmates or staff.

collateral attack A type of appeal that allows a prisoner to challenge a conviction or sentence after the first appeal is over.

collateral consequences Also known as *collateral costs*: more than monetary costs to governments and taxpayers expended due to mass incarceration practices.

common law English-based law that was known throughout the country and applied by local judges through the use of precedent.

community corrections The various sanctions and forms of supervision that occur within the community rather than in an institutional setting.

community-oriented policing The term devised for a reform movement that arose in the mid-1980s to ease racial tensions and increase police effectiveness in minority neighborhoods. The thrust of the movement was to break down old prejudices by placing officers in regular contact with citizens in nonemergency settings, building better information about community events and conditions, building mutual trust, and creating effective problem solving. The community-policing movement incorporates a wide range of tactical deployments, from walking beats to crime-prevention activities to community organizing. One of the features that distinguishes community policing from traditional law enforcement is a focus on a range of noncrime problems broadly known as "quality-of-life issues," in which police advocacy and leadership play more important roles than law enforcement.

community policing The current era of American policing, placing crime control on an equal footing with forging community partnerships and allowing communities greater ability to control their own affairs, incorporating crime prevention and crime analysis into an overall community effort to reduce crime and disorder.

community supervision A general term to denote a variety of circumstances and sanctions requiring an offender to abide by specific conditions in order to remain in the community rather than being placed in an institutional setting.

CompStat A management initiative of the New York City Police Department under Commissioner Bill Bratton in the 1990s. Named for a column in a crime statistics database, CompStat involved the use of up-to-date crime information to reinvigorate the NYPD's command staff's commitment to crime reduction. It was also criticized for the sometimes adversarial nature of the central administration's challenges to the precinct commands. The term *CompStat* has become synonymous with data-driven approaches to crime control and police accountability.

concerned parent role This approach often leads attorneys to push youths to admit to petitions in order to secure the help and assistance of the court.

concurrent cause two independent causes happen at the same time and either cause could have resulted in harm

conditions of supervision The specific requirements imposed by a court or correctional authority that an offender must agree to and abide by to remain in the community.

confidentiality In self-report surveys, a condition where the identity of a respondent is known by the researcher, but the researcher does not reveal that individual's identity. In confidential situations the information from a respondent can be traced back to an individual. Note that confidentiality differs from **anonymity.**

consent decrees Formal contracts between the US Department of Justice and local agencies or corporate entities to correct unlawful conditions. Usually an alternative to civil rights suits, consent decrees set out timetables and corrective measures to bring the agencies in line with acceptable practices.

constable An ancient English office of local police authority, with mandatory service on a rotating, annual basis under the 1285 Statute of Winchester; in contemporary America, a local office often attached to the court for service of papers and other writs; in modern-day England, a form of address to a police officer.

constitutional law Law that is found in the US Constitution and the various state constitutions.

contract cities Local municipalities who contact with the county sheriffs for a specified number of hours of service. Contracts guarantee basic police services while relieving smaller cities of part of the expense of maintaining their own departments.

convict leasing A Southern development that spread throughout the United States, where inmates were contracted out to work in the stone quarries and coal mines during the industrial era of punishment.

co-occurring disorders Refers to inmates who can be classified as having both substance abuse and mental health disorders.

correctional officers Individuals who supervise inmates in an institutional setting, sometimes referred to as guards.

corruption Generically, the misuse of a position of authority for personal gain. Police corruption in particular takes a variety of forms, from passive acceptance of gratuities to actively seeking bribes to accepting money from crime figures to destroy evidence or reveal police information. A subset, "corruption of noble cause," has emerged to describe the use of illegal means to achieve a legitimate crime-control end, with no personal benefit to the officers.

courtroom workgroup The collection of people who work in and around courthouses. The term *workgroup* is used because these people are employed by different organizations (prosecutor's offices, public defender's offices, probation, corrections, etc.) and the membership changes often, usually from one defendant's case to another.

crime-control model Philosophy of criminal justice that contends that the most important goal of the criminal justice system is to suppress crime. This goal is best achieved via the aggressive and quick apprehension, trial, and processing of criminals.

crime prevention A series of related actions, often promoted by the police, that reduce individual or collective risk of crime victimization. Target hardening through the use of locks or barriers, personal self-defense, property-marking records that reduce the resale value of stolen goods, collective actions such as Neighborhood Watch or other community organizing, educational programs in schools, and many more all fall under the crime prevention label.

crime rate The number of crimes committed (or reported to authorities), usually expressed as the number of events per 1,000 or 100,000 people (or residents) per year.

criminal law definition a definition in which a delinquent is any juvenile who violates the criminal code

cruel and unusual punishment Prohibits not only barbarous modes of punishment, like the rack and thumb screws, but also any punishment that is grossly disproportionate to the crime at hand.

D

dark figure of crime Term used by criminologists to refer to the total number of unreported crimes.

day–evening centers Provide educational programming, treatment programs, or other activities during the day, but send the youths home at night.

day reporting centers Nonresidential programs that require offenders to report on a daily or very frequent basis to a reporting center.

deadly force Force that has the potential for causing the death of an individual being apprehended.

death penalty Sanction that is reserved for the most serious offenders utilized in 38 states and in the federal system.

defense attorneys Attorneys with the job of defending the accused against prosecution by the government.

deinstitutionalization The release of individuals in secure care back into the community for supervision or outright release.

delinquency Term referring to juvenile misbehavior that could refer to criminal acts or status offenses.

detached worker program This type of program sought to place gang workers directly with the gangs in the communities. The workers were to spend time with the gangs and try to redirect their activities to noncriminal behavior.

detectives Investigators who do not answer calls. Their time is spent interviewing witnesses and following up on leads in unsolved crime cases. Detectives may specialize in a certain type of crime (homicide, burglary, robbery, sex crimes, etc.) or conduct all kinds of criminal investigation.

detention In the juvenile system, detention is the counterpart to the bail decision in adult court.

detention centers Facilities designed to hold a variety of offenders for a relatively brief period of time, usually for less than one year.

determinate sentencing Also referred to as "flat" or "fixed" sentences, results in a defendant knowing how long his or her sentence will be when a judge imposes it.

deterrence Contends that punishments should prevent crime by making potential offenders aware of the costs of crime. In effect, potential offenders will know that punishment will ensue if a crime is committed; thus, they will refrain from engaging in crime. Deterrence argues that the costs of crime outweigh its benefits.

deviance Human behaviors or actions that are considered by others to be wrong, bad, or inappropriate.

direct cause occurs when an individual's behavior is the direct cause of harm; essentially, but for an individual's behavior, harm would not have occurred

direct file refers to the ability of prosecutors to directly file the case in adult court

discretion It is not possible to write a law or rule that will cover every possible situation the police might encounter. The police combine their knowledge with the array of verbal and nonverbal information that attends each unique situation, make an accurate judgment about what's going on (the "situational exigencies"), and decide on the proper response.

disposition The equivalent to a sentence in an adult court.

disproportionate minority contact (DMC) Recognizes the overrepresentations of minority youth at almost all stages of the juvenile system, including arrest, court referral, detention, and probation.

district courts The trial courts of the federal system.

diversion programs Programs available for some first-time, youthful, or non-violent offenders that temporarily stop the prosecution of their cases in exchange for participation in preapproved programs. Upon successful completion of a program, the original charges are dismissed.

domestic violence courts Created to address a number of problems faced by the courts in domestic situations. For example, many domestic violence cases involve divorce proceedings or child custody issues, which can result in numerous cases being brought before different judges.

double jeopardy Constitutional provision that prohibits multiple prosecutions for the same offense.

drug courts Courts that focus on rehabilitation and treatment for drug offenders instead of criminal punishment.

dual court system Represented by the various state court systems and the federal courts. Individuals may be prosecuted by either state or federal courts (and sometimes both).

dual-entry tracks A term most often applied to progressive sheriffs' departments that hire separately for jail deputies and for patrol (road) deputies. It replaces the older single-entry system where all deputies began their careers as jail deputies and then moved up to patrol. *See also* **single-entry tracks**.

due-process model As opposed to the **crime-control model**, a model of criminal justice that emphasizes procedures and guidelines that the government must follow in order to adjudicate defendants.

duress another excuse from criminal liability. In this situation, a person must be under threat of death or serious bodily injury that causes the individual to commit a crime

E

electronic monitoring Use of technology to monitor offenders who are released into the community before trial or as a condition of a home-confinement sentence.

ex post facto A retroactive law that is prohibited by the US Constitution.

excessive bail Unreasonably high bail, prohibited by the Eighth Amendment to the US Constitution.

excessive fines Financial punishment deemed to be disproportionate to the offense, prohibited by the Eighth Amendment to the US Constitution.

exclusionary rule A constitutional protection for citizens against unlawful police actions; the rule requires that any evidence obtained illegally must be excluded from criminal trials. Originally a federal-level rule only, it was applied to the states and to local police departments in the landmark 1961 Supreme Court decision *Mapp v. Ohio*.

F

family group conferencing (FGC) Includes family members, close friends, and other support groups of the victims and offenders in mediation conferences. Facilitators lead the participants through a discussion of the facts of the cases, the impact of the events on all parties, the feelings of all participants toward the actions and the offenders, and the development of mutually agreed-upon resolutions.

felony Term applied to the most serious of crimes (including murder, robbery, and rape). Felonies usually carry a possible prison term of greater than one year.

Field Training (Officers and Programs) A process by which a newly hired police recruit makes the transition from academy learning to the street, under the tutelage and observation of an experienced police officer. Most programs involve a gradual increase in responsibilities, a formal grading process, and a series of tests on duty to determine whether the new officer is in fact an appropriate hire for the agency or should be dismissed because of conditions not revealed by the initial hiring process.

fines Punishment that requires payment of a monetary sum to the court. Usually used in conjunction with probation.

first responders Public employees in the emergency services who are the first to be called to the scene of an emergency, including Fire and EMS (Emergency Medical Services, ambulance and first-aid workers). Police patrol officers are considered first responders, while detectives and other investigators are not.

force continuum A training guide for police use of force, linking police levels of force to specific actions by the citizens.

Foreign Intelligence Surveillance (FISA) Court Federal court created by Congress in the Foreign Intelligence Surveillance Act of 1978. This court has jurisdiction over electronic surveillance of foreign agents.

Fourteenth Amendment Due-process clause specifies that no state shall "deprive any person of life, liberty, and property without due process of law."

G

Gang Resistance Education and Training (G.R.E.A.T.) Program involves using police officers to teach antigang, antiviolence lessons in middle schools. The thrust of G.R.E.A.T. is to provide youths with the necessary skills for identifying high-risk situations and resisting the peer pressure and allure to take part in gangs and gang activity.

general deterrence A subtype of deterrence theory that predicts that those contemplating the commission of a crime will be influenced by their understanding of the certainty and severity of the punishment and the speed at which that punishment will be administered. General deterrence contends that when laws entail sufficient certainty and severity and the punishment is quickly meted out, potential criminals will not commit crimes.

grand jury A proceeding featuring citizens who assess a prosecutor's evidence in order to determine if there is enough evidence to proceed to trial.

group hazard hypothesis The claim that society responds to group transgressions more strongly than to individual violations; thus, youth gangs are singled out for intervention more often than individual offenders.

H

habeas corpus Protection that allows defendants to challenge the legality of their confinement or incarceration.

halfway houses A term usually used to describe facilities that house recently released inmates or inmates in the transition process of approaching full release and that assist with their transition back into the community. May be privately operated or state-run.

harassment A common complaint against the police by youths and minority groups, who resent being the subject of police attention—which they consider extralegal attention—while going about their law-abiding business. Also, sometimes used by the police in sardonic fashion to describe their focused attention on known criminals and crime-producing locations.

HAZMAT An acronym for "hazardous materials," a broad category of harmful substances ranging from toxic chemicals to explosives to nuclear waste. First responders who respond to HAZMAT emergencies require special equipment and training.

home confinement The restriction of offenders to their residences except for preapproved activities. May be enforced by the use of various electronic monitoring equipment that can assist officials in knowing offenders' whereabouts. Also known as *house arrest.*

home detention Involves ordering youths to remain at home at all times, unless given permission by the court to leave the premises.

houses of refuge Early institutions handling youths in need, particularly the poor, which focused on education, skill training, religious training, hard work, and discipline.

hung jury The term used when a trial jury cannot come to a unanimous verdict.

I

impartial trial Protection that hopes to ensure an unbiased and neutral jury at trial.

incapacitation A philosophy of criminal justice that argues that the role of the criminal justice system is to separate or segregate criminals from the rest of society in order to protect it. If known criminals are removed from society, advocates argue, there will be less crime. Unlike **retribution**, incapacitation does not see segregation as a form of punishment. Rather, incapacitation also differs from **rehabilitation** in that it does not necessarily advocate treating offenders.

incorporation The process of requiring states to adopt the protections found in the federal Bill of Rights.

indeterminate sentencing A sentencing scheme that is characterized by a range of punishments; the exact amount of time served is determined by the parole board.

industrial era The period in correctional history when inmates spent their confinement involved in private and state industry craft- or factory-oriented labor, worked on state-run canal and road projects, and even constructed prisons.

informal adjustment Decision to handle youths in a manner that does not involve full formal court processing.

informal social control One of two methods by which society and the other individuals that make up society influence behavior (the other method is called *formal social control*). Examples of informal social control include staring, scorn, the cold shoulder, shunning, and telling people that they are doing something wrong. Societies rely very heavily upon informal social control to keep people in conformity.

initial appearance The first appearance of a defendant before a judge after arrest, when the defendant is notified of the charges against him or her, a bail decision, and the right to counsel. Also known as *first appearance*.

intake decision The juvenile system's counterpart to filing charges or a grand jury indictment in the adult system; at intake the decision is made to file a petition with the court to hear the case or to handle the youth in another way.

intensive supervision probation A form of probation (or parole) that requires more frequent contacts between offenders and their supervising officers than regular probation and typically involves more conditions of supervision.

intermediate sanctions A general term used to describe a variety of sanctions that fall between regular probation and jail or prison in severity.

Internal Affairs A special investigative unit within a police department, charged with investigating complaints against police officers. The current trend is toward redefining the unit as an "Office of Professional Responsibility" or similar title; other, less printable names are applied to it by police officers under investigation.

involuntary intoxication a defense in all criminal offenses due to the nature of the intoxication; an individual may not know that he or she had ingested the drug; an individual may be forced to consume a drug under duress; the intoxicating substance that was ingested by an individual may have unforeseeable side effects

J

jails Facilities designed to hold a variety of offenders for a relatively brief period of time, usually less than one year.

john details A form of sting operation directed against street prostitution in which undercover police officers pose as prostitutes to arrest "johns," men who solicit prostitutes for sex.

judges Individuals who are considered neutral figures among the courtroom workgroup. They make a number of decisions ranging from issuance of warrants to sentencing defendants.

judicial review The power of courts to declare laws unconstitutional.

judicial waiver Requires a waiver hearing in front of a judge who determines the suitability of removing the case to the adult court.

just desserts Appropriate punishment for a crime; an element of retribution.

justification A defense to criminal liability that states that an offender was justified in committing a crime (for example, self-defense).

K

Kansas City Preventive Patrol Experiment The first randomized test of police patrol's effectiveness as a deterrent of crime; preliminary results indicated that the number of police officers had little or no impact on crime or citizens' perceptions; subsequent developments in the field, notably the Minneapolis Hot Spots of Crime experiment, have refocused the issue with different results.

L

law compliance The voluntary observance by citizens of the requirements of law.

law enforcement The application of deterrence, rapid response, investigation, arrest, and prosecution against those who would or do violate the criminal law. Also applied to violators of traffic laws and local ordinances.

legal aid A form of appointed counsel that is considered nonprofit and is usually found in larger cities.

legislative waiver The legislature has dictated, through a statute, that certain youths must be tried in the adult court; the juvenile court is excluded from hearing the case. *See also* **statutory exclusion.**

M

mala in se Behaviors that are considered inherently bad and must be prohibited and punished (for example, murder).

mala prohibita Behaviors that are considered problematic, but not necessarily bad (for example, gambling).

mass incarceration The incarceration of larger and larger numbers of individuals serving longer prison sentences.

master jury list A list of individuals in the community deemed eligible for jury service, usually those who are registered voters or who possess drivers' licenses.

maximum-security prisons A prison classification that represents the highest level of security in many states, typically holding the most violent and disruptive prisoners in those jurisdictions without supermax facilities. Movement within such facilities is limited.

medium-security prisons A classification of prisons that hold a diverse inmate population and can have a variety of architectural styles. Inmates may have some degree of movement within the institutions during certain times of the day and participate in a range of activities.

mens rea The intent or "guilty mind" behind the commission of a crime.

mental capacity A defense to criminal liability in which offenders' mental states can reduce or absolve them of liability (for example, insanity).

mental-health courts Courts that work with corrections officials and the community to assist defendants who suffer from mental illness.

merit selection A form of judicial appointment in which a state governor selects a judge to serve a specified amount of time (usually one year) and asks voters to either retain or replace the judge at the end of that period.

minimum-security prisons A prison classification representing the most open and least restrictive type of institution. These facilities can house prisoners convicted of nonviolent offenses, those who pose a minimal security risk, and those nearing final release and allow the greatest freedom of movement for housed inmates.

Minneapolis Domestic Violence Experiment Project that provided evidence that arrests had a greater deterrent effect on subsequent marital violence than police believed, forging a new police response to a widespread social problem.

misdemeanor A class of less serious crimes, usually involving punishment of less than one year in prison. Misdemeanors often have different levels of seriousness (such as misdemeanor one, misdemeanor two, etc.).

M'Naghten Rule Under this rule, individuals must prove that they were in such a state of mind that they could not know what they were doing or that they did not know that what they were doing was wrong.

Monitoring the Future Survey A self-report survey that includes many more serious offenses than earlier self-report surveys and elicits significantly fewer positive responses. It includes questions on hitting teachers, group fighting, use of weapons, robbery, and aggravated assault.

multijurisdictional task forces Composite organizations made up of representatives of law enforcement personnel from many agencies across a wide geographical area that may include representatives from state and federal agencies. Task forces concentrate on crime problems that extend far beyond the jurisdictional boundaries of any single agency, such as organized crime, drug distribution networks, and counterterrorist intelligence work. Sometimes called *regional task forces*, *multijurisdictional* is the current preferred term, recognizing federal and state participation.

mutual aid Formal agreements between and among police agencies to assist each other in times of need. A system of legal compacts that provide law enforcement authority and civil protection to officers who are called upon to assist in jurisdictions other than their own.

N

National Incident-Based Reporting System (NIBRS) Replaces the UCR Summary Reporting System and provides much more detailed information on 23 categories of crimes with 52 total offenses.

National Youth Survey (NYS) Self-report survey that included many more serious offenses than other surveys and elicited significantly fewer positive responses.

needs principle one of the three principles of effective classification; two types of needs:: general needs which are more like deficiencies in conduct or life, such as lack of employment or educational skills, substance abuse problems, and relationship issues and criminogenic needs, which are anti-social attitudes, anti-social friends, substance abuse, lack of empathy, and impulsive behavior

Neighborhood Watch An organization for citizens to work together for community-based self-help activities.

net widening Term used to describe circumstances in which a correctional program is inadvertently used for a larger or different population than the one originally intended.

new-generation jails (NGJs) Newer facilities, often built to replace or modify existing jails, that house fewer inmates in what are known as pods or modules that contain anywhere from 16 to 30 separate cells with one or two inmates per cell.

new-offense violations Criminal offenses that violate offenders' community-supervision sanctions.

nonpartisan election A method of electing state judges in which candidates do not indicate a party affiliation on the ballot.

nonsecure detention The placement of youths in group homes, halfway houses, foster care, or other community-based alternatives to a secure facility.

nullification Refusal to enforce the law and sanctions against children.

O

official statistics One of three types of data society gathers on crime. Official statistics are gathered by or from criminal justice institutions and usually involve crimes brought to the attention of these institutions. The most famous of these official statistics are the FBI's Uniform Crime Reports (UCR), which record the number of crimes reported to the police and the number of arrests police make. *See also* **self-report statistics** and **victimization studies**.

once/always provision Once a youth has been adjudicated in adult court, the youth is permanently under the adult court's jurisdiction.

order maintenance A form of police activity that targets conduct that is less serious than predatory crime, but still disturbs the quality of life of citizens; generally low-level police interventions encourage law compliance, but law enforcement techniques may be used when necessary, to ensure general compliance with expected forms of conduct: "local rules" about the use of parks, loud music, self-expression through graffiti, and a wide range of other social expectations and violations.

original jurisdiction Jurisdiction in which a court serves as the entry point for cases, typically for initial appearances, trials, and so forth.

P

parens patriae Basic philosophy of the juvenile court emphasizing a role of the state as parent. The philosophy grew out of the English Chancery Court, which was tasked with looking after the property rights of orphaned children, among other things.

parole supervision The supervision of offenders who have been released from correctional institutions prior to the completion of their maximum terms of incarceration and must abide by their conditions of supervision to remain in the community. Used in jurisdictions with indeterminate sentencing.

partisan election A method of electing state judges in which candidates indicate a party affiliation on the ballot.

patrol A form of police deployment that puts officers on the streets as a visible presence, both to deter criminals and reassure law-abiding citizens and to discover crimes and unsafe conditions that require police intervention; although most patrolling is done in police cars, other types of patrol such as motorcycles, bicycles, and foot patrols are common.

penitentiary era The period in correctional history when a formal penal system was developed that relied heavily on incarceration as punishment.

peremptory challenge A method of removing jurors from the jury pool in which the prosecutors or defense attorneys do not specify reasons for the removal.

plea bargain An agreement between the prosecutor and defense attorney, approved by the judge, in which a defendant pleads guilty to a charge in hopes of lenient treatment.

police academy The "boot camp" for new or prospective police officers. A formal training setting in which the basic knowledge, skills, and responsibilities of police service are taught through formal instruction. Two models exist: **stress-based academies**, which emulate many features of the military boot camp, and **campus-based academies**, in which the training regimen is often integrated into an associate's degree program on the campus.

police subculture An outgrowth of studies of police in the 1960s, the concept of a "police subculture" assumes a broad allegiance to various philosophical beliefs and common concerns: danger, challenges to authority, political conservation (reactionary, in the 1960s), and the general division of the world into good and bad, with the police as a "thin blue line" separating tax-paying civilization from the anarchy of the criminal classes. In light of wholesale changes in the police occupation, including the inclusion of women and minorities and the changes in philosophy of **community-oriented policing** and **problem-oriented policing**, the assumptions of this notion are now being challenged.

Positivist school The Positivist school of criminal justice contends that human behavior is influenced by external conditions and situations that are beyond individuals' control; things such as poverty and abusive parenting influence the likelihood that a child will grow up poor and abusive as well.

postconviction review A form of appeal undertaken after the first appeal of right in which defendants challenge the constitutionality of the case process.

power shifts Special time slots, usually spanning the late evening and early morning hours, when additional police officers are on duty to handle expanded call load. Power shifts are often volunteer slots, selected by officers because of the greater likelihood of activity. They tend to be permanent or semipermanent hours, although some flexibility is possible in many agencies.

precedent The judicial practice of relying on previous decisions to make current ones, in order for the law to be stable and consistent.

precincts Administrative division of police agencies containing multiple beats and patrol areas; refers to both a specific geographical area and the police personnel assigned to it. A feature of larger communities where central command is cumbersome, precinct organization allows for more responsive policing services and a tighter chain of command for everyday operations. Both patrol and investigative services may be precinct based, though support services and some investigative units may operate from a single, central command center.

preliminary hearing The stage in a criminal case in which a judge determines if there is enough evidence against a defendant to proceed to trial. Used in place of a grand jury if a grand jury is not convened.

presentence investigation A report produced at the request of the court to assist in determining the most appropriate sentence for a particular offender.

preservice training In some states, individuals are permitted to seek their police-officer certification by putting themselves through a police-training academy before being hired by an agency; completion of the training does not give them police powers, however, which are only bestowed once they are hired by a municipality or other jurisdiction.

President's Commission on Law Enforcement and the Administration of Justice A widespread investigation of the deficiencies and needs of the criminal justice system in America ordered by President Johnson. Its February 1967 report, *The Challenge of Crime in a Free Society*, galvanized reform efforts and contributed to the passage of the 1968 Omnibus Crime Control and Safe Streets Act and to the creation of the **Law Enforcement Assistance Administration**.

principle of legality A principle of law that requires the existence of a law that prohibits conduct before a person can be found guilty of it.

prison A facility designed to hold offenders who have been convicted and sentenced to more than one year of incarceration of felony offenses.

prison programs Organized instruction designed to help offenders with rehabilitation, educational, and vocational needs and to guide the structure and activities involved in inmates' daily routines.

prison violence Coercive actions, threats made, and physical assaults against and between those living and working in prison.

prisoner reentry A general term used to denote a prisoner's transition from an institutional setting and the challenges in that process.

private police Uniformed security services that function as police protection for local interests. Some employ officers who have completed state-mandated police certification; others do not. The authority for private police typically derives from the property rights of their employers, but there are special legal provisions in some cases. Campus police officers serving colleges and universities, the Port Authority Police of New York and New Jersy Port Authority, railroad police, and others operate under particular legislative authorization.

private prison A correctional facility that is managed and operated by a private corporation.

pro bono A form of legal representation in which attorneys volunteer their time without compensation.

pro se A form of legal representation in which defendants serve as their own attorneys in court proceedings.

probable cause This standard is difficult to define, but the US Supreme Court, in *Brinegar v. United States* (1949), provided a definition: probable cause exists when "the facts and circumstances . . . [and] . . . reasonably trustworthy information [are] sufficient in themselves to warrant a man of reasonable caution in the belief that an offense has been or is being committed."

probation A form of community supervision in which an offender is allowed to remain in the community but must abide by certain restrictions, such as finding employment or abstaining from alcohol use.

problem-oriented policing An informal theory of police effectiveness first articulated by Herman Goldstein in 1979, which criticizes the police efforts at crime control as incident-based and emphasizing the means over the ends. It proposes the use of broader analysis to link multiple events that stem from common sources, redefining them as "problems" and bringing a wide spectrum of police and community resources to bear on the sources of the problem. The tactical equivalent is known as "problem solving," and both are united under the acronym POP.

procedural law The "how" of the law that outlines procedures that government officials must follow when adjudicating defendants.

property marking Prevention technique in which owners mark their property for protection and return of the property if stolen.

prosecutorial waiver The decision to try a juvenile in the adult court is made by the prosecutor, who has sole discretion in the matter.

prosecutors Attorneys who represent the state against the accused in criminal cases and are responsible for charging defendants and presenting evidence of their guilt.

proximate cause something other than the individual's behavior caused the harm, but the individual began the series of events that led to the harm

public defender A type of appointed counsel who provides indigent defense services only.

public trial Criminal proceeding open to the public, which acts as a "watchdog" over government practices. The right to a public trial is guaranteed by the Sixth Amendment to the US Constitution.

pulling levers Pulling levers simply sought to deter behavior by taking a zero-tolerance response with regards to any transgressions by any member of a gang. The entire gang was held responsible for the acts of all its members.

punishment Response given to those who violate group norms, rules, and laws.

R

racial profiling A contested practice, denied by the police but asserted by minority comunities, in which police aggressively stop Black and Hispanic motorists for trivial reasons in order to view and try to search their cars for drugs. It is premised upon an unsupported belief that minorities are more involved in the illegal drug trade than whites.

rebuttal when both sides in a trial have another chance to refute any evidence given by the other side

reentry The transition period of persons soon-to-be or recently released from prison or jail back into the community and involves providing services and assistance to these returning individuals and their families.

reform era The period in correctional history when a more humanitarian approach to the practice of incarceration was advocated. Practices such as purposeful labor, vocational and educational training, early release, and rewards for good behavior were utilized.

reformatories Early institutions for handling youths that largely supplanted houses of refuge. They focused on education, religious training, hard work, and discipline.

regional task forces *See* **multijurisdictional task forces.**

rehabilitation A philosophy of criminal justice that views criminals as "broken" and seeks to "repair" them by reformation and treatment. According to supporters of rehabilitation, once reformed, criminals will no longer engage in crime. Examples of rehabilitation include drug treatment, mental-health counseling, and job training.

residential community correctional program A general term used to describe a facility that houses offenders (typically for six months or less) who were either sentenced to or placed in the program as a condition of their community supervision. There is a considerable diversity in the populations served by these programs, the types of programs available, and the freedom of movement afforded residents.

responsivity principle one of the three principles of effective classification; amenability to a given treatment or programmatic approach, as well as to correctional placement

restorative (reparative) justice Programs that use interventions to return victims, offenders, and communities to their pre-offense states. They generally involve the voluntary participation of offenders, victims, and community members in seeking an outcome acceptable to all parties. Also known as *reparative justice.*

retribution A philosophy based on the belief that criminals should be punished because they have violated the law and that the criminal justice system exists to punish wrongdoers. Punishment should be commensurate with the harm committed by the criminal (an "eye for an eye"), which is in accord with the beliefs of those who follow the Classical school. Retribution, however, does not punish in order to prevent potential criminals from committing crime. Rather, advocates of retribution argue that punishment is the proper and just thing for a society to do, regardless of its effectiveness in preventing crime.

retributive era The period in correctional history when the response to law violators was more severe penalties and decreasing support for rehabilitative efforts, including lengthier prison sentences, more punitive sanctions such as "three strikes, you're out," and attempts to limit the discretion of judges and correctional administrators who make decisions on sentence lengths.

reverse waiver Where the adult court can return a waived youth to the juvenile system for processing.

right to counsel Protection guaranteed by the Sixth Amendment to the US Constitution that allows certain defendants the right to have attorneys assist them in their defense.

risk principle one of the three principles of effective classification; states that we only target offenders who are medium-high to high risk in terms of their propensity to reoffend

rotating shifts A means of providing around-the-clock police coverage in a manner that is fair to all employees. The burden of working the difficult hours of the midnight shift and weekends, and the benefits of working days, are equally distributed by assigning officers to work each shift in turn for a set period of time, then "rotating" or moving to another shift: days to evenings to midnights and then back to days to begin the cycle again. Rotating shifts tend to be defined in terms of weeks or months (usually no more than three months at the longest). Disruption of the "internal clock" of the body's circadian rhythm is one of the negative effects of rotating shifts. The alternative is **steady shifts** of longer duration.

S

safe havens Homes or businesses where youths can go for safety when they feel threatened, typically on the way to or from school.

school resource officers Sworn police officers who are assigned to schools or networks of schools, on either a full -or part-time basis. School resource officers usually work in uniform and monitor safety situations in the schools in addition to performing community-relations work with school-age children and with other school groups.

secure custody Involves several components: prisons must ensure that they are physically secure and can prevent the likelihood of escape and the introduction of contraband into the institution; reduce the occurrence of inmate assaults on staff; limit the frequency of inmate-on-inmate violence; and secure the efficient functioning of an institution.

secure detention The equivalent in the juvenile system of the local jail for adults.

self-incrimination Protection found in the Fifth Amendment to the US Constitution that specifies that an individual cannot be forced to confess to involvement in criminal activity.

self-report statistics One of three types of data collected on crime. Self-report statistics are gathered by asking people to report the number of times they have committed a crime during a set period of time. Self-report statistics are often better at discovering unreported crimes, victimless crimes, less serious crimes, and crimes where arrest is unlikely. *See also* **official statistics** and **victimization studies**.

sentencing guidelines Sentencing structures utilized in some states to determine sentences based on the offenses committed, the defendants' prior records, and other information in order to create more fairness and equity in sentencing.

service An umbrella term for a wide range of police assistance to citizens (e.g., directions, emergency transportation, escorts of funeral processions) that do not fall under either **law enforcement or order maintenance**.

sexting Involves the transmission of sexual images across an electronic medium.

sheriff The chief law enforcement officer of a country. Also an ancient office, first developed in England, and also an elected position and an office established in the state constitution of many states. Sheriffs' departments provide general policing services, court security and services, and correctional facilities of the country jail, although not all sheriffs' departments provide all three services.

shock incarceration Something used interchangeably with **boot camps**, but can also refer to a program in which judges or correctional authorities are given the authority to grant early conditional release (often after less than 180 days' incarceration) to low-risk offenders who had been originally sentenced to a term of incarceration and place them on a form of community supervision for the remainder of their sentences.

single-entry tracks A phrase referring to the practice of starting all sworn employees of an agency at the same level: patrol officer in police departments and frequently jail officer in sheriffs' departments. *See also* **dual-entry tracks**.

special conditions Conditions of community supervision that are tailored to the risks or needs of particular offenders and that are not used for all offenders in a jurisdiction. Common examples include drug treatment, work toward obtaining a GED, sex-offender counseling, and the payment of restitution to a victim.

specialized prisons Facilities that primarily house inmates with specific characteristics that pose unique challenges to institutions, such as substances abusers, sex offenders, and mentally handicapped or psychiatric prisoners.

specific deterrence One of the two types of deterrence. Specific deterrence refers to the deterring effect of punishing a particular offender and argues that offenders who are punished for a crime will be less likely to commit that crime again because they will remember the punishment they received the first time. *See also* **general deterrence**.

speedy trial Protection found in the Sixth Amendment to the US Constitution that guarantees that defendants have their trials commence within a certain amount of time after arrest.

split sentences Prisoners a period of probation following their release.

standard conditions Conditions of community supervision that are required for all offenders placed on community supervision in a given jurisdiction. Common examples include remaining law abiding, reporting to their supervising officers as directed, and notifying their officers of changes in residence.

state patrols/highway patrols Primarily enforce traffic laws on state highways; they have police powers and training, but no general police jurisdiction.

state police Police who have standard law enforcement duties and general jurisdiction throughout the state.

state training schools The juvenile justice system alternative to adult institutions.

status offense An action that is illegal only for juveniles. Typical status offences include the use of alcohol or tobacco, curfew violations, truancy, disobeying one's parents, running away, and swearing.

statutory exclusion The legislature has dictated, through a statute, that certain youths must be tried in the adult court; the juvenile court is excluded from hearing the case. *See also* **legislative waiver**.

statutory law The most common type of law, created by legislative bodies. Crimes and punishments are examples of statutory law.

steady shifts A means of providing around-the-clock police coverage that allows the body to adjust to shift work over longer periods, typically from six months to a year. Shift assignments are usually voluntary or assigned on a seniority-based lottery system. Officers spend a longer time on one shift.

sting operations Anticrime tactics in which police officers pose as criminals in order to arrest other criminal actors and discredit criminal market areas. Sting operations include officers posing as drug dealers in known drug locations, posing as prostitutes in areas known for street prostitution or gay cruising, posing as fences for stolen property, and impersonating other market-driven criminal enterprises.

stress-based academics Police recruit training facilities that function in a fashion similar to military boot camps, with a heavy emphasis on physical training, regimented military style discipline, and residential settings. The instructional curriculum is similar to that of the alternate model, **campus-based academics**, which forgo the boot-camp-style of inducing stress in favor of other values.

strict liability Crimes that do not require **mens rea**, or intent, for an individual to be held liable.

substantive law The "what" of the law. Describes what the law is rather than how the law should be enforced (i.e., **procedural law**).

supermax prisons The most restrictive and secure prisons in the country, generally reserved for the most incorrigible and dangerous prisoners in a correctional system.

supervised release A term of supervision following a prisoner's mandatory release from prison. While similar to parole, it is used in jurisdictions with **determinate sentencing** and does not involve a discretionary release by the parole authority.

supervision violations Violations of a condition of supervision. Depending on the seriousness of the violations, may result in consequences ranging from informal warnings to eventual revocation of offenders' community supervision and possible prison sentences.

T

technical violations Violations of conditions of supervision that do not involve the commission of new criminal offenses. Common examples include failure to pay financial conditions, failure to attend required treatment programs, or drug tests that indicate the use of illegal or prohibited substances.

teen courts (or youth courts) Rest on the restorative justice philosophy which seeks to help the offender, the victim, their families and friends, and society at large. These courts rely on youths to act as judges, attorneys, and jury members.

token economy Method for controlling or rewarding behavior in juvenile facilities. Youths receive points or tokens for acting appropriately and lose them for inappropriate behaviors. Tokens are good toward extra privileges or purchases from a store or vending machine.

transfer or waiver Process whereby youths are sent to the adult court for processing. It may take various forms, including judicial waiver, prosecutorial waiver, statutory exclusion/legislative waiver, or demand waiver.

transinstitutionalization Process whereby the mentally ill were first placed in secure confinement in a hospital setting, released, and then reconfined under the authority of the criminal justice system (i.e., prisons).

trial by jury Criminal proceedings heard by a jury made up of a defendant's peers. The right to a trial by jury is guaranteed by the US Constitution, but only applies to defendants facing six months' or more incarceration.

trial courts of general jurisdiction Usually, courts that handle felony trials.

trial courts of limited jurisdiction Courts that handle the early stages of criminal cases, such as first appearances, bail hearings, and so forth, as well as other cases such as traffic violations and minor civil actions.

troops Administrative divisions of a state police or state patrol agency, corresponding to precincts in local police departments. It refers to both a specific geographical area and the police personnel assigned to it.

U

Uniform Crime Reports (UCR) The most common official source of information on offending and offenders and reflect those offenses that came to the attention of the police.

use of force A general power of the police, used to gain compliance when other measures such as persuasion and direction fail. Use of force is a broad term covering any physical contact initiated by police against a resisting citizen, from a guiding hand to a firm restraining grip, to the application of chemical sprays, stun guns, or impact weapons like the nightstick, to the use of firearms. Use of firearms and some applications of impact weapons fall under the special category of **deadly force**, that which can produce death or serious bodily injury.

V

venire A group of individuals called for jury duty. After receiving a summons in the mail, these individuals must report to court for jury selection.

victimization studies One of the three types of crime data collected. Victimization studies ask people if they have been victims of a crime during a certain time period, and they mitigate some of the problems encountered by **official statistics** and **self-report statistics**.

victimless crime Class of crime in which there is no individual directly victimized, including crimes such as illegal drug use or underage drinking.

voir dire The questioning of potential jurors during jury selection to screen out those who may not be appropriate (for example, those who may be biased against the defendant or who may be relatives of the victim).

voluntary intoxication rarely an excuse to criminal liability and not usually a complete defense; it can be used to mitigate an individual's behavior and perhaps get charges reduced

W

wilderness programming Programs in which youths are placed in situations where they must learn survival skills and rely on one another to succeed. Can be either short-term or long-term and can take a variety of different forms, including sailing trips, wagon trains, or back-country camps. The underlying idea is to build self-esteem and show the youths that hard work and perseverance pay off.

Y

youthful offender statutes Provisions whereby the juvenile justice system can retain jurisdiction over individuals who were adjudicated in the system but have since passed the age of majority.

Z

zealous advocate role Emulate the role of an attorney found in the adult criminal court. The training of most attorneys and the move to more due-process concerns has resulted in attorneys fighting for their youthful clients, even when they know the child is guilty and in need of the help that could be provided by the court.

REFERENCES

Abadinsky, H. (1997). *Probation and parole: Theory and practice*, 6th ed. Upper Saddle River, NJ: Prentice Hall.

Adams, K. (1992). Adjusting to prison life. In M. Tonry (Ed.), *Crime and justice: A review of research*, 275–360. Chicago: University of Chicago Press.

Aday, R. (2003). *Aging prisoners: Crisis in American corrections*. Westport, CT: Praeger.

Alemagno, S., E. Shaffer-King, P. Tonkin, and R. Hammel. (2004). *Characteristics of arrestees at risk for co-existing substance abuse and mental disorder*. Washington, DC: National Institute of Justice.

Alm, S. A. (2015). HOPE Probation and the new drug court: A powerful combination. *Minnesota Law Review, 99*, 1665–96.

American Civil Liberties Union. (2012). *At America's expense: The mass incarceration of the elderly*. https://www.aclu.org/files/assets/elderlyprisonreport_20120613_1.pdf.

American Law Institute. (1962). *Model Penal Code*. Philadelphia: American Law Institute.

Anderson, J. (2003). *Public policymaking: An introduction*. Boston: Houghton Mifflin.

Andrews, D. A. (2006). Enhancing adherence to risk-need-responsivity: Making quality a matter of policy. *Criminology and Public Policy, 5*, 595–602.

Andrews, D. A., and J. Bonta. (2006). *The psychology of criminal conduct*. Cincinnati: Anderson Publishing.

Andrews, D., I. Zinger, R. Hoge, J. Bonta, P. Gendreau, and F. Cullen. (1990). Does correctional treatment work? A clinically relevant and psychologically informed meta-analysis. *Criminology, 28*, 369–404.

Aos, S., M. Miller, and E. Drake. (2006). *Evidence-based public policy options to reduce future prison construction, criminal justice costs, and crime rates*. Public Policy Report #06-10-1201. Olympia, WA: Washington State Institute for Public Policy.

Applegate, B., R. Surette, and B. McCarthy. (1999). Detention and desistance from crime: Evaluating the influence of a new generation jail on recidivism. *Journal of Criminal Justice, 27*, 539–48.

Argersinger v. Hamlin, 407 U.S. 25 (1972).

Arnold, E., P. Valentine, M. McInnis, and A. McNeece. (2000). Evaluating drug courts: An alternative to incarceration. In L. Mays and P. Gregware (Eds.), *Courts and justice: A reader*, 419–31. Prospect Heights, IL: Waveland Press.

Atkins v. Virginia, 536 U.S. 304 (2002).

Austin, J. (2014, April 5). *Key trends in national crime, arrests and jails* [video file]. https://www.youtube.com/watch?v=kAKat5OPA18.

Austin, J., and J. Irwin. (2001). *It's about time: America's imprisonment binge,* 3rd ed. Belmont, CA: Wadsworth Thompson.

Barron v. Baltimore (1833). 32 US 243 (1833)

Barrows, J., and C. R. Huff. (2009). Gangs and public policy: Constructing and deconstructing gang databases. *Criminology and Public Policy, 8,* 675–704.

Batson v. Kentucky, 476 U.S. 79 (1986).

Baumgartner, F. R., L. Christiani, D. A. Epp, K. Roach, and K. Shoub. (2017). Racial disparities in traffic stop outcomes. *Duke Forum for Law and Social Change, 9,* 21–54.

Bayens, G., J. Williams, and J. Smykla. (1997). Jail type makes a difference: Evaluating the transition from a traditional to a podular, direct supervision jail across ten years. *American Jails, 11,* 32–39.

Bazemore, G., and D. Maloney. (1994). Rehabilitating community service: Toward restorative service sanctions in a balanced justice system. *Federal Probation, 58,* 24–35.

Beck, A., and L. Maruschak. (2001). *Mental health treatment in state prisons, 2000.* Washington, DC: Bureau of Justice Statistics.

Belknap, J. (2001). *The invisible woman: Gender, crime, and justice.* Belmont, CA: Wadsworth.

Bennett, T., K. Holloway, and D. Farrington. (2008). The statistical association between drug misuse and crime: A meta-analysis. *Aggression and Violent Behavior, 13,* 107–18.

Berman, Mark (2017). Trump tells police not to worry about injuring suspects during arrest. *Washington Post,* July 28.

Bernfeld, G. A., D. P. Farrington, and A. W. Leschied (Eds.). (2001). *Offender rehabilitation in practice: Implementing and evaluating effective programs.* New York: John Wiley and Sons.

Biderman, A. D., and A. J. Reiss. (1967). On exploring the "dark figure" of crime. *The Annals, 374*(1), 1–15.

Bishop, D. M., and B. C. Feld. (2012). Trends in juvenile justice policy and practice. In B. C. Feld and D. M. Bishop (Eds.), *The Oxford handbook of juvenile crime and juvenile justice,* 898–926. New York: Oxford University Press.

Bittner, E. (1970). *The functions of the police in modern society: A review of background factors, current practices, and possible role models.* Cambridge, MA: MIT Press.

Black, D. (1981). *The manners and customs of the police.* New York: Academic Press.

Blackstone, W. (2002). *Commentaries on the laws of England.* Chicago: University of Chicago Press.

Blumstein, A. (1995). Crime and punishment in the United States over 20 years: A failure of deterrence and incapacitation? In P. Wikstrom, R. Clarke, and J. McCord (Eds.), *Integrating crime prevention strategies: Propensity and opportunity,* 123–40. Stockholm: National Council for Crime Prevention.

Bond, B. (2001). Principals and SROs: Defining roles. *Principal Leadership* (April), 51–55.

Bonta, J., S. Wallace-Capretta, and R. Rooney. (2000). A quasi-experimental evaluation of an intensive rehabilitation supervision program. *Criminal Justice and Behavior, 27,* 312–29.

Bostock v. Clayton County, Georgia _U.S._ (2020).

Bottomley, K. (1990). Parole in transition: A comparative study of origins, developments, and prospects for the 1990s. In M. Tonry and N. Morris (Eds.), *Crime and justice: A review of research*, 319–74. Chicago: University of Chicago Press.

Bottoms, A. (1999). Interpersonal violence and social order in prisons. In M. Tonry and J. Petersilia (Eds.), *Prisons*, 205–82. Chicago: University of Chicago Press.

Braga, A. A., D. M. Kennedy, A. M. Piehl, and E. J. Waring. (2001). *The Boston Gun Project: Impact evaluation findings*. Washington, DC: National Institute of Justice.

Brinegar v. U.S., 338 U.S. 160 (1949).

Brooks, K., and D. Kamine. (2003). *Justice cut short: An assessment of access to counsel and quality of representation in delinquency proceedings in Ohio*. Columbus: Ohio State Bar Association.

Brown, M. K. (1981). *Working the street: Police discretion and the dilemmas of reform*. New York: Russell Sage Foundation.

Brown, T. M. L., S. A. McCabe, and C. Wellford. (2007). *Global positioning system (GPS) technology for community supervision: Lessons learned*. Fall Church, VA: Noblis. https://www.ncjrs.gov/pdffiles1/nij/grants/219376.pdf.

Buckwalter-Poza, R. (2016). *Making justice equal*. Center for American Progress. https://www.americanprogress.org/issues/criminal-justice/reports/2016/12/08/294479/making-justice-equal/.

Burke, P. (1995). *Abolishing parole: Why the emperor has no clothes*. Lexington, KY: American Probation and Parole Association.

Burruss, G. W., and K. Kempf-Leonard. (2002). The questionable advantage of defense counsel in juvenile court. *Justice Quarterly, 19*, 37–68.

Bushnell, A. (2018, January 11). *Australia's Criminal Justice Costs: An International Comparison*. https://ipa.org.au/publications-ipa/research-papers/ipa-research-finds-australia-falling-behind-world-criminal-justice-costs-results-2.

Carp, R., and R. Stidham. (1990). *Judicial process in America*. Washington, DC: Congressional Quarterly Press.

Carroll, L. (1974). *Hacks, blacks, and cons*. Lexington, MA: Lexington Books.

Carson, E. A. (2020). *Prisoners in 2018*. Washington, DC: Bureau of Justice Statistics. https://www.bjs.gov/content/pub/pdf/p18.pdf.

Carson, E. A., and W. J. Sabol. (2012). *Prisoners in 2011*. Washington, DC: Bureau of Justice Statistics.

Casey, P., and D. Rottman. (2005). *Problem-solving courts: Models and trends*. Williamsburg, VA: National Center for State Courts.

Center for Substance Abuse Treatment. (2005). *Substance abuse treatment for adults in the criminal justice system*. Treatment Improvement Protocol (TIP) Series 44. Rockville, MD: Substance Abuse and Mental Health Services Administration.

Clark, J. (2009). U.S. and Europe jointly establish cyber-crime force. http://online.wsj.com/article/SB124632958157771629.html.

Clear, T., and H. Dammer. (2003). *The offender in the community*. Belmont, CA: Thompson Wadsworth.

Clear, T., P. Harris, and S. Baird. (1992). Probationer violations and officer response. *Journal of Criminal Justice, 20*, 1–12.

Cohen, S. (1985). *Visions of social control*. Cambridge, MA: Polity Press.

Coker v. Georgia, 433 U.S. 584 (1977).

Commonwealth v. Fisher, 213 Pa. 48 (1905).

Conley, J. (1980). Prisons, production, and profit: Reconsidering the importance of prison industries. *Journal of Social History, 14*, 257–75.

Cooper v. Pate (1964). 378 U.S. 546

Corbett, R. P. Jr. (2015). The burdens of leniency: The changing face of probation. *Minnesota Law Review, 99*, 1697–733.

Court Statistics Project. (2020). *State court caseload digest: 2018 data.* http://www.court-statistics.org/__data/assets/pdf_file/0014/40820/2018-Digest.pdf.

Crime and Justice Institute. (2004, April 24). *Implementing evidence-based practice in community corrections.* https://s3.amazonaws.com/static.nicic.gov/Library/019342.pdf

Crime Stoppers International (2015). http://csiworld.org/.

Cristall, J., and L. Forman-Echols. (2009). *Property abatements—the other gang injunction: Project T.O.U.G.H.* National Gang Center Bulletin 2. Washington, DC: Bureau of Justice Assistance.

Cullen, F. T., S. M. Manchak, and S. A. Duriez. (2014). Before adopting Project HOPE, read the warning label: A rejoinder to Kleiman, Kilmer, and Fisher's comment. *Federal Probation, 78*(2), 75–77.

Curry, G., and S. Decker (1998). *Confronting gangs: Crime and community.* Los Angeles: Roxbury Publishing.

Dawson-Edwards, C., R. Tewksbury, and N. T. Nelson. (2020). The causes and pervasiveness of DMC: Stakeholder perceptions of disproportionate minority contact in the juvenile justice system. *Race and Justice, 10*, 223–42.

DeMichele, M., and B. Payne. (2009). *Offender supervision with electronic technology: Community corrections resource,* 2nd ed. Washington, DC: U.S. Department of Justice. http://www.appa-net.org/eweb/docs/APPA/pubs/OSET_2.pdf.

Dentler, R. A., and L. J. Monroe. (1961). Social correlates of early adolescent theft. *American Sociological Review, 26*, 733–43.

Ditton, P. M. (1999). *Mental health and treatment of inmates and probationers.* Washington, DC: U.S. Department of Justice. www.ojp.usdoj.gov/bjs/pub/pdf/mhtip.pdf.

Downing, R. (2011). *Cybersecurity: Protecting America's new frontier.* https://www.justice.gov/sites/default/files/testimonies/witnesses/attachments/11/15/11//11-15-11-crm-downing-testimony-re-cyber-security---protecting-americas-new-frontier.pdf

Duriez, S.A., F. T. Cullen, and S. M. Manchak. (2014). Is Project HOPE creating a false sense of hope? A case student in correctional popularity. *Federal Probation, 78*(2), 57–70.

Edlin, B. R., B. J. Eckhardt, M. A. Shu, S. D. Holmberg, and T. Swan. (2015). Toward a more accurate estimate of the prevalence of hepatitis C in the United States. *Hepatology, 62*(5), 1353–63.

Egley, A., J. C. Howell, and M. Harris (2014) Highlights of the 2012 National Youth Gang Survey. Washington, DC: Office of Juvenile Justice and Delinquency Prevention. https://www.ojjdp.gov/pubs/248025.pdf.

Erickson, M. (1973). Group violations and official delinquency: The group hazard hypothesis. *Criminology, 11*, 127–60.

Esbensen, F., D. W. Osgood, D. Peterson, T. T. Taylor, and D. C. Carson. (2013). Short- and long-term outcome results from a multisite evaluation of the G.R.E.A.T. program. *Criminology and Public Policy, 12*, 375–412.

Ex parte Crouse, 4 Wheaton (Pa.) 9 (1838).

Fagan, J. (1995). Separating men from the boys: The comparative advantage of juvenile versus criminal court sanctions on recidivism among adolescent felony offenders.

In J. Howell, B. Krisberg, J. Hawkins, and J. Wilson (Eds.), *A sourcebook: Serious, violent, and chronic juvenile offenders*, 238–60. Thousand Oaks, CA: Sage Publications.

Faiver, K. (1998). *Health care management issues in corrections*. Lanham, MD: American Correctional Association.

Federal Bureau of Investigation (2019) 2018 NIBRS. https://ucr.fbi.gov/nibrs/2018/tables/data-tables.

Feld, B. C. (1988). In *re Gault* revisited: A cross-state comparison of the right to counsel in juvenile court. *Crime and Delinquency, 34*, 393–424.

Fletcher v. Peck, 10 U.S. 87 (1810).

Flitter, E. (2020, February 21). The price of Wells Fargo's fake account scandal grows by $3 billion. *New York Times.* https://www.nytimes.com/2020/02/21/business/wells-fargo-settlement.html.

Florida Department of Corrections. (2017 July). Florida's community supervision population: Monthly status report. http://www.dc.state.fl.us/pub/

Fontaine, J., D. Gilchrist-Scott, J. Roman, S. Taxy, and C. G. Roman. (2012). *Supportive housing for returning prisoners: Outcomes and impacts of the retuning home—Ohio Pilot Project.* Washington, DC: Urban Institute, Justice Policy Center. http://www.urban.org/publications/412632.html.

Gaes, G., T. Flanagan, L. Motiuk, and L. Stewart. (1999) Adult correctional treatment. In M. Tonry and J. Petersilia (Eds.), *Prisons.* (pp.361-426). Chicago: University of Chicago Press.

Gaes, G., and W. McGuire. (1985). Prison violence: The contribution of crowding versus other determinants of prison assault rates. *Journal of Research in Crime and Delinquency, 22*, 41–65.

Galassi, A., E. Mpofu, and J. Athanasou. (2015). Therapeutic community treatment of an inmate population with substance use disorders: Post-release trends in re-arrest, re-incarceration, and drug misuse relapse. *International journal of environmental research and public health, 12*(6), 7059–72.

Garland, B., E. J. Wodahl, and J. Mayfield. (2011). Prisoner reentry in a small metropolitan community: Obstacles and policy recommendations. *Criminal Justice Policy Review, 22*(1), 90–110.

Garofalo, J., and M. McLeod. (1988). Improving the use and effectiveness of neighborhood watch programs. *NIJ Research in Action.* Washington, DC: National Institute of Justice.

Gendreau, P. (1996). The principles of effective intervention with offenders. In A. T. Harland (Ed.), *Choosing correctional options that work: Defining the demand and evaluating the supply,* 117–30. Thousand Oaks, CA: Sage.

Gideon v. Wainwright, 372 U.S. 335 (1963).

Glaze, L. E., and D. Kaeble. (2014). *Correctional populations in the United States, 2013.* NCJ 248479. http://www.bjs.gov/content/pub/pdf/cpus13.pdf.

Gleicher, L., S. M. Manchak, and F. T. Cullen. (2012). Creating a supervision tool kit: How to improve probation and parole *Federal Probation, 77*(1), 22–27.

Gowdy, V. (2001). Should we privatize our prisons: The pros and cons. In E. Latessa, A. Holsinger, J. Marquart, and J. Sorenson (Eds.), *Correctional contexts: Contemporary and classical readings,* 198–208. Los Angeles: Roxbury Publishing.

Graham v. Connor, 490 U.S. 386 (1989).

Gray, M. K., M. Fields, and S. R. Maxwell. (2001). Examining probation violations: Who, what, and when. *Crime and Delinquency, 47*(4), 537–57.

Gregg v. Georgia, 428 U.S. 153 (1976).

Gressens, M. (2019). *FY19 private appointed counsel (PAC) effective pay rate study: Public defense attorney overhead rates and access to benefits.* http://www.ncids.org/FY19%20Effective%20Pay%20Rate%20Overhead%20Report.pdf.

Guevara, L., C. Spohn, and D. Herz. (2004). Race, legal representation, and juvenile justice: Issues and concerns. *Crime and Delinquency, 50,* 344–71.

Haas, K., and G. Alpert. (1989). American prisoners and the right of access to the courts: A vanishing concept of protection. In L. Goodstein and D. MacKenzie (Eds.), *The American prison: Issues in research and policy,* 65–87. New York: Plenum.

Hagan, J., and R. Dinovitzer. (1999). Collateral consequences of imprisonment for children, communities, and prisoners. In M. Tonry and J. Petersilia (Eds.), *Prisons,* 121–62. Chicago: University of Chicago Press.

Harer, M., and D. Steffensmeier. (1996). Race and prison violence. *Criminology, 34,* 323–55.

Harland, A. (1998). Defining a continuum of sanctions: Some research and policy development implications. In J. Petersilia (Ed.), *Community corrections: Probation, parole, and intermediate sanctions,* 70–79. New York: Oxford University Press.

Harmelin v. Michigan, 501 U.S. 957 (1991).

Harris, M. (1996). The goals of community sanctions. In T. Ellsworth (Ed.), *Contemporary community corrections,* 13–33. Prospect Heights, IL: Waveland Press.

Hartwell, S. (2010). Ex-inmates with psychiatric disabilities returning to the community from correctional custody: The forensic transition team approach after a decade. In Peyrot, M. and S.L. Burns (eds.), *New Approaches to Social Problems Treatment,* 263–83. Bingley, UK: Emerald Group Publishing Limited.

Hawken, A, and M. A. R. Kleiman. (2009). *Managing drug involved probationers with swift and certain sanctions: Evaluating Hawaii's HOPE* (No. 229023). Washington, DC: National Institute of Justice.

Hawkins, R., and G. Alpert. (1989). *American prison systems: Punishment and justice.* Englewood Cliffs, NJ: Prentice Hall.

Hemmens, C., J. Worrall, and A. Thompson. (2004). *Significant cases in criminal procedure.* Los Angeles: Roxbury Publishing.

Hennigan, K. M., and D. Sloane. (2013). Improving civil gang injunctions: How implementation can affect gang dynamics, crime, and violence. *Criminology and Public Policy, 12,* 7–42.

Hindelang, M., T. Hirschi, and J. Weis. (1979). Correlates of delinquency: The illusion of discrepancy between self-report and official measures. *American Sociological Review, 44,* 995–1014.

Hockenberry, S. and C. Puzzanchera (2020). *Juvenile court statistics, 2018.* Pittsburgh: National Center for Juvenile Justice.

Hockenberry, S., A. Wachter, and A. Sladky (2016). *Juvenile residential facility census, 2014: Selected findings.* Washington, DC: Office of Juvenile Justice and Delinquency Prevention. http://www.ncjj.org/Publication/Juvenile-Residential-Facility-Census-2014-Selected-Findings-.aspx.

Horwitz, A. (2010). The costs of abusing probationary sentences: Overincarceration and the erosion of due process. *Brooklyn Law Review, 75*(3), 753–90.

Hughes, T., and D. J. Wilson. (2002). *Reentry trends in the United States.* Washington, DC: U.S. Department of Justice, Bureau of Justice Assistance. bjs.ojp.usdoj.gov/content/pub/pdf/reentry.pdf.

Hyland, S. (2018). *Full-time employees in law enforcement agencies, 1997–2016*. Statistical Brief, NCJ 251762. Washington, DC: Bureau of Justice Statistics.

Hyland, S. S. (2019). *Justice Expenditure and Employment Extracts, 2016—Preliminary*. http://www.bjs.gov/index.cfm?ty=pbdetail.

In re Gault, 387 U.S. 1 (1967).

In re Winship, 397 U.S. 358 (1970).

International Association of Chiefs of Police (2014) *2013 Social Media Survey Results*. https://www.berkeleyside.com/wp-content/uploads/2014/02/2013SurveyResults.pdf

Irwin, J. (1980). *Prisons in turmoil*. Boston: Little, Brown.

Jacobs, J. (1982). Sentencing by prison personnel: Good time. *UCLA Law Review, 30*, 217–70.

Jacobson, M. P., V. Schiraldi, R. Daly, and E. Hotez, E. (2017). *Less is more: How reducing probation populations can improve outcomes*. Papers from the Executive Session on Community Corrections. https://www.hks.harvard.edu/sites/default/files/centers/wiener/programs/pcj/files/less_is_more_final.pdf.

James, D. J., and L. E. Glaze. (2006). *Mental health problems of prison and jail inmates*. Washington, DC: U.S. Department of Justice.

Johnson, H., and N. Wolfe. (1996). *History of criminal justice*, 2nd ed. Cincinnati, OH: Anderson Publishing.

Johnson, R. (2002). *Hard time: Understanding and reforming the prison*. Belmont, CA: Wadsworth.

Jones, A. (2018). Correctional control 2018: Incarceration and supervision by state. https://www.prisonpolicy.org/reports/correctionalcontrol2018.html.

Jones, M., and J. J. Kerbs. (2007). Probation and parole officers and discretionary decision-making: Responses to technical and criminal violations. *Federal Probation, 71*(1), 9–15.

Jordan, K. L., and D. Myers. (2011). Juvenile transfer and deterrence: re-examining the effectiveness of a "get tough" policy. *Crime and Delinquency, 57*(2), 247–70.

Justice Center. (2008). *Mental health courts: A primer for policy makers and practitioners*. New York: Justice Center/Council of State Governments.

Kaeble, D., and M. Alper. (2020). *Probation and parole in the United States, 2017–2018*. NCJ 252070. https://www.bjs.gov/content/pub/pdf/ppus1718.pdf.

Kaeble, D. and T. P. Bonczar. (2016). *Probation and parole in the United States, 2015*. NCJ 250230. https://www.bjs.gov/content/pub/pdf/ppus15.pdf.

Kempinen, C. A., and M. C. Kurlycheck. (2003). An outcome evaluation of Pennsylvania's boot camp: Does rehabilitative programming within a disciplinary setting reduce recidivism? *Crime and Delinquency, 49*, 581–602.

Kent v. U.S., 383 U.S. 541 (1966).

Kleiman, M. A. R. (2015). Substituting effective community supervision for incarceration. *Minnesota Law Review, 99*, 1621–30.

Kleiman, M. A. R. (2016). Swift-certain-fair: What do we know now, and what do we need to know? *Criminology & Public Policy, 15*(4), 1185–93.

Kleiman, M. A. R., B. Kilmer, and D. T. Fisher. (2014). A response to Stephanie A. Duriez, Francis T. Cullen, and Sarah M. Manchak: Theory and evidence on the swift-certain-fair approach to enforcing conditions of community supervision. *Federal Probation, 78*(2), 71–74.

Klingele, C. (2013). Rethinking the use of community supervision. *Journal of Criminal Law and Criminology, 103*(4), 1015–69.

Klingele, C. (2015). What are we hoping for? Defining purpose in deterrence-based correctional programs. *Minnesota Law Review, 99*, 1631–63.

Klockars, C. (1985). *The idea of police.* Newbury Park, CA: Sage Publications.

Knudsen, K., and S. Wingenfeld. (2015). A specialized treatment court for veterans with trauma exposure: Implications for the field. *Community Mental Health Journal, 52*, 127–35.

Kurki, L. (2000). Restorative and community justice in the United States. In M. Tonry (Ed.), *Crime and justice: A review of research*, vol. 27. (pp 235-303). Chicago: University of Chicago Press.

Kyllo v. U.S., 533 U.S. 27 (2001).

Lab, S. D. (2016). *Crime prevention: Approaches, practices, and evaluations*, 9th ed. New York: Routledge.

Laird, L. (2017). *Starved of money for too long, public defender offices are suing—and starting to win.* https://www.abajournal.com/magazine/article/the_gideon_revolution.

Langan, P., and D. Levin. (2002). *Recidivism of prisoners released in 1994.* Washington, DC: Bureau of Justice Statistics.

Larkin, P. J. (2015). Swift, certain, and fair punishment: 24/7 Sobriety and HOPE: Creative approaches to alcohol- and illicit drug-using offenders. *Journal of Criminal Law and Criminology, 105*(1), 39–94.

Latessa, E., and L. Travis. (1992). Residential community correctional programs. In J. Byrne, A. Lurrigo, and J. Petersilia (Eds.), *Smart sentencing: The emergence of intermediate sanctions*, 166–81. Newbury Park, CA: Sage Publications.

Latessa, E. J., S. J. Listwan, and D. Koetzle. (2013). *What works (and doesn't) in reducing recidivism.* New York: Routledge Pub

Lattimore, P. K., D. L. MacKenzie, G. Zajac, D. Dawes, E. Arsenault, and S. Tueller. (2016). Outcome findings from the HOPE demonstration field experiment: Is Swift, Certain, and Fair an effective supervision strategy? *Criminology & Public Policy, 15*(4), 1103–41.

Leiber, M. J., and R. Fix. (2019). Reflections on the impact of race and ethnicity on juvenile court outcomes and efforts to enact change. *American Journal of Criminal Justice, 44*(4), 581–608.

Lipsey, M., and D. Wilson. (1998). Effective intervention for serious juvenile offenders: A synthesis of research. In R. Loeber and D. Farrington (Eds.), *Serious and violent juvenile offenders: Risk factors and successful interventions*. Thousand Oaks, CA: Sage Publications.

Lipsey, M. W. (2009). The primary factors that characterize effective interventions with juvenile offenders: A meta-analytic overview. *Victims and Offenders, 4*, 124–47.

Los Angeles City Attorney's Office. (2009). *Gang injunctions: How they work (The City Attorney's report).* Los Angeles: City Attorney's Office.

Lowenkamp, C. T., A. W. Flores, A. M. Holsinger, M. D. Makarios, and E. J. Latessa. (2010). Intensive supervision programs: Does program philosophy and the principle of effective intervention matter? *Journal of Criminal Justice, 38*, 368–75.

Lowenkamp, C. T. and E. J. Latessa. (2005). Increasing the effectiveness of correctional programming through the risk principle: Identifying offenders for residential placement. *Criminology & Public Policy, 4*(2), 263–90.

Lowenkamp, C. T., E. J. Latessa, and A. M. Holsinger. (2006). The Risk Principle in action: What have we learned from 13,676 offenders and 97 correctional programs? *Crime and Delinquency, 52*, 77–93.

Lowenkamp, C. T., E. J. Latessa, and P. Smith. (2006). Does correctional program quality really matter? The impact of adhering to the principles of effective interventions. *Criminology and Public Policy, 5*(3), 575–94.

Lucas, P., and K. Hanrahan. (2016). No soldier left behind: The veterans court solution. *International Journal of Law & Psychiatry, 45*, 52–59.

Lurigio, A., and J. Petersilia. (1992). The emergence of intensive probation supervision programs in the United States. In J. Byrne, A. Lurigio, and J. Petersilia (Eds.), *Smart sentencing: The emergence of intermediate sanctions*, 3–18. Newbury Park, CA: Sage Publications.

Lurigio, A. J., A. Rollins, and J. Fallon. (2004). The effects of serious mental illness on offender reentry. *Federal Probation, 68*(2), 45–52.

M'Naughten's Case, 8 Eng. Rep. 718 (1843).

MacKenzie, D. L., and H. Donaldson. (1996). Boot camp for women offenders. *Criminal Justice Policy Review, 21*, 21–43.

MacKenzie, D. L., and R. Freeland. (2012). Examining the effectiveness of juvenile residential programs. In B. C. Feld and D. M. Bishop (Eds.), *The Oxford handbook of juvenile justice*, 771–98. New York: Oxford University Press.

Mai, C. and R. Subramanian. (2017). *Price of prisons 2015: Examining state spending trends, 2010–2015*. New York: Vera Institute of Justice.

Makarios, M., and E. J. Latessa, E. J. (2013). Developing a risk and needs assessment instrument for Prison Inmates: The Issue of Outcome. Criminal Justice and Behavior, 40, 1449-1471.

Maltz, M. (1999). *Bridging gaps in police crime data: A discussion paper from the BJS Fellows Program*. Washington, DC: U.S. Department of Justice.

Mancini, M. (1978). Race, economics, and the abandonment of convict leasing. *Journal of Negro History, 63*, 339–40.

Mapp v. Ohio, 367 U.S. 643 (1961).

Marbury v. Madison, 5 U.S. 137 (1803).

Marciniak, L. M. (1999). The use of day reporting as an intermediate sanction: A study of offender targeting and program termination. *The Prison Journal, 79*(2), 205–25.

Marshall Project (2020) A State-by-State Look at Coronavirus in Prisons https://www.themarshallproject.org/2020/05/01/a-state-by-state-look-at-coronavirus-in-prisons

Martin, C, D. E. Olson, and A. J. Lurigio. (2000). *An evaluation of the Cook County Sheriff's Day Reporting Center Program: Rearrest and reincarceration after discharge*. Chicago: Illinois Criminal Justice Information Authority. http://www.icjia.org/assets/pdf/researchreports/An%20Evaluation%20Rearrest%20and%20Reincarceration%20After%20Discharge.pdf.

Martinson, R. (1974). What works?—Questions and answers about prison reform. *The Public Interest, 42*, 22–54.

Maruna, S., and R. Immarigeon (Eds.). (2004). *After crime and punishment: Pathways to offender reintegration*. Portland, OR: Willan Publishing.

Maruschak, L. M., and J. Bronson. (2017). *HIV in prisons, 2015-statistical tables*. Washington, DC: Bureau of Justice Statistics.

Maruschak, L. M., and T. D. Minton. (2020). *Correctional populations in the United States, 2017-2018*. NCJ 252157. https://www.bjs.gov/content/pub/pdf/cpus1718.pdf.

Mastrofski, S. D., J. B. Snipes, and A. E. Supina. (1996). Compliance on demand: The public's response to specific police requests. *Journal of Research in Crime and Delinquency, 35*(3), 269–305.

McBride, D., and C. VanderWaal. (1997). Day reporting centers as an alternative for drug-using offenders. *Journal of Drug Issues, 27,* 379–97.

McCleary, R. (1992). *Dangerous men: The sociology of parole,* 2nd ed. New York: Harrow and Heston.

McCollister, K., M. French, M. Prendergast, E. Hall, and S. Sacks. (2004). Long-term cost effectiveness of addiction treatment for criminal offenders. *Justice Quarterly, 21,* 559–679.

McCulloch v. Maryland, 17 U.S. 316 (1819).

McGarrell, E. F., K. Olivares, K. Crawford, and N. Kroovand. (2000). *Returning justice to the community: The Indianapolis juvenile restorative justice experiment.* Indianapolis: Hudson Institute.

McGuire, J. (2001). What works in correctional intervention? Evidence and practical implications. In G. A. Bernfeld, D. P. Farrington, and A. W. Leschied (Eds.), *Offender rehabilitation in practice: Implementing and evaluating effective programs,* 25–43. New York: John Wiley and Sons.

McKeiver v. Pennsylvania, 403 U.S. 528 (1971).

McMann v. Richardson, 397 U.S. 759 (1970).

Miller v. Alabama (2012). 132 S. Ct. 2455

Miller-Wilson, L. S., and P. Puritz, P. (2003). *Pennsylvania: An assessment of access to counsel and quality of representation in delinquency proceedings.* Washington, DC, and Philadelphia: American Bar Association Juvenile Justice Center and Juvenile Law Center in collaboration with the National Juvenile Defender Center and the Northeast Juvenile Defender Center. http://www.jlc.org/sites/default/files/publication_pdfs/PA%20Assesment%20of%20Access%20to%20Counsel.pdf.

Mitchell, K. J., D. Finkelhor, L. M. Jones, and J. Wolak (2012). Prevalence and characteristics of youth sexting: A national study. *Pediatrics, 129,* 1–9.

Montgomery v. Louisiana (2016). 136 S. Ct. 718

Morgan, K. (1996). Factors influencing probation outcome: A review of the literature. In T. Ellsworth (Ed.), *Contemporary community corrections,* 327–40. Prospect Heights, IL: Waveland Press.

Morgan, R. E., and G. Kena. (2018). *Criminal victimization, 2016: Revised.* Washington, DC. US Department of Jusice, Office of Justice Programs.

Morris, N., and D. Rothman. (1995). *The Oxford history of the prison.* New York: Oxford University Press.

Morris, N., and M. Tonry. (1990). *Between prison and probation: Intermediate punishments in a rational sentencing system.* New York: Oxford University Press.

Mulvey, E. P., and C. A. Schubert. (2012). *Transfer of juveniles to adult court: Effects of a broad policy change in one court.* Washington, DC: Office of Juvenile Justice and Delinquency Prevention.

National Association of Youth Courts (2017). https://www.youthcourt.net/.

National Education Association (2019). *Ranking of the states 2018 and estimates of school statistics 2019.* https://www.nea.org/sites/default/files/2020-06/2019%20Rankings%20and%20Estimates%20Report.pdf.

National Gang Center (2016) *Brief review of federal and state definitions of the terms "gang," "gang crime," and "gang member."* https://www.hsdl.org/?view&did=682835

National Institute of Corrections. (2011). *Special challenges facing parole (NIC 024200).* Washington, DC: US Department of Justice.

National Institute of Justice. (2003). *Correctional boot camps: Lessons from a decade of research*. Washington, DC: U.S. Department of Justice.

Nellis, A. (2009). *Back on track: Supporting youth reentry from out-of-home placement to the community*. Washington, DC: Juvenile Justice and Delinquency Prevention Coalition, The Sentencing Project.

Neubauer, D., and H. Fradella. (2014). *America's courts and the criminal justice system*. Stanford, CA: Stanford University Press.

Newman, S. A., J. A. Fox, E. A. Flynn, and W. Christeson. (2000). *America's after-school choice: Prime time for juvenile crime, or enrichment and achievement*. Washington, DC: Invest in Kids.

O'Connell, D. J., J. J. Brent, and C. A. Visher. (2016). Decide your time: A randomized trial of a drug testing and graduated sanctions program for probationers. *Criminology & Public Policy*, *15*(4), 1073–102.

O'Neal v. Vermont, 144 U.S. 323 (1892).

Office of Juvenile Justice and Delinquency Prevention (2020). *Statistical briefing book*. https://www.ojjdp.gov/ojstatbb/.

Ohio Department of Rehabilitation and Corrections. (2007). *Best practices tool-kit: Sex offender assessment and treatment*. https://kb.osu.edu/bitstream/handle/1811/30140/Tool-Kit%20SO%20Assessment%20and%20Treatment.pdf?sequence=1&isAllowed=y

Osterman, M. (2009). An analysis of New Jersey's Day Reporting Center and Halfway Back Programs: Embracing the rehabilitative ideal through evidence based practices. *Journal of Offender Rehabilitation*, *48*(2), 139–53.

Packer, H. (1968). *The limits of the criminal sanction*. Stanford, CA: Stanford University Press.

Padgett, K. G., W. D. Bales, and T. G. Blomberg. (2006). Under surveillance: An empirical test of the effectiveness and consequences of electronic monitoring. *Criminology and Public Policy*, *5*, 61–91.

Palko v. Connecticut, 302 U.S. 319 (1937).

Paparozzi, M. A., and M. DeMichele. (2008). Probation and parole: Overworked, misunderstood, and under-appreciated: But why? *Howard Journal of Criminal Justice*, *47*(3), 275–96.

Paparozzi, M. A., and P. Gendreau. (2005) An intensive supervision program that worked: Service delivery, professional orientation, and organizational supportiveness. *The Prison Journal*, *85*, 445–66.

Petersilia, J. (1997). Probation in the United States. In M. Tonry (Ed.), *Crime and justice: A review of research*, 149–200. Chicago: University of Chicago Press.

Petersilia, J. (1998). A crime control rationale for reinvesting in community corrections. In J. Petersilia (Ed.), *Community corrections: Probation, parole, and intermediate sanctions*, 20–28. New York: Oxford University Press.

Petersilia, J. (2002). Community corrections. In J. Wilson and J. Petersilia (Eds.), *Crime: Public policies for crime control*, 483–508. Oakland, CA: Institute for Contemporary Studies.

Petersilia, J. (2003). *When prisoners return home: Parole and prisoner reentry*. New York: Oxford University Press.

Petersilia, J., and S. Turner. (1993). *Evaluating intensive supervision probation/parole: Results of a nationwide experiment. Research in brief: National Institute of Justice*. Washington, DC: U.S. Department of Justice.

Pew Center on the States. (2008). *One in 100: Behind bars in America 2008.* https://www.pewtrusts.org/-/media/legacy/uploadedfiles/pcs_assets/2008/one20in20100pdf.pdf

Pew Center on the States. (2011). *State of recidivism: The revolving door of America's prisons.* Washington, DC: The Pew Charitable Trusts.

Pew Charitable Trust (2014). *Max out: The rise in prison inmates released without supervision.*http://www.pewtrusts.org/en/research-and-analysis/reports/2014/06/04/max-out.

Pew Charitable Trusts (2018). *Probation and parole systems marked by high stakes, missed opportunities.* https://www.pewtrusts.org/en/research-and-analysis/issue-briefs/2018/09/probation-and-parole-systems-marked-by-high-stakes-missed-opportunities.

Pisciotta, A. (1994). *Benevolent repression: Social control and the American reformatory-prison movement.* New York: New York University Press.

Pollock, J. (2004). *Prisons and prison life: Costs and consequences.* Los Angeles: Roxbury Publishing.

President's Commission on Law Enforcement and the Administration of Justice. (1967). *The challenge of crime in a free society.* Washington, DC: U.S. Government Printing Office.

Prins, S. J., and L. Draper. (2009). *Improving outcomes for people with mental illnesses under community supervision: A guide to research-informed policy and practice.* New York: Justice Center/Council of State Governments. https://csgjusticecenter.org/publications/improving-outcomes-for-people-with-mental-illnesses-under-community-corrections-supervision-a-guide-to-research-informed-policy-and-practice/

Prison Policy Initiative. (2020). *Responses to the COVID-19 pandemic.* https://www.prisonpolicy.org/virus/virusresponse.html.

Procon.org. (2020) *Legal medical marijuana states and DC: Laws, fees, and possession limits.* https://medicalmarijuana.procon.org/legal-medical-marijuana-states-and-dc/.

Reaves, B. A. (2013). Felony defendants in large urban counties, 2009—statistical tables. NCJ 243777. https://www.bjs.gov/content/pub/pdf/fdluc09.pdf.

Reider, L. (1998). Towards a new test for the insanity defense: Incorporating the discoveries of neuroscience into moral and legal theories. *UCLA Law Review, 46,* 289–342.

Rembar, C. (1989). *The law of the land: The evolution of our legal system.* New York: Simon and Schuster.

Riley v. California 573 U.S._(2014).

Robles-Ramamurthy, B. and C. Watson. (2019). Examining racial disparities in juvenile justice. *Journal of the American Academy of Psychiatry and the Law, 47,* 48–52.

Roper, Superintendent, Potosi Correctional Center v. Simmons, 543 U.S. 551 (2005).

Rosen, A. (2019). High time for criminal justice reform: Marijuana expungement statutes in states with legalized or decriminalized marijuana laws. https://www.mpp.org/assets/pdf/issues/criminal-justice/high-time-for-criminal-justice-reform.pdf.

Rosenbaum, D. P. (1987). The theory and research behind neighborhood watch: Is it a sound fear and crime reduction strategy? *Crime and Delinquency, 33,* 103–34.

Rothman, D. (1971). *The discovery of the asylum.* Boston: Little, Brown.

Rothman, D. (1980). *Conscience and convenience: The asylum and its alternatives in progressive America.* Boston: Little, Brown.

Samaha, J. (2012). *Criminal procedure.* Belmont, CA: Wadsworth/Cengage Learning.

Sawyer, W., and P. Wagner. (2020). *Mass incarceration: The whole pie 2020.* https://www.prisonpolicy.org/reports/pie2020.html.

Schall v. Martin, 467 U.S. 253 (1984).

Schwartz, B. (1992). *The great rights of mankind: A history of the American Bill of Rights.* Madison, WI: Madison House.

Schwartzapfel, B. (2020, April 3). Probation and parole officers are rethinking their rules as coronavirus spreads. The Marshall Project. https://www.themarshallproject.org/2020/04/03/probation-and-parole-officers-are-rethinking-their-rules-as-coronavirus-spreads

Scott, D., and J. Kunselman. (2007). Social justice implications of domestic violence court processes. *Journal of Social Welfare and Family Law, 29,* 17–31.

Scott v. Illinois (1979). 440 US 367

Sellin, J. (1976). *Slavery and the penal system.* New York: Elsevier.

Sexton, G. (1995). *Work in American prisons: Joint ventures with the private sector.* Washington, DC: National Institute of Justice.

Shapland, J., A. Bottoms, S. Farrall, F. McNeil, C. Priede, and G. Robinson. (2012). *The quality of probation supervision: A literature review.* Sheffield, UK: University of Sheffield, Centre for Criminological Research.

Sheenan, R., G. McIvor, and C. Trotter (Eds.). (2011). *Working with women offenders in the community.* New York: Willan Publishing.

Sheldon, R. (2001). *Controlling the dangerous classes: An introduction to the history of criminal justice.* Needham Heights, MA: Allyn and Bacon.

Short, J., and I. Nye. (1958). Extent of unrecorded delinquency: Tentative conclusions. *Journal of Criminal Law, Criminology, and Police Science, 49,* 296–302.

Shy, Y. (2004). *Mandatory minimum sentencing in Massachusetts: Alternative approaches.* https://www.cjpc.org/mandatory-minimum-in-other-states.html

Sickmund, M., T. J. Sladky, W. Kang, and C. Puzzanchera. (2019). Easy access to the census of juveniles in residential placement. http://www.ojjdp.gov/ojstatbb/ezacjrp/.

Slate, R. (2000). Courts for mentally ill offenders: Necessity or abdication of responsibility? In L. Mays and P. Gregware (Eds.), *Crime and justice: A reader,* 432–50. Prospect Heights, IL: Waveland Press.

Smith, D., and C. Visher. (1981). Street-level justice: Situational determinants of police arrest decisions. *Social Problems, 29,* 167–77.

Spergel, I. A., and G. D. Curry. (1993). The National Youth Gang Survey: A research and development process. In A. P. Goldstein and C. R. Huff (Eds.), *The gang intervention handbook,* 359–400. Champaign, IL: Research Press.

Stanford v. Kentucky (1989). 492 US 361

Strickland v. Washington, 446 U.S. 668 (1984).

Swan, H., W. Campbell, and N. Lowe. (2020). *Pandemic preparedness and response among community supervision agencies: The importance of partnerships for future planning.* Abt White Paper. Rockville, MD: American Probation and Parole Association. https://www.appa-net.org/eweb/docs/APPA/pubs/PPRCSA.PDF.

Sykes, G. (1958). *The society of captives.* Princeton, NJ: Princeton University Press.

Taxman, F. S. (2008a). No illusions: Offender and organizational change in Maryland's proactive community supervision efforts. *Criminology & Public Policy, 7*(2), 275–302.

Taxman, F. S. (2008b). To be or not to be: Community supervision déjà vu. *Journal of Offender Rehabilitation, 47*(3), 209–19.

Tennessee v. Garner (1985). 471 U.S. 1

Tenzer, L. (2019). #MeToo, statutory rape laws, and the persistence of gender stereotypes. *Utah L. Rev. 117*, https://digitalcommons.pace.edu/lawfaculty/1116/

Tonry, M. (1990). Stated and latent functions of ISP. *Crime and Delinquency, 36*, 174–91.

Tonry, M. (1999). *The fragmentation of sentencing and corrections in America. Sentencing and corrections: Issues for the 21st century.* Papers from the Executive Sessions on Sentencing and Corrections, no. 1. Washington, DC: National Institute of Justice. https://www.ojp.gov/pdffiles1/nij/175721.pdf

Tonry, M., and M. Lynch. (1996). Intermediate sanctions. In M. Tonry (Ed.), *Crime and justice: A review of research*, 99–144. Chicago: University of Chicago Press.

Travis, J. (2004). Reentry and reintegration: New perspectives on the challenges of mass incarceration. In M. Pattillo, D. Weiman, and B. Western (Eds.), *Imprisoning America: The social effects of mass incarceration.* (pp. 247-268). New York: Russell Sage.

Travis, J. (2005). *But they all come back: Facing the challenges of prisoner reentry.* Washington, DC: Urban Institute Press.

Travis, J., and M. Waul (eds.). (2003). *Prisoners once removed: The impact of incarceration and reentry on children, families, and communities.* Washington, DC: The Urban Institute Press.

Treatment Advocacy Center. (2014). *The treatment of persons with mental illness in prisons and jails: A state survey* (abridged). https://www.treatmentadvocacycenter.org/storage/documents/treatment-behind-bars/treatment-behind-bars-abridged.pdf

Trotter, C. (2006). *Working with involuntary clients: A guide to practice.* Thousand Oaks, CA: Sage Publishing.

Trotter, C. (2013). Reducing recidivism through probation supervision: What we know and don't know from four decades for research. *Federal Probation, 77*(2), 43–48.

U.S. Department of Justice, Civil Rights Division (2015). *Investigation of the Ferguson Police Department.* Washington, DC: U.S. Department of Justice.

United State Courts (2020). *Officers innovate in the field during COVID-19 crisis.* https://www.uscourts.gov/news/2020/06/11/officers-innovate-field-during-covid-19-crisis.

United States v. Finley, 477 F.3d 250 (5th Circuit 2007).

United States v. Jones, (2012). 565 U.S. 400

United States v. Perrine, 518 F.3d 1196 (2008).

United States v. Salerno, 481 U.S. 739 (1987).

United States v. Smith, 155 F.3d 1051 (9th Circuit 1998).

Vaas, A., and A. Weston. (1990). Probation day centres as an alternative to custody. *British Journal of Criminology, 30*, 189–205.

Van Voorhis, P. (1994). *Psychological classification of the adult male prison inmate.* Albany: State University of New York Press.

Vanstone, M. (2008). The international origins and initial development of probation. *British Journal of Criminology, 48*, 735–55.

Varan, A. K., D. W. Mercer, M. S. Stein, and A. C. Spaulding. (2014). Hepatitis C seroprevalence among prison inmates since 2001: still high but declining. *Public Health Reports, 129*(2), 187–95.

Vigil, J. D. (2010). *Gang redux: A balanced anti-gang strategy.* Long Grove, IL: Waveland.

Visher, C. A., and J. Travis. (2011). Life on the outside: Returning home after incarceration. *The Prison Journal, 91*(3), 1025–195.

Von Hirsch, A. (1998). The ethics of community-based sanctions. In J. Petersilia (Ed.), *Community corrections: Probation, parole, and intermediate sanctions*, 89–98. New York: Oxford University Press.

Walker, S. (1993). *Taming the system: The control of discretion in criminal justice, 1950–1990*. New York: Oxford University Press.

Waslin, M. (2020). The use of executive orders and proclamations to create immigration policy: Trump in historical perspective. *Journal of Migration & Human Security, 8*, 54–67.

White, L .L. (2020). Probation conditions relaxed during the pandemic. Some say they should stay that way. *The Appeal*. https://theappeal.org/coronavirus-probation-parole-technical-violations/.

White, T. F. (2005). *Re-engineering probation towards greater public safety: A framework for recidivism reduction through evidence-based practice*. https://portal.ct.gov/-/media/OPM/CJPPD/CjResearch/ProjectBehaviorHealth/Resources/20050401Study ReegineerProbationCSSDpdf.pdf

Whitehead, J., and S. Lab. (2018). *Juvenile justice: An introduction*, 9th ed. New York: Routledge.

Wilson, D. B., D. L. MacKenzie, and F. N. Mitchell. (2005). *Effects of correctional boot camps on offending: A Campbell Collaboration systematic review*. https://www.campbellcollaboration.org/better-evidence/effects-of-correctional-boot-camps-on-offending.html

Wilson, J. A., and R. C. Davis. (2006). Good intentions meet hard realities: An evaluation of the Project Greenlight reentry program. *Criminology and Public Policy, 5*(2), 303–38.

Wodahl, E. J., R. Ogle, and C. Heck. (2011). Revocation trends: A threat to the legitimacy of community-based corrections. *The Prison Journal, 9*(2), 207–26.

Wooldredge, J. D. (1994). Inmate crime and victimization in a Southwestern correctional facility. *Journal of Criminal Justice, 22*, 367–81.

World Prison Brief data. (n.d.). https://www.prisonstudies.org/world-prison-brief-data.

Yoffe, Emily. (2017). Innocence Is Irrelevant: This is the age of the plea bargain—and millions of Americans are suffering the consequences. *The Atlantic*, September 2017. https://www.theatlantic.com/magazine/archive/2017/09/innocence-is-irrelevant/534171/

Zalman, M., and L. Siegel. (1997). *Criminal procedure*. Florence, KY: Cengage.

Zimmer, L. (1986). *Women guarding men*. Chicago: University of Chicago Press.

INDEX

Note: Page numbers followed by *b* or *t* refer to materials found in boxes or tables. Figures refer to graphs, shown by *f*. Definitions are found in the Glossary.